DATE DUE

UPI 261-2505 G   PRINTED IN U.S.A.

Object Persistence

Beyond Object-Oriented Databases

Object Persistence

Beyond Object-Oriented Databases

Roger Sessions

ObjectWatch, Incorporated
Austin, Texas

For book and bookstore information

http://www.prenhall.com

Prentice Hall PTR, Upper Saddle River, New Jersey 07458

Acquisitions editor: Gregory G. Doench
Editorial assistant: Leabe Berman
Production supervision: Mary Sudul
Cover design: Design Source
Cover design director: Jerry Votta
Copyeditor: Mary Lou Nohr
Manufacturing manager: Alexis R. Heydt

Cover Illustration: *The Disintegration of the Persistence of Memory*
(1952-54) Oil on canvas
10 x 13 inches
Collection of Mr. & Mrs. A. Reynolds Morse
on loan to The Salvador Dali Museum
St. Petersburg, Florida
Copyright 1994 Salvador Dali Museum, Inc.

©1996 Prentice Hall PTR
Prentice Hall, Inc.
A Simon & Schuster Company
Upper Saddle River, New Jersey 07458

The publisher offers discounts on this book when ordered in bulk
quantities. For more information, contact Corporate Sales Department,
Prentice Hall PTR, One Lake Street, Upper Saddle River, NJ 07458.
Phone: 800-382-3419; FAX: 201-236-7141; email: corpsales@prenhall.com.

Printed in the United States of America

10 9 8 7 6 5 4 3 2 1

ISBN 0-13-192436-2

Prentice-Hall International (UK) Limited, *London*
Prentice-Hall of Australia Pty. Limited, *Sydney*
Prentice-Hall Canada Inc., *Toronto*
Prentice-Hall Hispanoamericana, S.A., *Mexico*
Prentice-Hall of India Private Limited, *New Delhi*
Prentice-Hall of Japan, Inc., *Tokyo*
Simon & Schuster Asia Pte. Ltd., *Singapore*
Editora Prentice-Hall do Brasil, Ltda., *Rio de Janeiro*

Contents

Chapter 4   Introduction to IDL   47

Chapter 5   The Interfaces of Persistence   121

Chapter 8   The Datastore Vendor Perspective   203

Chapter 9   The Vision   235

F i g u r e s

Object Persistence

Beyond Object-Oriented Databases

Introduction

The Object Management Group (OMG) has adopted a specification for the Persistent Object Service (POS). The specification provides an industry standard for writing datastore independent code for storing and restoring objects and for plugging existing datastores into an object storage framework. The adoption of the POS standard by this large industry consortium will likely have a major impact on the way object-oriented storage systems are designed and used in the next few years.

This standard will impact most data storage industries. Traditional database vendors will find they can participate as first-class object datastores. Object-oriented databases will be reexamining their interfaces for conformance to this standard. The object-oriented community will start moving to an object-centric view of persistence rather than a data-centric view of datastores.

The POS (Persistent Object Service) specification provides important benefits. It allows object implementors to create objects that can be stored to any datastore, in any format. It allows clients to use a single interface regardless of whether the object is stored in file systems, relational databases, object-oriented databases, or other datastores. It allows existing corporate-centric datastores, such as relational databases, to be used as first-class object stores.

The standard also defines the components that must be implemented by datastore vendors to support the storage of objects. This book describes work in progress for support of the OMG standard with plug compatibility for DB2™, Stream files, and other datastores. This book describes the interfaces used for storing and restoring objects, and looks at code that implements the concept of datastore independence.

In short, this book gives you all the background you need to understand the Persistent Object Service standard and tells you everything you need to know about how this standard works. This book even tells you when the standard doesn't work and what might be done to fix it.

This book is for you, whether you are an end user running applications that store objects, an applications developer implementing persistent objects, a datastore provider wanting to plug into this service, or just a student trying to keep up with the latest theories on how to view object persistence.

Historical Perspective

Software, like many things, has undergone a huge transformation in the last twenty-five years. In the early 70s, programs were considered state of the art if they used some higher-level language. Our development techniques, however, were still firmly rooted in Assembly Language. A program to manage, say, a hospital emergency room, would contain code like the following:

```
        /* ... */
        pptr = 0;
        n = n1;
100     if (n == 0) goto 1000;
        if (n->type == "P") goto 200;
        if (n->type == "S") goto 300;
200     if (n->phys.ptype == ntype) goto 500
        goto 400;
300     if (n->spec.ptype == ntype) goto 500
400     n = n->next;
        goto 100;
500     if (n->type == "P") pptr = n->phys;
        goto 1000;
        if (n->type == "S") pptr = n->spec;
1000    /* ... */
```

By the 80s, we discovered structured programming. Gotos were out. Indented logic branches were in. Our emergency room code would now look like the following.

```
n = n1;
while (!n) {
  if (n->type == "P") &&
     (n->phys.ptype == ntype)
       pptr = n->phys;
  else if
     (n->type == "S") &&
     (n->spec.ptype == ntype)
     pptr = n->spec;
  n = n->next;
}
```

Structured programming promised to solve the software crisis by creating small, focused modules, which could be reused in many different programming situations. Unfortunately, the modules were invariably dependent on specific data types that were defined external to the modules. The modules encapsulated behavior, but not data. When programmers made minor changes to these data structures, the modules were no longer useful.

Programmers sought a technique for encapsulating both behavior *and* data structures. Thus were born objects. Our code started getting much more readable. By the late 80s, our hospital management program evolved to a fairly simple main program, which would now contain the following:

```
physician =
  getNextAvailablePhysician(WaitingRoom, Cardiologist);
```

This main program would make use of class libraries containing method implementations, such as:

```
Physician WaitingRoom::
  getNextAvailablePhysician (specialty_needed)
{
  return (findByKey(specialty_needed));
}
```

It was starting to look as if the age of software maintainability and reuse had actually arrived.

Unfortunately, what looked like a good idea in the academic world quickly ran into real-world problems. It is true that we had encapsulated both data and behavior, allowing both to be managed and extended as a coherent package. In the real world, data had to be stored, and existing data had to be read in. Our make-believe world of simple, encapsulated object methods quickly began to deteriorate. Our methods started getting ugly.

```
Physician WaitingRoom::
getNextAvailablePhysician (specialty_needed)
{
  Physician phys;
  EXEC SQL INCLUDE SQLCA;
  EXEC SQL BEGIN DECLARE SECTION;
    char Name[100];
    short Age;
  EXEC SQL END DECLARE SECTION;
  EXEC SQL SELECT NAME, AGE
  INTO :Name, :Age
  WHERE SPECIALITY = specialty_needed;

  if (sqlca ->sqlcode == NONE_FOUND) return NULL;
```

```
    if (Speciality == NULL)
        phys = new physician;
    else {
        phys = new specialist;
        setSpeciality(phys, speciality_needed);
    }
    setName(phys, Name);
    setAge(phys, Age);
}
```

Object-oriented database vendors gave us their solution. Simply throw away your terabytes of existing data, rewrite your millions of lines of code, bring your corporation to a halt for ten years while you update your system, and your problems will be solved!

Software was undergoing other changes as well. Problem domains were becoming more distributed. Our concept of process began as a deck of punch cards, evolved to executable programs, to multiple processes on a machine communicating with each other, to processes communicating over a homogenous network, to processes communicating over a corporate-wide network consisting of many manufacturers' machines. Watching the enormous advances in the Internet over the last few years, it is clear that we have just barely begun to understand the concept of distributed software.

So where is this driving the industry? The next generation of software will consist of components tied into a huge variety of database products. These components will be distributed over mega-networks that will literally extend throughout the known galaxy. If we think software was complicated before, we clearly ain't seen nothin' yet.

If objects are the answer, how do we get our objects back to a manageable state? How do we create objects that can be tied into *any* database, that can be distributed over *any* network, that can cooperate with other objects written in *any* programming language? These are the fundamental problems that must be solved if object-oriented programming will be of any value into the twenty-first century.

The OMG

Over 600 companies are members of OMG (Object Management Group) located in Framingham, Massachusetts. The purpose of the OMG is to create standards that will enable a distributed objects components industry. These standards range from low level, describing the interfaces for the underlying plumbing, to mid level, describing basic services object implementors can assume exist independent of their implementations, to high level, describing how objects within applications interact.

The members of OMG range from the giants of the hardware and software industry to tiny companies barely starting up. Members include companies seeking to dominate entire industries; companies seeking toeholds in developing markets; companies that want to find a niche developing software components; and companies desperately wanting to purchase existing components instead of continually having to write their own. Some of the OMG members are so large they have multiple representatives at the OMG, each representing a different, and sometimes competing, interest within the same company. Others are so small that sending a single representative to a few OMG meetings a year is a huge financial commitment.

Attendees at OMG meetings often include a who's who of the object industry. These people each have company loyalties, strong personal beliefs, and shifting allegiances within OMG. As one can imagine, attempts to reach consensus with such a group are well sprinkled with politics, personalities, and philosophical conflicts.

In the face of this daunting challenge, the OMG has done a remarkable job of achieving agreement on issues ranging from basic distributed object architecture to object interface definition language to object persistence. Despite the range of interests and loyalties, members believe that these are important issues. If the industry cannot collectively set its own standards, then it will be forced to deal with de facto standards set and controlled by a single, autocratic corporation.

We are all aware of the importance of standards to our customers. With standards, customers become less dependent on a single major supplier. With standards, customers are willing to take chances on smaller, start-up companies. With standards, customers are willing to try newer technologies.

For the industry of distributed objects, standards are more important than for any other industry. By its very nature, this is an industry that depends on interoperability. People must know how to describe, implement, and use objects that are distributed over unknown networks. People must be able to develop applications that work with different underlying frameworks. Objects from one company must be able to communicate and cooperate with objects from other companies. Whole systems must be able to make assumptions about basic object service infrastructures, just as today, programs can be written that are, to a large extent, ignorant of the underlying operating system.

For all its imperfections, the OMG is clearly the industry's best hope of achieving standards for object-based components. It has already achieved remarkable agreements in the following areas:

- How object interfaces are defined. The OMG has defined IDL (Interface Definition Language), which gives a language-independent way of describing the public interface objects present to the world.
- How operations are called on objects. The OMG has already defined language bindings for C and C++ and is working on other important languages.
- How objects are distributed. The OMG has defined the basic features of the underlying architecture for support of distribution of objects across processes or machines. This architecture is called the CORBA (Common Object

Request Broker Architecture). CORBA defines the ORB (Object Request Broker), which is the basic technology for distributing objects and routing method invocations. The OMG is now working on interoperability between ORBs, so that different implementations of the ORB can work cooperatively.

- What types of object services are used. The OMG has voted on standards for many object services, including Life Cycle (how objects are created and destroyed), Naming (how objects are located by name in a multiuser context), Events (how objects create and respond to external events), and, of course, Persistence (how objects are stored on a long-term basis). It is the last of these services that is the focus of this book.

Outline of This Book

0. Introduction

This chapter provides an introduction to this book, a background to the OMG, a historical perspective on the problems of the object components industry, and biographical information about the author.

1. The Making of a Standard

Chapter 1 describes some of the political intrigue that went into this standard. This chapter will be of interest to people who like knowing about the politics of standards and who like to know the personalities involved in this kind of decision-making process. This chapter can be skipped by those who just want to understand the standard itself. For those of us who lived through the making of the Persistence Standard, this chapter is probably the most interesting in the book, and possibly the most controversial.

2. The Goals of Persistence

Chapter 2 describes the goals of the Persistent Object Service specification. It describes the concept of datastore independence, giving code examples. It also discusses the idea of datastore plugability, or how datastore vendors plug their products into this service. This chapter presents a high-level view of the POS architecture, especially as it relates to the client API (Application Programming Interface) and the datastore pluggable interface, the SPI (Service Provider Interface).

3. The OMG Object Model

Chapter 3 describes the OMG Object Model. It contains sections on location independence, implementation independence, and the Object Request Broker (ORB). It also describes the concepts of IDL, the OMG Interface Definition Language, which is described more fully in Chapter 4. Chapter 3 defines the basic concepts of interface, operations, and method implementations. It describes some of the major object services related to Persistence with sections on Life Cycle, Naming, Transactions, Concurrency, Security, and Query.

4. Introduction to IDL

Chapter 4 is an introduction to IDL. It describes the major components of an IDL definition, including method prototypes, most supported data types, environment, operations, attributes, and exceptions. It also describes the C bindings, which show how methods are implemented in C. Examples are given in the SOM implementation of the CORBA specification.

5. The Interfaces of Persistence

Chapter 5 describes each of the interfaces of Persistence, with detailed discussions on each of the operations. This chapter also points out problem areas in the specification and possible solutions.

6. The Application Developer Perspective

There are three major perspectives from which Persistence can be viewed. The highest view is as seen by the application developer, the person using object components to develop an application. Chapter 6 describes what application developers need to understand. It describes how Persistence can be related to Transactions, how embedded objects are managed, how persistent IDs are used, and how persistent IDs relate to object references.

7. The Object Implementor Perspective

Chapter 7 describes Persistence as seen by the object implementor, the person who is implementing object components that will serve as the building blocks for applications. Chapter 7 discusses the concept of protocol, that is, how data is moved in and out of an object. It describes the protocol based on the Externalization Service and gives the arguments for making this the universal protocol for all objects.

8. The Datastore Vendor Perspective

Chapter 8 describes Persistence as seen by a datastore provider wanting to plug into the service. This chapter describes exactly what such a datastore must implement in order to be an OMG compatible datastore. The chapter looks at some case studies of existing datastore products that are plugging into this service, including relational databases and POSIX files.

9. The Vision

Chapter 9 puts the Persistent Object Service in an overall context of software development, present and future.

One might ask why this book is necessary. After all, the OMG has published this standard, and it is freely available. Many products will soon be hitting the market, all claiming to be compliant with the OMG Persistence Proposal.

The official Persistent Object Service specification is sparse. It includes less than fifty pages and a large number of superfluous interfaces, interfaces that are included as examples on how something might be done, not requirements for how things must be done. Some of these examples were added not to elucidate, but to placate, as is often the case with a document that is as much a historical record of political compromise as it is an attempt to define a standard.

I have spoken to dozens of software developers who have tried to make sense out of the Persistence Specification and failed. These are highly intelligent engineers with many years of experience reading and interpreting technical documents. If engineers like these cannot make sense out of the specification, what hope has the application developer?

Yet it is my belief that the ideas of the Persistence Specification are simple. When I have explained the standard, I have had few problems. It is the specification that is obviously complicated, not the ideas behind it.

I believe this book will fulfill a critical need. I hope it will accomplish the following purposes:

- Give enough background about the overall OMG architecture and object programming model so that readers can understand how Persistence fits into the overall picture.
- Describe the architectural goals the POS was intended to accomplish.
- Describe the client programming model, showing exactly how client code stores and restores objects.
- Describe how objects should be written so that they can be stored in any OMG compliant datastore.
- Describe how datastore products plug into the service, with examples of existing datastore products that have already been integrated into this service.
- Describe some of the problems with the standard and show how these might be resolved in the future.

If you are either a client of persistence, a producer of persistence products, or just one who is interested in a major standard, one that will have a dramatic influence on object persistence products and the industry as a whole over the next ten years, this book is for you. If you work for a company that is using, or expects to be using object technology over the next few years, you cannot possibly afford to be unaware of this work. If you are considering buying an object-oriented database in the near future, you need to understand this important alternative.

Acknowledgments

I am always nurtured by the constant faith and encouragement of my wife, Alice Sessions. She is a natural-born teacher and realizes the value of a good book, especially a good book that has actually been finished. Like all great teachers, she knows when to prod, when to encourage, and when to lie low.

My children, Emily and Michael, are both intrigued by the book-writing process. They have learned to put up with the eccentricities of a father who carries a computer more often than a wallet and who will whip out his laptop at a birthday party (never my own children's, I do have some sense of priorities!), at a skating rink, or at a fast food stop, and just "jot down a few notes."

Many people have been part of the Persistence Specification, and I owe all of them a debt of thanks. The most important is Dan Chang, of IBM Santa Theresa. Dan worked closely with me for over a year, developing the ideas that became the OMG specification and convincing the world that these ideas were important. In *The Wisdom of Teams*, Katzenbach and Smith describe these characteristics of high performance teams:

- They are obsessive about their goals.
- They are composed of team members who are exceptionally committed to each other.
- They outperform all reasonable expectations.

Dan and I were such a team, and it was one of the great experiences of my professional career.

Others contributed to the OMG Persistence Specification. George Copeland, of IBM Austin and Mike Powell, of SunSoft edited the final compromise and added several good technical ideas. Rick Cattell, of SunSoft was involved in some of the early discussions. Don Belisle, of IBM Austin, coauthored my original OMG Persistence proposal. Alan Synder and Mark Hepner, both from SunSoft, were part of the original IBM/SunSoft team trying to work out a common architecture. We received good review comments from Steve Munroe, Mike Conner, and Ashok Malhatra (all IBMers), among others. We received management support from Jerry Ronga, Jo Cheng, Larry Loucks, and Don Haderle. Guylaine Cantin worked closely on the first implementation of the Persistence Specification and contributed many original ideas on plugging relational databases into the persistence framework. Bob Orfali, coauthor of *The Client/Server Survival Guide* and many other books on my essential reading list, has been a great supporter and special advisor over the years.

I like to write in coffeehouses. Fortunately, Austin has a wonderful collection of coffeehouses that will let you unfold your laptop, spread out your papers, and lose yourself in the process of writing, all for the cost of a cup of coffee. The one where I have written more of this book than any other is "Texpresso." I appreciate Dave and Scott's good-natured tolerance of my activities and their constant refueling of my creativity with the best cappuccino in Texas.

This book has benefited from many careful reviewers. I especially thank Guylaine Cantin, who gave an extraordinary line-by-line review. Also, George Copeland, Mark Hapner, John Henekel, Bob Orfali, Charlie Redlin, and Clovis Tondo have all given a thorough reading and have contributed many excellent suggestions.

Prentice-Hall is, as always, a pleasure to work with. I am very grateful to my ever supportive editor, Greg Doench, and for the careful work of my copy editor, Mary Lou Nohr, who also created the index.

Although this book discusses the work of many people and work done during my tenure at IBM, nothing in this book should be taken as representing the opinion of anybody other than myself, and nothing in this book should be taken as a commitment by IBM to produce any particular product or to add any particular features to any product.

About the Author

Roger Sessions was one of the principal architects of the OMG Persistent Object Service Specification and was the technical lead for the first IBM Persistent Object Service Implementation. He was the Architect and Lead Programmer for the Persistence Framework of SOM version 1.0, one of the IBM products on which the POS specification is based. He was on the IBM SOM programming team since its inception in 1990 until 1995, when Roger left IBM to found Object-Watch, Inc., a company specializing in offering training, consulting, and mentoring to companies starting to adopt Distributed Object Technology. He now travels throughout the world teaching and consulting.

Roger is the author of two other books: *Class Construction in C and C++; Object-Oriented Programming Fundamentals* and *Reusable Data Structures for C.* He is the coauthor of many papers on the System Object Model (SOM), IBM's implementation of the OMG CORBA specification. He has spoken at over thirty conferences throughout the world on the principles of object-oriented programming, C++, SOM, and object persistence. He has given SOM tutorials at OOP-SLA, OS/2 World, IBM OO conferences, and others, and has consulted on many large-scale SOM projects. He is widely considered the world's leading expert in SOM and DSOM technology.

He can be reached through ObjectWatch, Inc., in Austin Texas.

The Making of a Standard

To the casual reader, the Persistent Object Service specification is a dry, technical document. Like many such documents, it is tedious to read and difficult to understand. To those of us who lived through its creation, it is a story of romance, intrigue, determination, and triumph.

This chapter is my own personal memoir, a time of history as seen through the eyes of one of the participants. I don't pretend this narrative is unbiased and detached. For over a year of my life, the pursuit of this standard was the all-encompassing quest of my professional life. I could no more be unbiased about its history than I could be clinically disinterested in the life of my children.

I hope this chapter adds some human warmth to a cold document, and I hope it gives some insight into how an organization like OMG accomplishes its work.

1.1   Product Background: SOM

In 1992 IBM came out with a product implementing OMG's CORBA specification. This product was called the System Object Model (SOM) and gave programmers the ability to define and implement objects in a language-neutral manner.

SOM was considered by many to be an important advance in the state of the art of object-oriented programming. It defined an architecture for implementing objects in one language and using them from a different language. Programmers could implement objects in C, for example, and use these implementations as the basis for implementations in some other language, say, Smalltalk. The new object implementations could even override methods of the original objects.

Let's consider a simple example to see how this works. We will give this example in Interface Definition Language (IDL), the accepted interface specification language of the OMG. We will describe IDL in more detail later, but we will keep this example simple enough so that most object-oriented programmers can follow without a prior understanding of IDL.

Let's say we have four classes: `animal`, `dog`, `littleDog`, and `bigDog`. animal defines the concept of "nameability" by defining the methods `set_name` and `get_name` and the concept of "printability" by defining the method `print`. The `print` method will display the name of the animal.

The IDL for animal looks like:

```
interface animal : Object {
  void set_name(in string newName);
  string get_name();
  void print();
  implementation {
    string name;    /* Data member */
  };
};
```

The pseudocode implementation of these animal methods looks like:

```
void animal::set_name(string newName)
{
  set datamember name to newName;
}
string animal::get_name()
{
  return datamember name;
}
void animal::print()
{
  print string "My name is: ";
  print datamember name;
}
```

The dog class is derived from animal. It adds a new method, bark, and overrides the animal print method. IDL does not give a syntax for specifying method overrides, so we will use the SOM-specific syntax.

The IDL for dog looks like:

```
interface dog : animal {
  void bark();
  implementation {
    override print;
  };
};
```

The pseudocode implementation of dog looks like:

```
void dog::bark()
{
  print string "unknown dog noise";
}
void dog::print()
{
  invoke animal::print()
  invoke dog::bark()
}
```

The classes littleDog and bigDog are both derived from dog and do nothing more than override the dog bark method. Their IDL definitions look like:

```
interface littleDog : dog {
  implementation {
    override bark;
  };
};
interface bigDog : dog {
  implementation {
    override bark;
  };
};
```

The pseudocode implementation of littleDog and bigDog is:

```
void littleDog::bark()
{
  print string "woof woof";
}
void bigDog::bark()
{
  print string "WOOF WOOF";
}
```

The pseudocode for a SOM client program could look like this:

```
declare pooh animal;
declare Snoopy dog;
declare toto littleDog;
declare lassie bigDog;

invoke set_name on pooh with "Pooh";
invoke set_name on Snoopy with "Snoopy";
invoke set_name on toto with "Toto";
invoke set_name on lassie with "Lassie";

invoke print on pooh;
invoke print on Snoopy;
invoke print on toto;
invoke print on lassie;
```

The output we expect from this program is:

```
1. My name is Pooh
2. My name is Snoopy
3. unknown dog noise
4. My name is Toto
5. woof woof
6. My name is Lassie
7. WOOF WOOF
```

The most interesting part of this example is the comparison between lines 3, 5, and 7. They are all being generated by the dog::print method, in particular, line 4:

```
1. void dog::print()
2. {
3.   invoke animal::print()
4.   invoke dog::bark()
5. }
```

This shows the ability of the bark method to resolve dynamically—depending not on a compile-time awareness of the class of the object associated with the method, but on a runtime awareness of the class of the object on which the method was invoked.

This, of course, is not a unique feature of SOM. All object-oriented programming languages support this feature, usually called dynamic method resolution. In fact, this capability is at the very heart of framework design.

What is unique about SOM is the ability to support inheritance and dynamic method resolution in a language-independent manner. The SOM architecture supports animal being implemented in one language, dog in another, littleDog and bigDog in other languages, and clients of all the classes working in yet some other language.

The choice of a language for one class implementation has no impact on the language choices for the other implementations, and clients neither know nor care which language(s) were used.

This is a remarkable architecture and is designed to address one of the fundamental stumbling blocks to object-oriented code reuse. It basically gives class libraries the reuse characteristics of procedural libraries, which have long enjoyed a separation between the language of the library implementation and the language of the client code.

SOM was first released with three major frameworks. A distributed framework, often called DSOM, was designed to implement the distributed characteristics of the CORBA specification, namely the ORB features. A replication framework, often called RSOM, was designed to facilitate the development of workgroup applications. And a persistent framework, often called PSOM, was designed to allow SOM objects to be stored in a variety of datastores.

1.2 The History

Against this background, OMG issued in October of 1992 their Request for Proposals (RFP) for a Persistent Object Service (POS). The rules were simple. Companies had until March 1993 to submit preliminary Persistence proposals. Companies would then have until May to examine each other's proposals, decide which companies had compatible proposals and, if desired, prepare new merged proposals. Final proposals were due in May, at which time evaluations and final voting would begin. The winning proposal would be the official OMG specification for object persistence, one of a suite of related OMG standards.

1.2.1 The Beginning

Mike Conner suggested that perhaps I should respond to the RFP by submitting a specification based on the Persistence Framework of SOM. Mike was the chief architect and visionary for the SOM project, and I was the technical lead of the Persistence Framework. From this offhand suggestion began an unpredictable and all-consuming saga that would not come to a close for over eighteen months and would end up changing forever the way the world would think of object persistence.

Although OMG had been in existence for some time by now, IBM had only recently become an active member and had never officially participated in the process of an OMG specification. I was fortunate to enlist the aid of Don Belisle, who was IBM's official OMG representative and who, more than anybody else at IBM, understood the political ins and outs of OMG. Together we prepared to submit what we believed to be the official IBM response to the Persistence RFP.

Our proposal was based on the SOM Persistence Framework, an open framework with support for storing objects in both traditional databases and file systems. This was driven by our analysis of the market, which indicated that most customers wanted to store object data in their existing corporate-centric databases, in particular, their relational databases, and relatively few cared about storing data in the so-called object-oriented databases.

Shortly before the deadline, we learned that we were not the only group within IBM planning on submitting the "official" IBM response. Dan Chang and Floyd Schakelford were submitting a specification based on a mainframe IBM product called CICS. This precipitated weeks of high-level phone calls and political maneuvering as each group believed that it truly represented the real interests of IBM. My own prejudicial belief that anybody working on mainframe products couldn't know anything about object-oriented programming probably did not contribute to a fast resolution.

Dan, Floyd, Don, and I met in Atlanta about a week before the OMG deadline. After a full day of face-to-face debate, I had to acknowledge that not only did Dan and Floyd know how to spell object-oriented, but they actually had some important insights into the special problems faced by storing object data in traditional datastores. Although we did not have time to prepare a joint response to the OMG, we did meet long enough to commit to preparing a revised joint proposal when the second round of proposals was due, and we agreed to announce this at the San Diego OMG meeting in March.

The proposals were due a week before the San Diego meeting. As the March deadline approached, we became increasingly anxious to see what our competition would be. We soon found out.

1.2.2   Round 1

Four Persistence proposals were submitted. Two were from IBM, my proposal and the Chang/Schakelford proposal. One was submitted from NCR/AT&T and was based on the C++ streams package. We did not see this as a major threat. The fourth proposal was a very different thing. This was submitted by SunSoft, and cosponsored by DEC, Groupe Bull, Itasco Systems, Novell, O2, ODI, Objectivity, Ontos, Oracle, Servio, Tivoli, and Versant. These names included all of the important players in object-oriented databases. This proposal was spearheaded by Rick Cattell, one of the best-known individuals in the field.

The SunSoft proposal was nicknamed JOSS (Joint Object Services Submission) to reflect the fact that it was cosubmitted by many companies and included sections for multiple object services, not just Persistence. The Persistence portion of the JOSS proposal was based on work done by the Object Database Management Group (ODMG).

The ODMG is a group of object-oriented database companies who were trying to agree on an industry standard for object-oriented databases. Their hope was that an industry standard would lead to more widespread acceptance of OODBs, much like the SQL standard led to widespread acceptance of relational databases. This consortium included many of the names that were part of the JOSS proposal and was also led by Rick Cattell of SunSoft. The ODMG companies controlled between them more than ninety per cent of the object-oriented database market.

The JOSS proposal was based largely on the architecture of one company, ODI. ODI is the most successful object-oriented database company and therefore in the best position to call the shots.

It is hard to describe the feeling one has after six months of focused, isolated effort on a project and then finds he is competing with a phalanx composed of a who's who in the object persistence industry. The situation was not lost on my management, who suggested that discretion might be the better part of valor, and perhaps we should accept the SunSoft offer of withdrawing our proposal and joining them for the next round.

As we examined the JOSS proposal, we decided it was a much weaker proposal than we might have expected, given the large number of highly visible companies supposedly involved in the effort. Its most glaring weakness was that it was completely biased toward using object-oriented databases as datastores, a strategy that we believed was out of touch with industry reality. Of course, this is not surprising, considering the proposal was prepared by object-oriented database companies.

Basing an industry standard for object persistence on object-oriented databases would have been a serious problem for an industry that has little interest in object-oriented databases. At that time, object-oriented databases accounted for only about one-seventh of the OO industry. The combined revenues of all object-oriented database companies put together was dwarfed by the revenue of any one of the major relational DB vendors. And the amount of corporate-centric data (the data companies rely on to run their companies) stored in object-oriented databases was minuscule, measured in tenths of one percent.

The proposal also had several technical flaws. One was lack of support for CORBA objects, the very objects OMG was trying to standardize. Another was its closed architecture, which prevented people from adding or modifying functionality. Another was lack of support for storing and restoring objects whose type is not known at compile time. This would eliminate its use for compound documents, which often contain objects whose types are unknown until run time.

The San Diego meeting contained little drama. The various groups made their pitches. This was considered by most to be just the preliminary round when everybody sizes up the competition and forms new alliances for the final round of proposals. I was a little intimidated by the steady stream of dignitaries. Here I was presenting directly to people whom I had before only seen as speakers in major conferences: Rick Cattell, Drew Wade, and one of my most admired writers, Mary Loomis.

The low point (literally) of my whole OMG experience occurred in San Diego. I decided I would sneak out of a particularly boring presentation. I found an unobtrusive side aisle and made my way as quietly as possible to the back of the room. In one sickening instant, I found myself hurtling to the floor. The presentation came to a dead halt as the participants focused their full attention on trying to figure out who was the klutz who had tripped over a PC cord and wondering just how badly he had damaged Mary Loomis's brand-new laptop computer, now dangling precariously on the edge of the table.

1.2.3   Round 2

Convinced of the superiority of our proposal, Dan Chang and I, with the support of our management, decided to press ahead. Floyd Schakelford had decided to focus his efforts on the Life Cycle Proposal, which was also being decided. As Dan and I had promised, we worked together to combine our two proposals, incorporating the best features of each. We redoubled our efforts to make sure we defined the most open architecture possible, with support for as many different datastore products as we could imagine. We microscopically examined every parameter of every operation of every interface. By the time the revised proposals were due in May, we were convinced we had a proposal that achieved the following goals:

- Support for relational databases and other corporate-centric datastores.
- A single client-level API for storing objects regardless of the underlying datastore.

- A technology allowing completely datastore-neutral objects.
- An open architecture that would allow new datastore products to plug in at any time.

We had no idea what was going on with the JOSS proposal during this time. We assumed they were addressing the weaknesses in their proposal. We had certainly taken advantage of every opportunity to point out the lack of support for corporate-centric datastores and the many technical deficiencies. In May 1993, we saw their revised proposal, and what we saw was the one thing we never anticipated.

I first received the revised JOSS proposal as a PostScript® file. I immediately sent it to the printer and watched as the sheets came off one by one. Even from this cursory examination, one fact seemed clear. The proposal was almost unchanged from the original version. It was still a closed-architecture, OODB proposal.

The new JOSS proposal was not completely devoid of surprises, however. The most interesting one was that NCR/AT&T had withdrawn their proposal and signed on as cosubmitters of the JOSS proposal. Three new companies had also signed on, increasing the JOSS consortium from 13 to 17.

This meant that it would be just Dan and me against JOSS. Although we continued to believe in the technical superiority of our proposal, it was clear that SunSoft had been doing their political homework. Most people gave us little chance for success. Even IBMers would ask us for copies of the JOSS proposal, assuming that our proposal was on its last breath of life and that JOSS would soon be setting the standard for object persistence.

1.2.4   Paris

On a beautiful May morning in Paris, Dan and I presented the fruits of our efforts to the Technical Task Force of the Object Management Group. It was immediately obvious that our direct support for storing standard CORBA objects, our open architecture, and our support for traditional datastores struck a responsive chord with the audience. In our trip report, we gave this description:

> We received our first major breakthrough on Wednesday afternoon. Since the evaluation process remained quite chaotic with the SunSoft and IBM teams occasionally attacking each other, a motion was made to form a neutral Persistence Service Evaluation subgroup. We raised the question about the neutrality of SunSoft cosubmitters in joining the subgroup. This started a debate over the nature of cosubmissions in the SunSoft Persistence Proposal. It was agreed that any company that so desired could withdraw as a cosubmitter from the SunSoft proposal and be allowed to join the Persistence Service Evaluation subgroup.

The next five minutes were mayhem, as companies were literally shout-
ing for recognition from the chair so they could withdraw their cosubmitter status. During that period, as best as we could tell, every cosubmitter
present at the meeting had withdrawn cosubmitter status.

That evening, in a small Parisian bistro, Dan and I drank *cafe au lait* and discussed for the first time the possibility that we were going to win.

As we left Paris we began a two-month period during which the two Persistence proposals were to be evaluated. Rick Cattell was as devoted to his proposal
as we were to ours, and one can imagine the heated exchange of claims, charges,
and countercharges that flew back and forth across the OMG email network.

By June, it was clear that Dan and I were being taken seriously. Within
IBM, people who only months ago couldn't be cajoled to take copies of our proposal were now poring over the minutest details. Suddenly it seemed that everybody at IBM had an opinion on what we were doing and how we should deal with
SunSoft. And suddenly, what had started as a minor, throwaway effort by some
rogue engineers within IBM had turned into a major political intrigue with corporate ramifications that to this day I can only guess at.

1.2.5   Chicago

The next OMG meeting was just outside Chicago in July. This was to be the
meeting at which the evaluation committee was to present its report, and the
Task Force would vote on Persistence. Dan and I had arrived a day early to com-
pose a formal response to the latest network mail from Rick Cattell. At eleven
o'clock we received a phone call from Mike Conner.

Mike Conner reported directly to Larry Loucks, the Vice President of Software Architecture for Personal Systems Products. In addition to being the chief
architect for the SOM product line, Mike was probably the most highly regarded
OO strategist within the IBM corporation. He said that he was meeting with representatives from SunSoft and that they wanted to try to work out a compromise. He asked Dan and me to join a meeting with himself and Mike Powell of
SunSoft. Mike Powell was the chief Object Architect in SunSoft and probably the
most powerful individual in the SunSoft organization. He was widely rumored to
be one of only three or four people in the world who had the number to the car
phone of the Sun president.

At first, Dan and I refused to attend the meeting. We were working on a
very tight deadline and felt we had been burned before in attempts to reach compromises with SunSoft. We finally agreed to meet for one hour. We said that at
the end of the hour we would decide if SunSoft was serious about working
together. If so, we would stay. If not, we would leave and resume working on our
mail response. Mike agreed to these conditions.

The meeting was conducted in one of the private conference rooms of the
Pheasant Run Hotel. It was attended by Mike Powell and Rick Cattell of Sun-
Soft; and Mike Conner, Dan, and me from IBM. The meeting was very cordial.
Mike Powell appeared to genuinely respect the work Dan and I had done and

made it clear he would personally guarantee the cooperation of others at Sun-Soft. At the end of the meeting, we agreed to formally request that the OMG grant us a four-month extension to allow us to work out our differences and submit a joint proposal from IBM and SunSoft.

The OMG was only too happy to grant this extension, since they are heavily biased toward any action that might lead to consensus rather than voting. And so began the next phase of the saga, as we worked to define how these two architectures that appeared to have little in common other than both claiming to support Object Persistence could be merged into a meaningful unit.

Dan and I had long advocated treating the SunSoft™ architecture as a specialization of our Persistent Data Service, our standard plug for datastores, and continued to insist that the POS had to support all datastores. SunSoft, on the other hand, thought our architecture should be treated as a special case for their own storage mechanisms, with the OODB architecture the norm.

Mike Powell had assigned two very capable engineers to work with Dan and me: Mark Hepner, who had been involved in the original JOSS proposal, and Alan Snyder, who is well recognized in the object world. Although the next three months were stress filled, we were making good progress and were close to arriving at a meeting of the minds.

1.2.6   Stockholm

In September, 1993, Mark, Dan, and I prepared a joint presentation for the Stockholm OMG meeting. (Alan was on vacation.) We showed how we proposed to put together the two architectures and described the remaining issues. We were all feeling good as we prepared for our trip.

The night before I was to leave I found out that Mike Powell had been shown the presentation and had a major problem with our work. He wanted the presentation stopped, his own team withdrawn from the project, and would personally take over the negotiations. I never saw Mark or Alan again.

The months of stress reached a crisis during the flight to Stockholm. Dan and I knew we had done an excellent job merging the two proposals and believed our work would be warmly received by the OMG. We certainly did not want to report that Mike Powell had reduced two months of close technical collaboration to rubble in less than twelve hours.

As the flight landed in Stockholm, a strategy came clearly to my mind. We would do the presentation, with or without SunSoft. If they refused, we would present the work as our own thoughts and let SunSoft explain their position.

The next evening we met with Geoff Lewis and Rick Cattell of SunSoft. Geoff had been closely associated with OMG since the beginning and was highly respected for his contributions to the standards activity. It was clear that in this case, however, Mike Powell was calling the shots.

Geoff explained that Mike was not happy with our work and had called off the presentation. I told Geoff that we had decided to do the presentation, with or without them. If they didn't like it, they could do their own presentation, explaining their position and what issues they felt remained. I was met with stunned disbelief. Geoff said we could not do this. He reminded me that Dan and I had agreed not to make any unilateral public statements. I reminded him that we had committed to an accurate status presentation in Stockholm. For a full minute, nobody uttered a word.

Two points were obvious. First, neither Geoff nor Rick Cattell *could* explain SunSoft's position, since neither had a clue as to what it was that had so upset Mike Powell. Second, they couldn't possibly put together a credible presentation in twelve hours, given they were thousands of miles from home, equipment, and technical expertise, and were operating with little sleep and under severe jet lag.

After an eternal silence, Geoff asked me a single question. "Do you have the authority to make this decision on behalf of IBM?" Now anybody who knows IBM knows how ridiculous this question is. A decision like this would have to go through twelve committees, require input from most of the lawyers in the corporation, take six months to finalize, and, at the end, would hardly be recognizable as to what the question had been in the first place. So I gave Geoff the only logical answer I could think of: "I have the full authority of IBM to make this decision. If you want to question this, you may contact my management."

Telling Geoff he could contact my management was a safe risk. We had crossed the international dateline, he had no access to electronic mail, and it was now two o'clock on Saturday morning back in Austin. The earliest he could possibly reach anybody would be twelve hours after we had already finished the presentation. As we left the meeting, we told Geoff to let us know the next morning whether he would be with us or against us.

The next day we were told SunSoft would be part of our presentation. They asked only that we remove two slides and slightly modify another, to which we readily agreed. And another strange chapter in the Object Persistence story had come to an end.

As we had expected, our presentation was warmly received by the OMG, with most participants marveling at how much progress had been made and how well IBM and SunSoft were cooperating with each other.

1.2.7 The Denouement

Having Mike Powell directly involved required us to change strategies in a hurry. No longer would this be a reasonable technical discussion between four, like-minded engineers. We were going to need a very heavy hitter. The obvious choice would have been Mike Conner, but he was unavailable for several months. The next best choice was George Copeland.

George was another of Larry Loucks's direct reports. He was an expert in the implementation of both relational and object-oriented databases. He was a founder and chief architect of Servio, the first of the OODB vendors. Even more important, he was a Senior Technical Staff Member, which gave him the necessary credentials to go against Mike Powell. I had talked to George several times about the OMG work, and I knew he understood and agreed with our technical direction. For the next several weeks, I worked closely with George, going through every interface, every operation, and every algorithm, until he understood the proposal as well as I did.

As little as two weeks before the November deadline, it was still not clear that the merger was going to work. Little communication had occurred between Mike and George. Dan and I shifted our focus from trying to work out a joint proposal to updating our own proposal, on the theory that the joint negotiation was likely to fail. Our new proposal was essentially our original proposal with more details on how specializations could accommodate the SunSoft architecture. This proposal had been rejected many times by SunSoft, but it was the only way we could see of achieving our original architectural goals.

The weekend the proposal was due, Mike and George finally started working together. As far as I could tell, neither slept for the next 48 hours. On the day of the OMG deadline, George was able to announce a compromise had been reached: IBM and SunSoft would make a joint Persistence submission.

The document George and Mike wrote described the high-level architecture Dan and I had developed and for which we had advocated for a year. It include full support for traditional datastores and a description on how the architecture could be specialized to support SunSoft architecture. The changes they made were almost entirely editorial in nature.

The saga that had begun over a year earlier was over. A new standard for Object Persistence had been born, and it was a standard that offered true persistence for CORBA objects, first-class support for traditional datastores, and run-time typing. The standard still required approval by OMG, but its passage was virtually guaranteed.

In November 1993, the OMG taskforce voted to recommend the new standard. In January, the required two-thirds majority of the member companies voted to accept this recommendation. In February, the OMG board of directors voted to accept the new proposal for Object Persistence and publish it in the next edition of the Object Services standards.

The Goals of Persistence

There are three important goals of Persistent Object Service (POS). They are:

- Support for corporate-centric datastores — Including relational databases, hierarchical databases, record-based file systems, and other datastores typical of those used to store the critical data of corporations.
- Datastore independence — A single, client-level API for storing objects regardless of the underlying datastore, and a single mechanism for object implementors to support.
- Open architecture — One that allows new datastore products to plug in at any time.

This chapter describes each of these goals in more detail and shows how the POS addresses each.

2.1 Support for Corporate-centric Datastores

Object-oriented database vendors sell their datastore products as the datastore of choice for objects. The world, according to the OODB vendors, is depicted in Figure 1. POS is all about storing objects. Why, then, do we care about datastores other than OODBs?

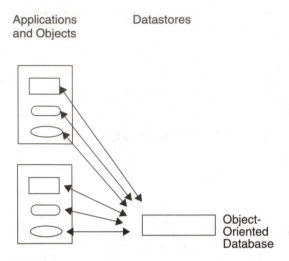

Figure 1. The World As Depicted by OODB Vendor

The fact is that the real world is very different from the vision projected by the OODB vendors. Very few corporations are storing any corporate-critical data in OODBs. The world they are facing is the object storage labyrinth shown in Figure 2.

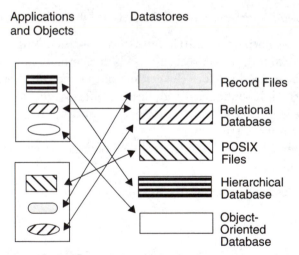

Figure 2. The World Faced by Applications Developers

So what does POS offer over OODBs? POS offers a simplifying solution to the object storage labyrinth. POS offers a single, industry-standard interface for storing objects to any underlying datastore. The POS vision is shown in Figure 3.

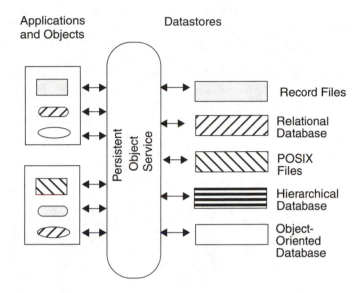

Figure 3. The POS Vision

With the rapidly increasing interest in corporate applications developers in object-oriented programming, why is there such a lag in adoption of object-oriented databases? The reason is that the vast bulk of the world's data is stored in traditional datastores, and the vast bulk of the world's programs are written under this assumption.

I believe that a fair estimate of today's data storage patterns is shown in Figure 4. As shown in this figure, the percentage of data currently stored in object-oriented databases is minuscule. This figure has been widely shown before most datastore vendors and many customers, and I have yet to hear anybody dispute the figures.

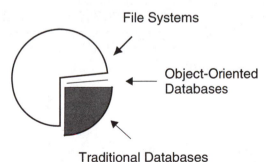

Figure 4. Percentage of World's Data in Different Datastores

As another estimate of the importance of the different datastores, we can look at actual product revenues. Figure 5 shows 1993 revenues of combined relational database vendors compared to combined object-oriented database vendors. As the figure shows, relational database revenues exceeded object-oriented database revenues by over 40 to 1. In fact, all of the object-oriented companies put together don't even approach the revenues of one of the major relational database companies.

This is not to say that object-oriented databases do not have an important niche in the market. It is not to say that they will not grow in importance over the next five years. But it is clear that any vision of them becoming the repository of choice for object data is at least ten years away, if it will ever come at all.

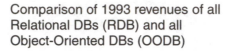

Comparison of 1993 revenues of all
Relational DBs (RDB) and all
Object-Oriented DBs (OODB)

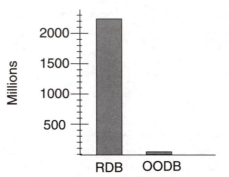

Figure 5. Comparison of Revenues

2.2 Client Datastore Independence

To understand the meaning of client-level, datastore-independent code, let's compare two programs that store their objects in two different datastores, using POS. The first saves its objects in a POSIX file using the POS. A POSIX file is the standard kind of file a C programmer sees, that is, a file created by `fopen` and written to by `fwrite` and referred to by a pathname. This code, with lines numbered for future reference, is:

```
1.   main()
2.   {
3.   /* Set up.
4.      ------- */
5.      somPersistencePOSIX_PID_POSIX pid;
6.      Account accnt;
7.      boolean done;
8.      string accntNo;
9.      Environment *ev = SOMEnvironmentNew();
10.     AccountNewClass(0,0);
```

```
11.
12. /* Get PID.
13.     -------- */
14.     pid = somPersistencePOSIX_PID_POSIXNew();
15.     __set_path(pid, ev, "/u/sherlock/accnts.dat");
16.
17. /* Main program loop.
18.     ----------------- */
19.     done = FALSE;
20.     while (!done) {
21.
22. /*    Restore account for updating.
23.       --------------------------- */
24.         accnt = _create(_Account, ev, pid);
25.         accntNo = readAccntNumber();
26.         _write_string(pid, ev, accntNo);
27.         _restore(accnt, ev, pid);
28.
29. /*    Update and store.
30.       ----------------- */
31.         updateAccount(accnt);
32.         _store(accnt, ev, pid);
33.
34.         _somFree(accnt);
35.         if(nomore()) done = TRUE;
36.     }
37.
38. /* Close up.
39.     --------- */
40.     _somFree(pid);
41.     SOMfree(ev);
42. }
```

Since this is the first program using POS that most readers have seen, we will look at the code in depth. The first two significant lines are:

```
5.      somPersistencePOSIX_PID_POSIX pid;
6.      Account accnt;
```

These lines declare objects of various types. The string "somPersistence" is in front of each of the SOM implementations of the POS defined types. This string distinguishes the object service to which a given interface belongs. The substring that follows this, "POSIX," "POF," "PO," or "PID," distinguishes the module in which a given type is defined. The remainder of the string (e.g., "PID_POSIX") is one of the standard types defined by the SOM POS implementation. We will omit the "somPersistence" and module name in this discussion.

Line 5 declares a `pid` of type PID_POSIX. A PID is an object that identifies the storage location of the persistent state for some object. Various specializations of PID exist for each of the different datastores. PID_POSIX is the PID we are using to describe simple POSIX files.

Line 6 declares an `accnt` of type `Account`, which is the object we will be storing. Although one cannot tell by looking at this line, Account is derived from the SOM implementation of the PO (Persistent Object).

```
7.      boolean done;
8.      string accntNo;
```

Lines 7 and 8 declare variables `done` and `accntNo`, a `boolean` and a `string`, respectively. A `boolean` is a standard IDL type that can be TRUE or FALSE. A string is a standard IDL type that maps to a C `char * ` type.

```
9.      Environment *ev = SOMEnvironmentNew();
```

Line 9 declares a variable of type pointer to `Environment`, allocates memory, and sets the pointer to the allocated memory. `Environment` is a predefined type in IDL. It contains various information, the most important of which is error return codes, called *exceptions* in IDL terminology. Exceptions are described in Section 4.10 on page 68. The IDL standard for C bindings says that the second parameter to a method call is always a pointer to an `Environment`. The first parameter is a reference to the target object.

```
10.     AccountNewClass(0,0);
```

Line 10 initializes the Account class.

```
14.     pid = somPersistencePOSIX_PID_POSIXNew();
```

Line 14 is one of many possible ways of instantiating objects. It uses a special macro of the form <classname>_new, where classname is the name of the class of the object that we are instantiating.

```
15.     __set_path(pid, ev, "/u/sherlock/accnts.dat");
```

Line 15 will be, for many readers, the first experience with an IDL operation invocation in C. IDL is intended to be language neutral; it defines only how interface operations are specified, not implemented or invoked. The invocation of an IDL operation in the C language is defined as looking like:

```
InterfaceName_OperationName(target_object,
   environment_pointer, additional parameters);
```

For the method invocation shown in line 15, the normal syntax would be:

```
15.     Account_set_path(pid, ev, "/u/sherlock/accnts.dat");
```

Since having to specify the InterfaceName as part of each method call becomes cumbersome, SOM allows the simplified syntax of

```
_OperationName(target_object,environment_pointer, additional parameters);
```

when the operation is unambiguous, that is, unique among all the interfaces used by this compilation unit. This syntax has the further advantage of more or less clearly distinguishing method invocations from procedure calls, since the former are preceded by the underscore character ("_") and the latter aren't.

Line 15 shows the one line of datastore-dependent code in the program. The POS intends the PID to be specialized for different datastores. The PID used here is specialized for POSIX files, as shown in line 17. When a PID is specialized, we can either add or modify behaviors. In this case we are going to add an attribute for the path of the file. An attribute is essentially a data member of an object with an associated set and get method. This is discussed in more detail in Section 4.9 on page 64.

```
19.     done = FALSE;
20.     while (!done) {
```

Lines 19 and 20 just start a while loop. Nothing special here.

```
24.       accnt = _create(_Account, ev, pid);
```

Line 24 illustrates another technique for instantiating objects. This line uses a special object called the class object. The class object is often called a class factory, because it knows, among other things, how to instantiate objects of a given class. The class object for any class, say, Account, is referenced by _<className>, say, _Account. We will not show the interface for the Account object at this point. For now, assume it is an object that represents an account record in a bank.

Notice the instantiation is done by using a standard method invocation on a normal object, in this case, the class object. This is clear if you remember two points. The first is that _create is a method invocation; the second is that the target object of a method invocation in the C bindings is always the first parameter of the method call. The second parameter of the invocation is the ubiquitous environment pointer. The third parameter is the pid associated with this object.

```
25.       accntNo = readAccntNumber();
26.       _write_string(pid, ev, accntNo);
```

Line 25 calls a procedure to read the desired account number and return the address of the resulting string. Line 26 places this string in the pid where it can be retrieved during the restore processing to locate the appropriate account record. How one places such information in the PID is undefined by POS. The method shown here is the IBM prototype implementation.

```
27.       _restore(accnt, ev, pid);
```

Line 27 shows the actual POS request to restore the object. Notice the target object is the object itself, which was already instantiated in line 24.

```
31.       updateAccount(accnt);
```

Line 31 calls some unspecified procedure to modify the account, probably through some object-oriented user interface.

```
32.         _store(accnt, ev, pid);
34.         _somFree(accnt);
```

Line 32 stores the newly updated account record back to the persistent store. Like the restore request, the target object of the method is the object being stored. Line 34 then frees the account object, since it has fulfilled its purpose. The next iteration of the loop will reinstantiate a new account object (see line 24).

It is not the purpose of this section to give a full discourse on the use of POS. We are just trying to give a feel for one of the ways this interface might be used at the client level. Later, we will discuss how the Transaction Service can be used to store and restore objects automatically on an as-needed basis.

When we examine the changes needed in this program to store our account object to a relational database, we start to get a sense of what we mean by client-level data independence. The example here shows code used to store objects to DB2/2™ and DB2/6000™, the first relational databases to fully exploit the POS architecture. We will show the new version of the program here, then just walk through the modified lines. Modified lines are shown in boldface.

```
1.   main()
2.   {
3.   /* Set up.
4.       ------- */
5.       somPersistenceDB2_PID_DB2 pid;
6.       Account accnt;
7.       boolean done;
8.       string accntNo;
9.       Environment *ev = SOMEnvironmentNew();
10.      AccountNewClass(0,0);
11.
12.  /* Get pid.
13.      -------- */
14.      pid = somPersistenceDB2_PID_DB2New();
15.      __set_dbalias(pid, ev, "corporate");
16.
17.  /* Main program loop.
18.      ------------------ */
19.      done = FALSE;
20.      while (!done) {
21.
22.  /*   Restore account for updating.
23.       --------------------------- */
24.      accnt = _create(_Account, ev, pid);
25.      accntNo = readAccntNumber();
26.      _write_string(pid, ev, accntNo);
27.      _restore(accnt, ev, pid);
28.
```

```
29.  /*    Update and store.
30.        ----------------- */
31.        updateAccount(accnt);
32.        _store(accnt, ev, pid);
33.
34.        _somFree(accnt);
35.        if(nomore()) done = TRUE;
36.      }
37.
38.  /* Close up.
39.      --------- */
40.      _somFree(pid);
41.      SOMfree(ev);
42.  }
```

Notice that the only code changes are in lines 5, 14, and 15. These lines are:

```
5.         somPersistenceDB2_PID_DB2 pid;
14.        pid = somPersistenceDB2_PID_DB2New();
15.        __set_dbalias(pid, ev, "corporate");
```

Line 5 now declares the pid to be a type specialized for DB2. Line 14 uses the new class instantiator. And Line 15 puts some DB2-specific information in the pid (rather than the POSIX file-specific information). Other than these changes, everything remains the same.

In general, any client-level datastore specific code is isolated to the PID. If we wish, we can remove even the little datastore-specific code we have in our program. The next version is completely datastore independent and is compatible at the binary level with any datastore.

```
1.   main()
2.   {
3.   /* Set up.
4.       ------- */
5.       somPersistencePID_PID_DS pid;
6.       string pidType;
7.       string pidString;
8.       Account accnt;
9.       boolean done;
10.      string accntNo;
11.      Environment *ev = SOMEnvironmentNew();
12.      AccountNewClass(0,0);
13.
14.  /* Get pid.
15.      -------- */
16.      pidType = determinePidType();
17.      pid = dynamicallyAllocateObject(pidType);
18.      pidString = getPIDString();
19.      _set_PIDString(pid, ev, pidString);
20.
```

```
21. /* Main program loop.
22.       ----------------- */
23.     done = FALSE;
24.     while (!done) {
25.
26. /*    Restore account for updating.
27.       -------------------------- */
28.         accnt = _create(_Account, ev, pid);
29.         accntNo = readAccntNumber();
30.         _write_string(pid, ev, accntNo);
31.         _restore(accnt, ev, pid);
32.
33. /*    Update and store.
34.       ---------------- */
35.         updateAccount(accnt);
36.         _store(accnt, ev, pid);
37.
38.         _somFree(accnt);
39.         if(nomore()) done = TRUE;
40.     }
41.
42. /* Close up.
43.     --------- */
44.     _somFree(pid);
45.     SOMfree(ev);
46. }
```

The lines that have been changed or added are those shown in bold. They are:

```
5.      somPersistencePID_PID_DS pid;
6.      string pidType;
7.      string pidString;
        /* ... */
16.     pidType = determinePidType();
17.     pid = dynamicallyAllocateObject(pidType);
18.     pidString = getPIDString();
19.     _set_PIDString(pid, ev, pidString);
```

Line 5 had declared a specialization of the PID. Now it declares the most generic PID. Lines 6 and 7 both declare strings that will be filled in at run time. The first is a string that will contain the type of the PID, and the second is the data values to which the PID must be set.

```
16.     pidType = determinePidType();
17.     pid = dynamicallyAllocateObject(pidType);
```

Line 16 invokes some function (not method) to determine the type of the PID. This may be done be reading a value stored in a file, by interacting with a human being, or by some other heuristic. Line 17 then dynamically instantiates a PID of the correct type. This, too, is a function invocation. This function can be implemented with any of several advanced techniques, most of which are discussed in Section 4.20 on page 118.

```
18.     pidString = getPIDString();
19.     _set_PIDString(pid, ev, pidString);
```

Lines 18 and 19 are critical lines from the perspective of datastore independence. Line 18 gets a string value from someplace. This someplace might be a user typing in a string, a read from a file, or an automatic generation by some other code fragment. Line 19 now sets the PID internal data to values that are somehow part of this string. Clearly, the value of this string must be carefully defined. What should the value of the string be?

According to POS, any `PID` supports a `get_PIDString` operation. This operation returns a string. What this string contains is not defined. What is implied is that the string can be passed into a new `PID` and used to recreate a data state identical to the data state that originally produced the string. A logical expectation is that the string contains the type of the `PID` (e.g., "PID_POSIX"), the values of the `PID` attributes (e.g., "/u/sherlock/accnts.dat"), and the values of any other data placed into the `PID` (e.g., the account number).

As you can see, client code using objects that support POS can be, to a large degree, independent of the underlying datastore that is holding the object's data. It is even possible to write code that is completely independent of the underlying datastore. And although this is an important goal of POS, it is by no means the most important goal. A much more important goal is to maintain datastore independence at the object level. This is the topic of the next section.

2.3   Object Datastore Independence

As important as datastore independence is to client code, it is far more critical to object code. The fundamental goal of CORBA is to enable a distributed objects industry. This means object implementors must be able to sell their class implementations to the widest possible audience. If they have to add any datastore-dependent code, even a few lines, they will suddenly find their audience sharply limited.

The implementor of our Account class would have most likely done the following, all of which are explored in depth in later chapters:

- Derived the Account class from some implementation of the POS-defined PO (PersistentObject) class. This derivation ensures that the object can be stored to any POS-compliant datastore.
- Derived the Account class from some protocol defining class, probably Streamable, which is described in Section 7.2 on page 173.
- Implemented whatever overridden methods are required by the chosen protocol.

All of these steps are described later. The important point now is that none are datastore dependent.

2.4   Open Architecture

The POS can be thought of as the glue between two unrelated systems. The first is the object and the object mechanisms. The second is the datastore.

The POS, as shown in Figure 6, includes two plugs, or sets of interfaces. The first is the interface used by client code, the interface that guarantees datastore independence. The second is the set into which datastores plug. These interfaces guarantee an open architecture, which invites any and all datastores to participate.

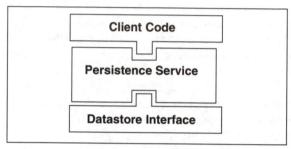

Figure 6. High-Level Overview of Persistence Service

The client plug shown in Figure 6 is composed primarily of the following interfaces:

- PO (Persistent Object) — An optional interface that clients use to store/ restore objects.
- PID (Persistent ID) — The identifier for the storage location of the persistent state of an object. This class is an abstract class. Clients will use specializations of this class.
- POM (Persistent Object Manager) — The interface for an object that manages store/restore requests. The design of the POS assumes the POM operations will be invoked by implementations of the PO, but other interpretations (which we discuss later) are possible.

The datastore plug shown in Figure 6 is composed primarily of one interface:

- PDS (Persistent Data Service) — An abstract definition of an object that knows how to store persistent data in some datastore. In general, there will be a collection of PDSs, each specialized for some datastore.

The relationships between these four primary components are shown in Figure 7. Let's follow the flow of a typical persistence request, say, a store invocation.

The client sets up the PID (1) and invokes the store on the persistent object (2). The persistent object passes on the store request to the POM (3). The POM looks at the PID and the object to determine which PDS can handle the restore. The POM forwards the store request to the appropriate PDS (4). The PDS then takes over the store, interacting directly with the persistent object and the datastore (5). Other scenarios are possible, but this is a typical one.

The PDS interface defines expectations of the POM. Since the POM uses only those operations defined in the PDS interface, it can make use of any specialization of the PDS. The only purpose of the PDS is to move data between an object and a datastore.

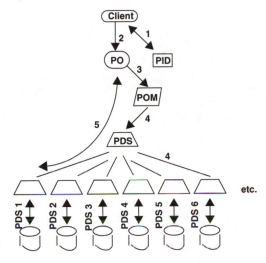

Figure 7. Components of POS

2.5 Summary

This chapter introduced the important interfaces of POS—how they are organized, how they interact, how they are used by clients, and how they are specialized by datastore providers. In the next chapters, we look at these interfaces in much more detail.

The OMG Object Model

OMG's CORBA specification defines an architecture that allows clients and objects to interact with each other. There are six main parts of the architecture, which we discuss in this section. These main pieces are object, clients, interfaces, the Object Request Broker, the Object Adapter, and the Language Bindings.

3.1 The Distributed Architecture

Let's start by looking at some basic definitions.

An *object* contains state (data) and methods (behaviors). An object method corresponds to some segment of code that will be executed against the state (if any) associated with the object.

A *client* is a segment of code that makes requests of objects. These requests may include input parameters and may return information as either updated parameters or return values.

The valid requests a client can make on a given object are defined by the interface(s) that the object supports. An *interface* contains some number of operations, any of which can be requested by the client.

When a client makes a request of an object, it does so by issuing that request to an *Object Request Broker* (ORB). The ORB must keep track of all the objects available and see to it that the request is routed to the correct one.

Once the correct object has been located, the ORB transfers the request to the object through an *Object Adapter* (OA). The Object Adapter is responsible for mapping the requested operation to a specific chunk of executable code. That code may correspond to a C++ method, a C procedure, an executable program, an interpreted ASCII file, or any other executable. Once the code executes, it processes any return values back through the Object Adapter, back to the ORB, and then back to the client.

When client code passes requests through to the ORB, it must do so through one of two mechanisms. The first is through ORB *procedures* that are defined in the CORBA architecture. This is a generally difficult interface. Much easier to use are the *language bindings*, which allow requests to the ORB to be made in a way more or less natural to a language. The language bindings for C++ make ORB requests look like C++ method calls. The language bindings for C make these same requests look like C procedure invocations.

Let's look at an example. We will look much more closely at the Interface Definition Language (IDL) in the next chapter. For now, consider a very simple object, a dog, which supports only one operation, getBark, which returns a string. In the SOM implementation of CORBA, the interface for this dog is

```
interface dog : SOMObject {
  string getBark();
}
```

Let's say Lassie is an object supporting the dog interface. This means that clients can request that the getBark operation be performed on Lassie and expect a string as a return value. In SOM, our client code, say, test, can look like this:

```
dog lassie;
string lassieBark;
/* ... */
lassieBark = _getBark(lassie);
```

We are simplifying this code a bit by not showing any instantiating code and by removing extraneous parameters from the operation.

Our C language implementation of dog can look like:

```
#include "dog.ih"

SOM_Scope string  SOMLINK getBark(dog somSelf,  Environment *ev)
{
    static string myBarkString = "Unknown Dog Noise\n";
    dogMethodDebug("dog","getBark");
    return myBarkString;
}
```

```
SOM_Scope string   SOMLINK bark(dog somSelf,   Environment *ev)
{
    static string myBarkString = "woof woof";
    string myBark;
    dogMethodDebug("dog","bark");

    myBark = (string) SOMMalloc(strlen(myBarkString) + 1);
    strcpy(myBark, myBarkString);
    return myBark;
}
```

We can picture the architecture as shown in Figure 8.

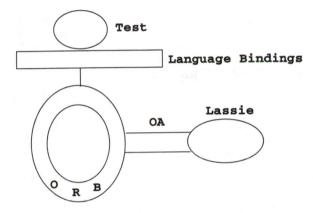

Figure 8. Client/Lassie Architecture

When the client invokes getBark, the following sequence of events occurs. Refer to Figure 9 for the flow from client to object and to Figure 10 for the flow back to the client. The steps are as follows:

1. Test requests getBark on Lassie.
2. The request is processed by the language bindings, turning it into a request that can be processed by the ORB.
3. The ORB transfers the request to the appropriate object adapter for Lassie.
4. The object adapter translates the request into a call of the getBark procedure.
5. The procedure executes.
6. At the end of the procedure, a string is returned to the object adapter.
7. The object adapter packages the string into a form the ORB can transmit and passes it on to the ORB.
8. The ORB transmits the return value back to test.
9. The C language bindings turn the ORB value into a form expected from method returns.
10. The language bindings return to the test code.

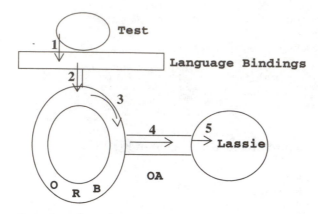

Figure 9. Events from Client to Object

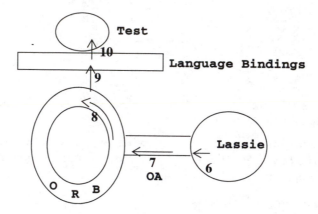

Figure 10. Flow from Object Back to Client

This basic architecture is highly adaptable. At the low end, ORBs can short-circuit the whole system when processing requests to local objects. At the high end, ORBs can sit on top of sophisticated transport mechanisms capable of invoking methods on objects living on the other side of the world.

3.2   Introduction to Object Services

Beyond this basic architecture for managing interactions between clients and objects, OMG is in the process of defining a series of Object Services that can make object components easier to program and to use. These services include Persistence (the topic of this book), Life Cycle (which describes how to create and destroy objects), Transactions (which describes how to commit and roll back changes to objects), Query (which describes how to find specific objects), Naming (which says how objects are located with naming contexts), and others.

One might ask why these object services are necessary. In fact, one might ask why CORBA is necessary, since one could distribute C++ objects simply by adding distribution code inside the C++ method bodies. Similarly, one could add code to the C++ object, which knows how to get data in and out of a datastore.

This approach has a major disadvantage. It specializes the object to the point where its reuse is sharply limited. One can imagine a generally useful business object, say, a company. If, for example, this company object contains specialized code for a particular datastore, then that object cannot be used in similar programming situations that happen not to use that same datastore. Similarly, if the company object contains code which knows how its data is distributed, that object cannot be used when a different distribution mechanism is used.

Effective reuse requires that we limit object implementation code to only that which is fundamental to the purpose of the object. An account object should know how balances are calculated, not know how an ORB ensures a client is authorized to invoke a particular method.

One of the goals of the CORBA architecture is to enable an Object Components industry, analogous to what we have today in the various vertical applications industries. In the future world envisioned by OMG, we can purchase objects much like we currently buy packaged software. Since objects will be built assuming the various OMG object services, they need none of the complex and application limiting code, for example, that says which datastore we are using as a repository for the object data. The next sections look briefly at a few of the object services closely related to persistence.

For a more detailed look at these and other services, see the very well done book by Robert Orfali, Dan Harkey, and Jeri Edwards titled *The Essential Distributed Objects Survival Guide*, published by John Wiley and Sons (1996).

3.3   Life Cycle

Although most distributed applications will be using existing applications, every object has to be instantiated by somebody, and many applications, even though instantiation will be greatly reduced, will have to instantiate some objects. Closely related to instantiation are copying, moving, and removing objects. Life Cycle is the service that defines how all this is accomplished.

The Life Cycle Service uses special objects called *factories* to create objects. A given instance of a factory can be used to create a particular type of object in a particular process. If we want to create a dog in a particular process on a particular machine, we find a factory that can accomplish this and ask it to create the object.

In order to find a factory of interest, we use a *FactoryFinder*, an object that knows about all the possible factories and, based on a particular search criterion, can find the one of interest. We look at factories, FactoryFinders and possible implementations of them, in Section 4.19 on page 112.

3.4   Naming

In the new world of distributed objects, objects will be everywhere. Applications will have to find those objects they need. In general, applications will not create new objects, they will borrow existing objects. They will not destroy objects when finished, they will simply stop using them.

The CORBA ORB supports methods to create strings from object references. These strings can be passed over to other processes, which can then use other ORB methods to reconstitute object references from these strings. One standard mechanism for passing these strings around is via shared files.

The use of stringified object references is a cumbersome process. The naming service provides a simpler interface for processes to find each other's objects. One process (usually the instantiating process) registers the objects and their associated name with the Name Service. Other processes can then ask the Name Service to find those objects by their name.

The Name Service provides various techniques for finding objects. It allows one to query and navigate through a hierarchical name space. Name/object mappings are assumed to live within contexts, and names within the Name Service can refer either to objects or contexts.

3.5   Transactions

Transaction Managers have been around for a long time. They are the basic backbone of computerized commerce. They allow a sequence of interactions occurring over an arbitrarily long sequence of time to behave as though the entire sequence had executed at the exact same instant. If something goes wrong before that instant, none of the interactions occur. Once we move past that instant, the interactions all behave as if they have all been irrevocably executed. That instant at which all interactions conceptually execute is called the commit point.

This functionality is very important to commerce. It ensures that when a purchase is made, either both the product and the payment are exchanged or neither is exchanged. It ensures that when money is transferred, either both the deposit and the withdrawal occur or neither occurs. It ensures that when a message is routed, either the message is delivered and the delivery is confirmed or the message is not delivered and the delivery is not confirmed.

The Transaction Manager needs to know when the sequence of interactions begins and when, or if, it ends. Transaction Managers supply client interfaces to define events. The client event to begin the sequence is called the *begin of the transaction*. The client event to execute the commit point is called the *commit of the transaction*. The client event to specify the sequence is to be forgotten *in toto* is called the *rollback of the transaction*.

A traditional Transaction Manager works with *resources*. A resource is something that can participate in the transaction. At the commit point, either all updates to all resources will be executed or all updates will be undone. Traditional Transaction Managers limit the ability to be a resource to large, monolithic databases.

The OMG Transaction Service has extended the concept of resources to include objects. Now, method invocations on objects can be part of the sequence of interactions that are part of the transaction. They either become committed or rolled back along with all the other transaction pieces. Similarly, method invocations to objects can now be undone should the transaction fail to commit.

There are a few nonobvious ramifications of including objects as transactional resources.

First, resources have shrunk in size. We might guess that the size of a typical distributed object will be in the range of thousands to tens of thousands of lines of code. This contrasts to database resource managers, which contain millions of lines of code.

Second, the number of resources has increased. A typical distributed application might need to coordinate the activity of dozens to hundreds of resource objects. Traditional transactional systems coordinate activity between two or three database resources.

Third, a lot more people need to know how to create a resource. Many distributed objects will need to include "whatever it takes" to be a resource. In traditional systems, the art of writing resources was limited to a few highly specialized database kernel programmers. Implementations of the Transaction Service will have to focus careful attention on simplifying the task of writing resources.

3.6 Concurrency

Closely associated with transactions is the idea of concurrency. The OMG Concurrency Control Service defines how objects can be locked so that multiuser access to objects can be coordinated. Again, this is a natural idea from databases, and OMG has taken two new steps: applying time-tested ideas to objects and decoupling systems into component services.

3.7 Security

The OMG Security Service says who can do what with which objects. Since people interact with objects (at least, distributed objects) through method invocations, the Security Service must therefore control access to methods.

This is different from what we traditionally think of as security. Security is usually thought of as defining access to data in a database. We say that a particular person is allowed to view, update, or delete data. We may even say that a person is allowed to run a particular program. But the Security Service assumes that objects are all-powerful. An object can do whatever it must to implement its behavior. It is the use of the object that is regulated, not the access to the stored data.

Regulating the use of objects can be very complicated. Some of the questions that must be answered include:

- How does the Distributed Object Administrator know what the impact of invoking a method is?
- If we define access for a particular method, based on assumptions about how that method is implemented, what happens if that method is overridden?
- When an object implements a method by invoking a method on another object, how is the security of the two objects coordinated?
- How can all this be accomplished without a huge impact on performance?

Since there are currently no implementations of an OMG Security Service, most of these questions are yet to be answered.

3.8 Query

The Query Service defines how we find objects within collections. The concept of a collection is very broad. We can think of a collection as being a physical collection object that actually contains object references. We can also think of a collection as a virtual collection, with actual objects stored in some datastore and turned back into objects if they satisfy a particular query.

One queries a collection and gets back either a single object or a collection of objects. The query itself can be in any of a number of query languages, and the Query Service defines hooks for arbitrary query languages.

The acceptance of the Query Service Specification is relatively recent, and I am not aware of any actual implementations. Based on my reading of the specification, I believe that Query has a close relationship with Persistence. For many applications, the Query Service may provide the dominant client interface to Persistent objects. These applications will use queries to "find" objects. The Query service will "find" these objects by instantiating them, using Life Cycle, and reading in their data, using Persistence. In these cases, Persistence will not be apparent to the clients but will be more of interest to the object implementor and the datastore provider.

However until we see some actual implementations of Query, we can only speculate.

3.9   Summary

The OMG Object Model is composed of two different levels. The lower level is concerned with the definition and distribution of objects. The higher level is concerned with a series of interrelated Object Services.

It is often said that OMG is not concerned with implementations, only with interfaces. We can see this by looking at the two layers. At the lower level, we have a language for defining interfaces objects support, called Interface Definition Language (IDL). Also at the lower level, we have an interface that defines a distribution mechanism. At the higher level, we have interfaces defined by the object services.

The OMG Object Services include Persistence, Queries, Security, Transactions, and others. It is interesting to compare the philosophy of these services to the philosophy of databases, which support these same types of functions.

Database vendors typically assume they own the universe. When you run a transaction, you use their transaction system. When you query, you use their query processor. When you store an object, you do so with their persistence engine.

OMG, on the other hand, assumes the universe is made up of many implementations of these object services provided by many different vendors. OMG assumes people will pick and choose those implementations that best solve their individual problems. You may choose a Transaction Service from one vendor, a Query Service from another, and a Persistence Service from another. Because they all support the OMG-defined interfaces and have well-defined interactions, they can be treated as plug-compatible components.

This represents a radical restructuring of the software universe. It opens the way for small companies to specialize in their own areas of expertise and will more and more relegate large companies to the role of system integrators or end-user solution providers. Since small companies often nurture creativity better than large companies, we may see the whole field of software development affected in a very positive way. This, at least, is the world we can hope for.

Introduction to IDL

This chapter is a general introduction to OMG's Interface Definition Language (IDL), as implemented in SOM. It does not cover every possible construct but gives an overview and discusses the most common elements of IDL in depth.

This chapter describes enough of IDL and SOM to enable you to follow all of the discussions in this book. Some of the material in this chapter is relatively advanced (e.g., Section 4.17 on page 103.) You might skim this chapter to make sure you understand the basics and come back to the more advanced material if you need it later.

4.1   Anatomy of an IDL Implementation

The SOM implementation of CORBA consists of three main components:

- The SOM run time, which knows how to register classes and invoke methods and perform the other tasks related to using objects.
- The Language Bindings, which make it convenient for clients and objects to interface with the SOM library.
- The DSOM enhancements to SOM, which allow clients and objects to be in different processes. Future versions of SOM are expected to de-emphasize the distinction between SOM and DSOM.

The general SOM architecture is shown in Figure 11. The DSOM enhanced architecture is shown in Figure 12.

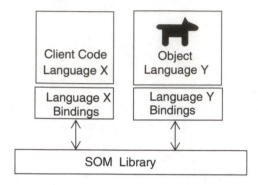

Figure 11. SOM Architecture— Single Process

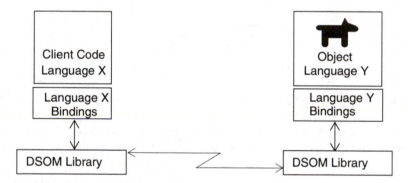

Figure 12. DSOM Architecture — Multiprocess

The process of creating and using an object is somewhat dependent on the object's implementation language. For an object written in C, the object implementor follows these steps:

1. Define the object's behavior in the IDL language. The file dog.idl, for example, might describe the behavior of a dog.
2. Compile the IDL file. Depending on the options used, any of several files are created. For a first compile, we might generate a language-specific template file (dog.c in our example), a header file containing the dog bindings for a C client (dog.h), and a header file containing the dog bindings for the implementor of the dog (dog.ih).
3. Fill in the template file with actual code. The template created by the IDL compiler will contain the skeleton of the methods, to which the object implementor adds implementation code.

4. Compile and link the objects in libraries.

In the next section, we look at this process in more detail.

4.2   Interfaces

We said the process of implementing an object involves four steps:

1. Creating an IDL file.
2. Compiling the IDL file, creating a language-specific template and language-specific bindings.
3. Filling in the language-specific template.
4. Compiling and linking the object.

Let's go through an example. The following IDL defines yet another simple dog type:

```
1. #include <somobj.idl>
2. interface dog : SOMObject {
3.   void bark();
4.   void print();
5.   implementation {
6.     releaseorder: bark, print;
7.   };
8. };
```

Going through this IDL file line by line, we start with line 1, which includes the IDL file(s) describing base interface(s) to this interface. In this case, we have only one base interface, SOMObject. Line 2 defines the interface and its base interface(s), that is, interfaces from which it is derived. Lines 3 and 4 declare the operations of this interface. Both are declared to return void and to take no parameters. Lines 5–7 are SOM IDL enhancements to standard IDL. The implementation section allows us to give implementation-specific information about this interface. In this case, the only such information we have is the release order of the operations.

The release order of operations allows SOM to ensure that binary code is kept in an upward compatible state. Upward binary compatibility is a somewhat complex issue. Essentially, it has to do with allowing changes to be made in base class definitions without forcing recompiles of derived classes. An in-depth discussion of this problem with respect to C++ code is given in *Class Construction in C and C++*[*]

We compile the dog.idl file specifying that dog.c, dog.h, and dog.ih files should be generated.

---

[*] Roger Sessions. *Class Construction in C and C++*. Prentice Hall (1992).

```
sc -sc;h;ih dog
```

The generated dog.c template file looks like this:

```
#define dog_Class_Source
#include <dog.ih>

SOM_Scope void SOMLINK bark(dog somSelf, Environment *ev)
{
/* dogData *somThis = dogGetData(somSelf); */
    dogMethodDebug("dog","bark");
}

SOM_Scope void SOMLINK print(dog somSelf, Environment *e v)
{
/* dogData *somThis = dogGetData(somSelf); */
    dogMethodDebug("dog","print");
}
```

The strings SOM_Scope and SOMLINK are defined via the dog.ih header file, which was generated by the SOM precompiler. SOM_Scope is defined to be equal to "static." This ensures that the procedures cannot be called directly, but must be invoked through the SOM method resolution process. SOMLINK is defined to be the null string and is basically a placeholder to be used if any link options need be specified. For the purposes of this discussion, we can treat the line

```
SOM_Scope void SOMLINK bark(dog somSelf, Environment *ev)
```

as being equivalent to

```
void bark(dog somSelf, Environment *ev)
```

Since SOM_Scope and SOMLINK are not relevant to this discussion, we will rewrite each of the emitted definitions in this simpler form. The emitted line

```
/* dogData *somThis = dogGetData(somSelf); */
```

which the emitter has commented out is needed only when the class has instance data. Our dog doesn't have instance data, so the emitter "omits" the line but leaves it in a commented-out form as a reminder that should we add instance data to dog, we will have to uncomment out this line. For our purposes, we will delete this line whenever it is not needed.
    The line

```
    dogMethodDebug("dog","bark");
```

is used for runtime tracing. It is also superfluous to normal coding, and we will remove it wherever it appears.
    When we are finished with these changes, our emitted code looks like:

```
#define dog_Class_Source
#include <dog.ih>

void bark(dog somSelf, Environment *ev)
{
}
void print(dog somSelf, Environment *e v)
{
}
```

Typically, we do not bother making these purely cosmetic changes, but for the purposes of examining code in this book, these changes will simplify the explanations.

The line in our dog implementation

```
#define dog_Class_Source
```

is used to create a definition that is used by the dog.ih file. The dog.ih file contains the C language bindings generated by the IDL compiler specifically for the dog implementation code. The lines that define the operations, such as

```
void bark(dog somSelf, Environment *ev)
```

contain two parameters in addition to any needed by the operation. The first parameter is always a reference to the object receiving the request, what we usually describe as the *receiving object*. The second parameter is always a pointer to an Environment structure. The most important use of the Environment structure is to return error information to the caller. These error return codes are called *exceptions* in CORBA parlance, and they are discussed in Section 4.10 on page 68.

Now that we have our dog C template, we are ready to start writing code. We will look at this in the next section.

4.3   C Implementations

Implementing our dog class consists of adding the body of the methods to the template created by the IDL compiler. Our completed dog, with added lines shown in bold, looks like this:

```
#define dog_Class_Source
#include <dog.ih>
#include <stdio.h>

void bark(dog somSelf,  Environment *ev)
{
  printf("unknown dog noise\n");
}
```

```
void print(dog somSelf,  Environment *ev)
{
  printf("\ndog says...\n");
  _bark(somSelf, ev);
}
```

The only added line that may not be obvious is the last, the one that looks like

```
  _bark(somSelf, ev);
```

The IDL compiler automatically creates a macro corresponding to each operation defined in the dog.idl file. The macro corresponding to <operation> always takes the form <_operation>. Therefore, the macro corresponding to bark is _bark. This macro is defined in the dog.h file, which is indirectly included via the dog.ih file. The purpose of this macro is to invoke SOM's operation resolution facilities to properly get to the right operation. For our purposes, this macro is the appropriate way to invoke an operation on an object.

Having completed the definition of dog (dog.idl) and the implementation of the dog operations (dog.c), we are ready to examine client code that instantiates and uses a dog object. Some code that does this is:

```
1. #include <dog.h>
2. void main()
3. {
4.   dog snoopy;
5.   Environment *ev;
6.   snoopy = dogNew();
7.   _print(snoopy, ev);
8.   _somFree(snoopy);
9. }
```

In line 1, the client code includes the dog binding file created by the IDL compiler, dog.h. In line 4, the client declares a dog object reference named snoopy. In line 5, the client declares a pointer to an Environment structure. In line 6, the client instantiates snoopy, using the SOM-provided dog instantiator. In line 7, the client asks snoopy to print himself. In line 8, the client frees the object pointed to by snoopy. The output from this program is:

```
dog says...
unknown dog noise
```

In the current version of SOM, the decision about whether an object is a SOM object (i.e., a nondistributed object) or a DSOM object (i.e., a distributed object) is made at instantiation. If the macro <_classnameNew> is used, as in line 6, the object will be nondistributed. If the object is to be distributed, the DSOM instantiation operations are used. To keep this discussion simple, we will only look at nondistributed objects. Later (in Section 4.19 on page 112) we will discuss techniques for unifying the instantiation code, some variants of which may find their way into the official SOM product.

4.4 C++ Implementations

Class implementors are not limited to implementing in C. They can implement in any language that has a process of creating SOM language bindings. In practice, this means any language that has a SOM IDL compiler.

SOM supports C++ bindings, but at press time they were not compliant with the official OMG standard C++ binding, and no plans to make them so had been announced by IBM. This section discusses the SOM C++ bindings.

If we take our dog idl file shown in Section 4.2 on page 49 and ask the SOM compiler to generate a C++ template and header files, we get files designed for a C++ implementor and client. The C++ dog implementation, with implementor-added lines shown in bold, is:

```
#define dog_Class_Source
#include <dog.xih>
#include <iostream.h>

void bark(dog *somSelf,  Environment *ev)
{
  cout << "unknown dog noise\n";
}

void print(dog *somSelf,  Environment *ev)
{
  cout << "\ndog says...\n";
  somSelf->bark(ev);
}
```

All of these lines will be obvious to the C++ programmer except perhaps the last. The line

```
somSelf->bark(ev);
```

is essentially the same as

```
this->bark();
```

which is one of the techniques a "normal" C++ method could use to invoke a method.

The C++ client, using the C++ language bindings, looks like this:

```
#include <dog.xh>
void main()
{
  dog *snoopy;
  Environment *ev;
  snoopy = new dog;
  snoopy->print(ev);
  delete snoopy;
}
```

These lines are equivalent to the C client, and the output this C++ client produces is exactly the same as that produced by the C client:

```
dog says...
unknown dog noise
```

4.5   Language Neutrality

One of the important design goals of SOM, and to a lesser extent of CORBA, was the concept of language neutrality.

From a class implementors's perspective, language neutrality means a class can be used as a base class, even when the derived class is implemented in a different language than the base class. This would allow, say, a Smalltalk programmer to derive a new Smalltalk class from a C++ base class.

From the client's perspective, language neutrality means not having to be aware of what language was used for implementing a class. This would allow, say, a C programmer to instantiate and manipulate classes implemented in, say, Smalltalk.

First we will demonstrate language neutrality from the client perspective. We will look at both C and C++ implemented dogs and show how both can be used from either a C or a C++ program. So that we can keep track of which dog implementation is which, we will call the C-implemented dog dog_c. Its IDL file is:

```
#include <somobj.idl>
interface dog_c : SOMObject {
  void bark_c();
  void print_c();
  implementation {
    releaseorder: bark_c, print_c;
  };
};
```

Notice we have renamed each of the operations to include a language postfix, so we can easily tell if we are invoking a C or C++ method. The C implementation of dog_c is:

```
#define dog_c_Class_Source
#include <dog_c.ih>
#include <stdio.h>

void bark_c(dog_c somSelf,  Environment *ev)
{
  printf("unknown c dog noise\n");
}
```

```
void print_c(dog_c somSelf,  Environment *ev)
{
  printf("\nc dog says...\n");
  _bark_c(somSelf, ev);
}
```

Next we define a C++ dog class, again using a language prefix so we can easily tell the C from the C++ dog. Its IDL is:

```
#include <somobj.idl>
interface dog_cpp : SOMObject {
  void bark_cpp();
  void print_cpp();
  implementation {
    releaseorder: bark_cpp, print_cpp;
  };
};
```

The C++ dog implementation is:

```
#define dog_cpp_Class_Source
#include <dog_cpp.xih>
#include <iostream.h>

void bark_cpp(dog_cpp *somSelf,  Environment *ev)
{
  cout << "unknown c++ dog noise\n";
}

void print_cpp(dog_cpp *somSelf,  Environment *ev)
{
  cout << "\nc++ dog says...\n";
  somSelf->bark_cpp(ev);
}
```

We will next look at a C client, using both the C and the C++ dog implementations.

```
#include <dog_c.h>
#include <dog_cpp.h>

void main()
{
  dog_c snoopy_c;
  dog_cpp snoopy_cpp;

  Environment *ev;

  snoopy_c = dog_cNew();
  snoopy_cpp = dog_cppNew();
```

```
   _print_c(snoopy_c, ev);
   _print_cpp(snoopy_cpp, ev);

   _somFree(snoopy_c);
   _somFree(snoopy_cpp);
}
```

This program gives the following output:

```
c++ dog says...
unknown c++ dog noise

c dog says...
unknown c dog noise
```

Notice that from the client's perspective, there is absolutely no difference between instantiating or using the C and C++ dogs. If it weren't for the fact that we purposely added language-identifying information to the class and operations identifiers, the client would have no way knowing which language was used for implementing the dog objects. From the client's perspective, all of the information needed for using dogs is contained in the appropriate IDL files, and this information is strictly language neutral.

The next program is the C++ client. From this program's perspective, both dog_c and dog_cpp appear for all the world as C++ objects.

```
#include <dog_cpp.xh>
#include <dog_c.xh>
void main()
{
  dog_c *snoopy_c;
  dog_cpp *snoopy_cpp;

  Environment *ev;

  snoopy_c = new dog_c();
  snoopy_cpp = new dog_cpp();

  snoopy_c->print_c(ev);
  snoopy_cpp->print_cpp(ev);

  delete snoopy_c;
  delete snoopy_cpp;
}
```

The output generated here is identical to the previous program:

```
c++ dog says...
unknown c++ dog noise

c dog says...
unknown c dog noise
```

Next, let's look at language neutrality from the class implementor's perspective. We will look at two new classes derived from our dog_c and dog_cpp. The first is littleDog, a new C++ class derived from our C dog. The IDL file for this is:

```
#include <dog_c.idl>
interface littleDog_cpp : dog_c {
  implementation {
    override: bark_c;
  };
};
```

Notice things are getting a little confusing. The C++ littleDog is overriding a C dog method, namely bark_c. But the override is going to be implemented in C++. Therefore, the bark_c override is actually a C++ method, even though its name maintains roots of its C heritage.

The C++ implementation of this class is:

```
#define littleDog_cpp_Class_Source
#include <ldog_cpp.xih>
#include <iostream.h>
#include <stdio.h>

void bark_c(littleDog_cpp *somSelf,  Environment *ev)
{
    cout << "woof woof (cpp)\n";
}
```

Next is a C bigDog derived from a C++ dog. The IDL is:

```
#include <dog_cpp.idl>
interface bigDog_c : dog_cpp {
  implementation {
    override: bark_cpp;
  };
};
```

The C implementation of bigDog is:

```
#define bigDog_c_Class_Source
#include <bdog_c.ih>
#include <stdio.h>

void bark_cpp(bigDog_c somSelf,  Environment *ev)
{
  printf("WOOF WOOF (c)\n");
}
```

Now we have a C client using the C++ littleDog derived from the C dog, and the C bigDog derived from the C++ dog. This could have just as easily been a C++ client using both dogs. The client code is as follows.

```
#include <ldog_cpp.h>
#include <bdog_c.h>

void main()
{
  littleDog_cpp toto;
  bigDog_c lassie;

  Environment *ev;

  toto = littleDog_cppNew();
  lassie = bigDog_cNew();

  _print_c(toto, ev);
  _print_cpp(lassie, ev);

  _somFree(toto);
  _somFree(lassie);
}
```

Let's look at the line

```
  _print_c(toto, ev);
```

This is invoking a C method on toto, a C++ littleDog. The code for this method was:

```
void print_c(dog_c somSelf,  Environment *ev)
{
  printf("\nc dog says...\n");
  _bark_c(somSelf, ev);
}
```

Notice the C print_c method is invoking a C _bark_c method, which has been overridden by a C++ class and a C++ method implementation. And as we can see from the output, this all works regardless of which language method is invoking which language override. The program output is:

```
c dog says...
woof woof (cpp)

c++ dog says...
WOOF WOOF (c)
```

These language-neutral mechanisms work for any SOM-supported language. Currently, there are several variants of C++ SOM support, and C, Smalltalk, COBOL and Object Rexx support. The list is continuing to grow.

4.6   Instance Variables

The OMG specification for IDL does not define how to describe instance data, that is, data associated with individual objects. The SOM extensions do provide this important functionality. The following dog IDL file shows a dog that contains a long integer as instance data. This variable will contain a count of the number of times the dog was asked to bark. The IDL is:

```
#include <somobj.idl>
interface dog : SOMObject {
  void bark();
  void print();
  implementation {
    long ntimes;
    releaseorder: bark, print;
  };
};
```

The C implementation of this dog is:

```
#define dog_Class_Source
#include <dog.ih>
#include <stdio.h>
#define MAX_TIMES 2

void bark(dog somSelf,  Environment *ev)
{
  dogData *somThis = dogGetData(somSelf);
  printf("woof woof\n");
}

void print(dog somSelf,  Environment *ev)
{
  dogData *somThis = dogGetData(somSelf);
  _ntimes++;
  printf("\ndog says...\n");
  if (_ntimes <= MAX_TIMES) _bark(somSelf, ev);
  else printf("Grrr\n");
}
```

Notice how the count is used to see if this dog has barked too many times. The C client code for this is as follows.

```
#include <dog.h>
void main()
{
  dog snoopy;
  Environment *ev;
  snoopy = dogNew();

  _print(snoopy, ev);
  _print(snoopy, ev);
  _print(snoopy, ev);

  _somFree(snoopy);
}
```

And the output, showing that snoopy will bark only twice, and then revert to growling, is:

```
dog says...
woof woof

dog says...
woof woof

dog says...
Grrr
```

4.7   Constants

In the dog IDL file shown in Section 4.6, we used a standard C define statement to document how many times a dog was allowed to bark. A better way to do this is with the IDL constant. The following IDL shows how the constant is used. The new line is shown in bold.

```
#include <somobj.idl>
interface dog : SOMObject {
  const long max_barks = 2;
  void bark();
  void print();
  implementation {
    long ntimes;
    releaseorder: bark, print;
  };
};
```

The declaration of a constant uses the keyword "const" followed by the type of the constant followed by "=" followed by the value the constant should have. It is not legal to change the value of a constant. The dog implementation is identical to that shown in Section 4.6, with the one change shown in bold:

```
void print(dog somSelf,  Environment *ev)
{
  dogData *somThis = dogGetData(somSelf);
  _ntimes++;
  printf("\ndog says...\n");
  if (_ntimes <= max_barks) _bark(somSelf, ev);
  else printf("Grrr\n");
}
```

4.8   Operations, Return Values, and Parameters

So far we have been looking at very simple operations that take no parameters and return no values. Now we will complicate the dog definition slightly by adding a string instance variable (noise), an operation to set this data (set_bark), an operation to return the number of characters in the dog's noise, and an operation to return the actual value of noise (get_bark). The instance variable will contain the noise the dog makes on barking.

As we can see from the IDL, when specifying a parameter, one must declare its type and declare whether it is input only ("in"), output only ("out"), or both ("inout"). Forgetting to declare the direction of a parameter is a common IDL programming error, since neither C nor C++ provides similar constructs.

We can also see from the declaration of get_bark how one declares the type of a return value. This is identical to C and C++.

```
#include <somobj.idl>
interface dog : SOMObject {

  void set_bark(in string newBark);
  string get_bark();
  void get_bark_length(out long length);

  void bark();
  void print();

  implementation {
    string noise;
    releaseorder: get_bark, set_bark,
                  get_bark_length, bark, print;
  };
};
```

A comparison of get_bark and get_bark_length shows the two different ways information can be returned from IDL operations. The operation get_bark returns its information as a return value. The operation get_bark_length returns its information as an output parameter. Either is legal.

The implementation of these operations is:

```
#define dog_Class_Source
#include <dog.ih>
#include <stdio.h>

void bark(dog somSelf,  Environment *ev)
{
  dogData *somThis = dogGetData(somSelf);
  if (!_noise) printf("unknown dog noise\n");
  else printf("%s\n", _noise);
}

void set_bark(dog somSelf, Environment *ev, string newBark)
{
  long length;
  dogData *somThis = dogGetData(somSelf);
  if(_noise) SOMFree(_noise);
  length = strlen(newBark) + 1;
  _noise = (string) SOMMalloc(length);
  strcpy(_noise, newBark);;
}

string get_bark(dog somSelf,  Environment *ev)
{
  dogData *somThis = dogGetData(somSelf);
  long length;
  string noise;

  if (!_noise) _set_bark(somSelf, ev, "unknown dog noise");

  length = strlen(_noise) + 1;
  noise = (string)SOMMalloc(length);
  strcpy(noise, _noise);
  return noise;
}

void get_bark_length(dog somSelf, Environment *ev,
long* length)
{
  dogData *somThis = dogGetData(somSelf);
  *length = strlen(_noise);
}

void print(dog somSelf,  Environment *ev)
{
  dogData *somThis = dogGetData(somSelf);
  printf("\ndog says...\n");
  _bark(somSelf, ev);
}
```

In the code of get_bark_length, we can see how output parameters are treated from the C implementation perspective. Although this operation had been declared in the IDL file as:

```
void get_bark_length(out long length);
```

when the C template was created, this turned into:

```
void get_bark_length(dog somSelf, Environment *ev,
long* length);
```

And as we can see, the length, which started out as an out long, has been transformed into a long *. This is not surprising to C and C++ programmers who are used to returning information through parameters as pointers to whatever type is to be returned.

Here is a C client:

```
#include <dog.h>
#include <stdio.h>
void main()
{
  dog snoopy;
  string snoopyBark;
  long barkLength;
  Environment *ev;

  snoopy = dogNew();
  _set_bark(snoopy, ev, "woof woof");

  _print(snoopy, ev);

  snoopyBark = _get_bark(snoopy, ev);
  _get_bark_length(snoopy, ev, &barkLength);

  printf("\nSnoopy's Bark: %s Length: %d\n",
     snoopyBark, barkLength);
  SOMFree(snoopyBark);
  _somFree(snoopy);
}
```

This program produces this output:

```
dog says...
woof woof

Snoopy's Bark: woof woof Length: 9
```

Notice the distinction between SOMFree and _somFree. The former is a procedure used for deallocating memory allocated with SOMMalloc. The latter is a method used to free an object.

4.9   Attributes

In the last example, we had an instance variable, noise. We also had an operation, set_bark, to set this variable, and an operation, get_bark, to read this variable. Whenever we have an instance variable and associated set and get
methods, we can naturally model this as an attribute. An attribute can be
thought of as an instance variable, a set method to set the value of the variable
and a get method to read the value of the variable.

As we discussed in Section 4.6 on page 59, pure IDL does not include the
concept of instance variables. Instance variables are considered part of the
implementation details of the class and, as such, are not described in IDL, which
is strictly a behavioral definition. Attributes, then, can be thought of as related
set and get methods, and the issue of what they set and get is left as an open
issue.

SOM goes beyond standard IDL and does include instance variables. SOM
is trying to offer a complete programming solution, and instance variables are
part of this. However, one should realize that the data being set and gotten may
be anywhere, including in a database, an associated object, global memory, or
any number of other sources.

SOM supports attributes both with and without associated data. The
nodata keyword is used to note that an attribute does not have associated data.
The example we show here is with associated data.

The following example rewrites the previous example to replace the noise
data and set_bark/get_bark operations all by a single noise attribute. Note that
an attribute is defined by the word "attribute" followed by the attribute type followed by the attribute identifier. Here is the attribute rewrite of our dog:

```
#include <somobj.idl>
interface dog : SOMObject {

  attribute string noise;
  void bark();
  void print();

  implementation {
    releaseorder: _get_noise, _set_noise,
                  bark, print;
  };
};
```

Next is the dog implementation:

```
#define dog_Class_Source
#include <dog.ih>
#include <stdio.h>
```

```
void bark(dog somSelf,  Environment *ev)
{
  dogData *somThis = dogGetData(somSelf);
  if (!_noise) printf("unknown dog noise\n");
  else printf("%s\n", _noise);
}

void print(dog somSelf,  Environment *ev)
{
  dogData *somThis = dogGetData(somSelf);
  printf("\ndog says...\n");
  _bark(somSelf, ev);
}
```

Notice there is something missing here. After all the discussion of get/set methods, there are none to be seen. The reason for this is that SOM automatically generates get/set methods for attributes, and these are placed in the dog.ih header file. If we examine this file, we find the following method implementations, with the most relevant sections shown in bold:

```
SOM_Scope string  SOMLINK _get_noise(dog somSelf,
Environment *ev)
{
    dogData *somThis = dogGetData(somSelf);
    dogMethodDebug("dog","_get_noise");
    SOM_IgnoreWarning(ev);

    return (somThis->noise);
}
SOM_Scope void  SOMLINK _set_noise(dog somSelf,
Environment *ev, string noise)
{
    dogData *somThis = dogGetData(somSelf);
    dogMethodDebug("dog","_set_noise");
    SOM_IgnoreWarning(ev);

    somThis->noise = noise;
}
```

Notice that these implementations do nothing more than set the instance variable to the parameter value. This might be acceptable in some cases, but when the attribute in question is a string (or any other pointer), this is not very helpful. To see why, consider the following main program.

```
#include <dog.h>
void main()
{
  dog snoopy, toto;
  Environment *ev;
  char bark[100];

  snoopy = dogNew();
  toto = dogNew();

  strcpy(bark, "WOOF WOOF");
  __set_noise(snoopy, ev, bark);
  strcpy(bark, "woof woof");
  __set_noise(toto, ev, bark);

  _print(snoopy, ev);
  _print(toto, ev);

  _somFree(snoopy);
  _somFree(toto);
}
```

The output from this program should have snoopy saying "WOOF WOOF," but see what we get:

```
dog says...
woof woof

dog says...
woof woof
```

The problem is that no local memory is being allocated for the instance data. We are simply setting two different instance variables (one in snoopy and one in toto) to the same block of memory. This is a pretty useless way to implement a set method, so in almost all cases we will need to create our own implementations. The way we do this is by declaring the noise attribute to be "noset and noget," which means SOM will not create default implementations and we will take responsibility for implementing these operations ourselves. The following dog definition does exactly that:

```
#include <somobj.idl>
interface dog : SOMObject {

  attribute string noise;
  void bark();
  void print();

  implementation {
    noise: noset, noget;
    releaseorder: _get_noise, _set_noise,
                  bark, print;
  };
};
```

Next is the dog implementation, with the proper set/get methods added. Note that the get method returns a copy of the attribute's memory rather than a direct pointer into the object's memory space, as the default get would have done.

```
#define dog_Class_Source
#include <dog.ih>
#include <stdio.h>
string _get_noise(dog somSelf,  Environment *ev)
{
  dogData *somThis = dogGetData(somSelf);
  long length;
  string noise;

  if (!_noise) __set_noise(somSelf, ev, "unknown dog noise");

  length = strlen(_noise) + 1;
  noise = (string)SOMMalloc(length);
  strcpy(noise, _noise);
  return noise;
}

void _set_noise(dog somSelf, Environment *ev, string noise)
{
  long length;
  dogData *somThis = dogGetData(somSelf);
  if(_noise) SOMFree(_noise);
  length = strlen(noise) + 1;
  _noise = (string) SOMMalloc(length);
  strcpy(_noise, noise);
}
```

The bark and print implementations are the same as shown earlier and are not repeated. With these changes, the test program works as expected:

```
dog says...
WOOF WOOF

dog says...
woof woof
```

When you define an attribute, say, noise, the name of the generated set and get method is _set_noise and _get_noise. Notice the leading underscores. This is required by the OMG standard for IDL. In SOM, one typically invokes a method by putting an underscore in front of the method name. This means that when invoking a set/get attribute method, the client will use two underscores, one for the CORBA-defined method name and one for the SOM method invocation.

4.10 Exceptions

Exceptions are the defined mechanism for returning error conditions to callers. They are not exceptions in the way most programmers think of exceptions, in that they do not define code segments that will automatically gain control in the case of defined conditions. Programmers who are expecting this type of exception will be sorely disappointed.

Exceptions are set and returned via the Environment parameter, that second implicit parameter to all CORBA operations. So far we have been ignoring the Environment parameter and, in fact, haven't even been bothering to allocate it. That will all change from now on.

An exception consists of two parts: a generic part and an exception-specific part. The generic part contains information that is common to all exceptions. This information is placed directly in the Environment structure. This is the exception category, the exception name, and a pointer to an exception-specific structure. The exception-specific information is placed in an exception-specific structure, and the exception structure pointer in the Environment structure is set to this structure. Exceptions are not required to define exception-specific information, and many return no information beyond the name of the exception, which is part of the generic information.

There are four distinct exception-related steps. First, we define the exception in an IDL file. Second, we identify which operations return which exceptions. Third, we set the exception based on some event having occurred in an operation. Fourth, we act on the exception in the client code.

In general, an exception declaration follows the form

```
exception exceptionName {
  type Element1;
  type Element2;
  ...
};
```

The information inside the brackets following the exceptionName are the elements, if any, of the structure that will contain the exception-specific information.

The following dog.idl defines two exceptions. The first occurs when an operation finds missing information in the receiving object. The second occurs when an operation is asked to place invalid information in the receiving object.

```
#include <somobj.idl>
interface dog : SOMObject {

  exception missing_info {
    string attribute_name; /* The missing attribute */
  };
  exception invalid_info {
    string attribute_name; /* The invalid attribute */
    string value;          /* The invalid value */
  };
```

```
  void set_bark(in string newBark)
  raises (invalid_info);

  string get_bark()
  raises(missing_info);

  void bark()
  raises (missing_info, invalid_info);

  void print()
  raises (missing_info, invalid_info);

  implementation {
    string noise;
    releaseorder: get_bark, set_bark,
                  bark, print;
  };
};
```

Notice that the syntax used to declare an operation raises an exception. The name of the method is followed by a clause that defines the exceptions. This clause precedes the semicolon which terminates the operation definition.

An operation can raise one or more exceptions and can also raise any of a number of predefined CORBA exceptions without so declaring.

In the dog implementation file, we see how exceptions are set. We have defined procedures for setting each of the exceptions, although this is just a coding style preference. The procedures set_ii_exception and set_mi_exception will set the invalid information and missing exceptions, respectively. Keep in mind that set_ii_exception and set_mi_exception are procedures, not operations; thus, they do not take a receiving object reference as a first parameter.

```
#define dog_Class_Source
#include <dog.ih>
#include <stdio.h>
#define set_exception somSetException

void set_ii_exception(Environment *ev, string att,
  string value);
void set_mi_exception(Environment *ev, string att);

void set_ii_exception(Environment *ev, string att,
string value)
{
  invalid_info *except;
  except = (invalid_info *) SOMMalloc (sizeof(invalid_info));
  except->attribute_name = (string) SOMMalloc(strlen(att)+1);
  except->value = (string) SOMMalloc(strlen(value)+1);
  strcpy(except->attribute_name, att);
  strcpy(except->value, value);
  set_exception(ev, USER_EXCEPTION, ex_invalid_info, except);
}
```

```
void set_mi_exception(Environment *ev, string att)
{
  missing_info *except;
  except = (missing_info *) SOMMalloc (sizeof(missing_info));
  except->attribute_name = (string) SOMMalloc(sizeof(att));
  strcpy(except->attribute_name, att);
  set_exception(ev, USER_EXCEPTION, ex_missing_info, except);
}
void bark(dog somSelf,  Environment *ev)
{
/* Set up.
   ------- */
   dogData *somThis = dogGetData(somSelf);

/* Check exceptions.
   ---------------- */
   if (!_noise) {
      set_mi_exception(ev, "noise");
      return;
   }
   if (!strcmp(_noise, "meow")) {
      set_ii_exception(ev, "noise", "meow");
      return;
   }
/* Print information.
   ----------------- */
   printf("%s\n", _noise);
}

void set_bark(dog somSelf, Environment *ev, string newBark)
{
/* Set up.
   ------- */
   long length;
   dogData *somThis = dogGetData(somSelf);

/* Check for invalid info exception.
   -------------------------------- */
   if(!strcmp("meow", newBark)) {
     set_ii_exception(ev, "noise", "meow");
     return;
   }
/* Release old memory, if necessary.
   -------------------------------- */
   if(_noise) SOMFree(_noise);

/* Copy in new value.
   ----------------- */
   length = strlen(newBark) + 1;
   _noise = (string) SOMMalloc(length);
   strcpy(_noise, newBark);
}
```

```
string get_bark(dog somSelf,  Environment *ev)
{
/* Set up.
   ------- */
   dogData *somThis = dogGetData(somSelf);
   long length;
   string noise;

/* Check for missing information exception.
   ---------------------------------------- */
   if (!_noise) {
       set_mi_exception(ev, "noise");
       return;
   }
/* Get noise information.
   --------------------- */
   length = strlen(_noise) + 1;
   noise = (string)SOMMalloc(length);
   strcpy(noise, _noise);
   return noise;
}

void print(dog somSelf,  Environment *ev)
{
  dogData *somThis = dogGetData(somSelf);
  printf("\ndog says...\n");
  _bark(somSelf, ev);
}
```

Let's look at set_mi_exception in detail.

```
void set_mi_exception(Environment *ev, string att)
```

The first line declares the procedure. We pass in two parameters. The first is a pointer to an Environment structure. The structure must have already been allocated in the client code. The second parameter is the name of the attribute, which will be copied into the eventual exception-specific structure.

```
missing_info *except;
```

The line above declares a local variable, which is a pointer to a missing_info structure. This structure is automatically declared as a result of the exception being defined in the dog.idl file. The declaration can be located in dog.h, if you are interested.

```
except = (missing_info *) SOMMalloc (sizeof(missing_info));
```

In the above line, the missing_info variable is now set to a block of dynamically allocated memory.

```
except->attribute_name = (string) SOMMalloc(sizeof(att));
```

Next, we dynamically allocate the string inside the missing_info structure. This string needs to be big enough to contain the string passed in as the second parameter.

```
strcpy(except->attribute_name, att);
```

In line 6 above, we copy the string parameter into the string reference contained in our exception structure.

```
set_exception(ev, USER_EXCEPTION, ex_missing_info, except);
```

Now comes the official setting of the exception. The set_exception procedure contains four parameters: an environment in which to set the exception, an exception category, the name of the exception, and a pointer to the exception-specific structure. The exception category can be either of SYSTEM_EXCEPTION or USER_EXCEPTION. In most cases, the SYSTEM_EXCEPTION is reserved for major system events, and most interfaces define their exceptions as USER_EXCEPTION. The name of the exception is predefined in dog.h as ex_exception_name. Finally, we pass in a pointer to the structure we have been setting up.

The client code demonstrates how exceptions are checked and cleared. We have consolidated this code into the check_error procedure. Notice that now that we are actually going to use the Environment structure, we have taken the trouble to allocate memory, using the SOM macro SOM_CreateLocalEnvironment, and free it, using the SOM macro SOM_DestroyLocalEnvironment.

```
#include <dog.h>
#include <stdio.h>

void check_error(Environment *ev);

void main()
{
  dog snoopy, lassie, toto;
  Environment *ev;

  ev = SOM_CreateLocalEnvironment();

  snoopy = dogNew();
  lassie = dogNew();
  toto =  dogNew();

  _set_bark(snoopy, ev, "woof woof");
  check_error(ev);

  _set_bark(lassie, ev, "meow");
  check_error(ev);

  _print(snoopy, ev);
  check_error(ev);
```

```
  _print(toto, ev);
  check_error(ev);

  _somFree(snoopy);
  SOM_DestroyLocalEnvironment(ev);
}
void check_error(Environment *ev)
{
/* Set up.
   ------- */
  string exceptName;
  missing_info *mi_except;
  invalid_info *ii_except;

/* If no exception, return.
   ---------------------- */
  if(ev->_major != USER_EXCEPTION) return;
  exceptName = exception_id(ev);

/* Deal with missing information exception.
   ------------------------------------- */
  if (!strcmp(exceptName, ex_missing_info)) {
      mi_except = (missing_info *) somExceptionValue(ev);
      printf("Missing Attribute %s\n",
        mi_except->attribute_name);
      SOMFree(mi_except->attribute_name);

  }
/* Deal with invalid information exception.
   ------------------------------------- */
  if (!strcmp(exceptName, ex_invalid_info)) {
      ii_except = (invalid_info *) exception_value(ev);
      printf("Invalid Attribute %s\n",
        ii_except->attribute_name);
      printf("Value: %s\n", ii_except->value);
      SOMFree(ii_except->attribute_name);
      SOMFree(ii_except->value);
  }
/* Free exception resources.
   ---------------------- */
  exception_free(ev);
}
```

The output demonstrates the two exceptions being raised. The first occurs from trying to get Lassie to meow and the second from having Toto print himself without first having his bark set.

```
Invalid Attribute noise
Value: meow
```

```
dog says...
woof woof
```

```
dog says...
Missing Attribute noise
```

To see what is necessary to deal with error conditions, let's look at check_error in more detail. We will look only at those lines that are related to the missing_info exception.

```
void check_error(Environment *ev)
```

The first line is the procedure declaration. We are passed in the Environment parameter, which may or may not have had an exception raised.

```
string exceptName;
```

The variable exceptName will eventually be used to contain the name of the exception.

```
missing_info *mi_except;
```

The variable mi_except will eventually be set to the value of the missing_info exception-specific structure.

```
if(ev->_major != USER_EXCEPTION) return;
```

The data member _major of the Exception structure receives the exception category. This could also have checked for NO_EXCEPTION, since an Environment that has not had an exception set will contain _major equal to NO_EXCEPTION. At this point in the code, if we have not returned, we are dealing with a bona-fide exception.

```
exceptName = exception_id(ev);
```

The macro exception_id will retrieve the exception name.

```
if (!strcmp(exceptName, ex_missing_info)) {
```

Now that we know we have an exception, the next question is, which exception. The above line checks to see if this is the missing_info exception by checking the exception name against the predefined string containing the name of the missing exception.

```
mi_except = (missing_info *) somExceptionValue(ev);
```

Since we have determined this as a missing_info exception, we need to retrieve a pointer to the exception-specific structure through the SOM macro somExceptionValue.

```
printf("Missing Attribute %s\n", mi_except->attribute_name);
```

The above prints out the name of the attribute.

```
SOMFree(mi_except->attribute_name);
```

The above frees the string containing the attribute name.

```
    exception_free(ev);
```

The exception_free macro takes care of freeing any exception resources associated with the Environment and resetting the exception category back to NO_EXCEPTION.

4.11 Valid Types

There are two categories of types: basic and constructed. Any valid type can be used anywhere a type is expected in IDL. This includes types of arguments to operations, return types of operations, types of elements in exceptions, and types of attributes. We will look separately at the basic and constructed types.

4.11.1 Basic Types

The basic data types and their C equivalents are shown in Table 1. Most correspond to C data types of the same name. The exceptions are octet, which is treated as an uninterpreted byte, a boolean, which can contain either of the two predefined values TRUE or FALSE, and string, which corresponds to char *.

Table 1 Basic Data Types and C Equivalents

IDL	C
float	float
double	double
long	long
short	short
unsigned long	unsigned long
unsigned short	unsigned short
char	char
boolean	unsigned char
octet	unsigned char
string	char *

We have already seen many examples of the string type. We will give one more example of a basic type. We will show a long type, as a representative basic type, used in the following dog definition:

```
#include <somobj.idl>
interface dog : SOMObject {
  attribute long age;
  void print();
  implementation {
    releaseorder: print, _set_age, _get_age;
  };
};
```

The following shows the dog implementation:

```
#define dog_Class_Source
#include <dog.ih>
#include <stdio.h>

void print(dog somSelf,  Environment *ev)
{
  dogData *somThis = dogGetData(somSelf);
  printf("My age is: %d\n", __get_age(somSelf, ev));
}
```

Notice we are using the default set/get methods for the long age attribute. The default set/get methods are usually acceptable for nonpointer attributes.

The client code, which uses this implementation, is:

```
#include <dog.h>
void main()
{
  dog snoopy;
  Environment *ev;
  snoopy = dogNew();
  __set_age(snoopy, ev, 100);
  _print(snoopy, ev);
  _somFree(snoopy);
}
```

The output from this program is:

```
My age is: 100
```

4.11.2   struct

A struct can be declared the same as in C. The only difference is that in IDL, the structure declaration becomes typedef'ed at the same time. As in all object-oriented programming languages, structures in IDL are used infrequently. They are almost always replaced by a class or interface. We will not cover them here in any depth.

4.11.3   enum

An enum type is a variable that can contain one of several constant values. The constant values are referred to by human-friendly names. The following dog has an enum breed variable that can take any of three values: collie, beagle, or all_of_above. Notice that once the enum is declared, it is used as if it had been typdef'ed.

```
#include <somobj.idl>
interface dog : SOMObject {
  enum breeds {collie, beagle, all_of_above};
  attribute breeds breed;
  void print();
  implementation {
    releaseorder: _set_breed, _get_breed, print;
  };
};
```

The dog implementation shows how a dog method checks to see to which constant the variable was set:

```
#define dog_Class_Source
#include <dog.ih>

void print(dog somSelf,  Environment *ev)
{
   dogData *somThis = dogGetData(somSelf);
   printf("My breed is: ");
   switch (_breed) {
     case dog_collie:
       printf("Collie\n");
       break;
     case dog_beagle:
       printf("Retriever\n");
       break;
     case dog_all_of_above:
       printf("A little of everything\n");
       break;
     default:
       printf("Unknown\n");
   }
}
```

Notice that once we get into the C bindings, the names of the constants are preceded by the name of the interface, dog. Similarly, the client code also uses the interface name before each of the constants.

```
#include <dog.h>
void main()
{
  dog snoopy, lassie, sam;
  Environment *ev;

  snoopy = dogNew();
  lassie = dogNew();
  sam = dogNew();

  __set_breed(snoopy, ev, dog_beagle);
  __set_breed(sam, ev, dog_all_of_above);

  _print(snoopy, ev);
  _print(lassie, ev);
  _print(sam, ev);

  _somFree(snoopy);
}
```

The output from this program is:

```
My breed is: Retriever
My breed is: Unknown
My breed is: A little of everything
```

4.11.4   union

A union is a type that can contain any of a number of possible types. It is similar to the C concept of union, but we have a discriminator automatically built in. The following dog definition declares a variable, dogInfo, which can contain either a long or a string. It also uses an enum (see Section 4.11.3) to discriminate between the possible value types.

```
#include <somobj.idl>
interface dog : SOMObject {

  enum infoTypes {age, name};
  union dogInfo switch (infoTypes) {
    case age:  long myAge;
    case name: string myName;
  };
  attribute dogInfo myInfo;

  void setAgeValue(in long newAge);
  void setNameValue(in string newName);

  void print();
  implementation {
    releaseorder: _set_myInfo, _get_myInfo,
                  setAgeValue, setNameValue, print;
  };
};
```

You can see the C binding for a union type by looking in the dog implementation. Keep in mind that myInfo was declared to be an attribute of a dog. The _d is automatically a data member of myInfo, and _u is automatically set to contain the actual value.

```
#define dog_Class_Source
#include <dog.ih>

void setAgeValue(dog somSelf, Environment *ev, long newAge)
{
   dogData *somThis = dogGetData(somSelf);
   if (_myInfo._d == dog_name && _myInfo._u.myName)
      SOMFree(_myInfo._u.myName);
   _myInfo._d = dog_age;
   _myInfo._u.myAge = newAge;
}

void setNameValue(dog somSelf, Environment *ev,
string newName)
{
   dogData *somThis = dogGetData(somSelf);
   if (_myInfo._d == dog_name && _myInfo._u.myName)
      SOMFree(_myInfo._u.myName);
   _myInfo._d = dog_name;
   _myInfo._u.myName = (string)
      SOMMalloc(strlen(newName) + 1);
   strcpy(_myInfo._u.myName, newName);
}
```

```
void print(dog somSelf, Environment *ev)
{
   dogData *somThis = dogGetData(somSelf);
   printf("My information type: ");
   switch(_myInfo._d) {
     case dog_age:
       printf("Age     Value: %d\n", _myInfo._u.myAge);
       break;
     case dog_name:
       printf("Name    Value: %s\n", _myInfo._u.myName);
       break;
   }
}
```

The client code in this particular case is not aware of the union.

```
#include <dog.h>
void main()
{
  dog snoopy, lassie;
  Environment *ev;

  snoopy = dogNew();
  lassie = dogNew();

  _setAgeValue(snoopy, ev, 10);
  _setNameValue(lassie, ev, "Lassie");

  _print(snoopy, ev);
  _print(lassie, ev);

  _somFree(snoopy);
  _somFree(lassie);
}
```

The output from this program is:

```
My information type: Age     Value: 10
My information type: Name    Value: Lassie
```

4.11.5   sequence

A sequence is a very common constructed data type in IDL. Like the other con-structed types, it acts as a typedef once declared. The following dog definition makes use of a sequence to store a set of strings. A sequence is declared by "sequence" followed by "<" followed by any valid type followed by the maximum number of items that can be placed in the sequence followed by ">" followed by the name of the variable. The maximum for items is optional. Notice we have used a constant to declare the maximum size of the sequence.

```
#include <somobj.idl>
interface dog : SOMObject {
  const long maxSize = 20;
  void set_item(in string newItem);
  void print();
  implementation {
    sequence<string,maxSize> items;
    releaseorder: set_item, print;
  };
};
```

As one can guess by looking at the dog implementation, a sequence maps to a C structure with three data members. Their names and purposes are as follows:

- _maximum (type long) — The maximum number of items that can be stored in the sequence. Although this was initially set with a constant in dog.idl, _maximum itself is not a constant. It may change through the life of the program if the code reallocates more space as needed.
- _length (type long) — The actual number of items currently stored in the sequence.
- _buffer (type void *) — The buffer containing the items. _buffer[n] contains the nth item in the sequence.

```
#define dog_Class_Source
#include <dog.ih>

void set_item(dog somSelf, Environment *ev, string newItems)
{
/* Set up.
   ------- */
   dogData *somThis = dogGetData(somSelf);
   string next;

/* Set up items, if unallocated.
   ----------------------------- */
   if (!_items._buffer) {
       _items._maximum = dog_maxSize;
       _items._length = 0;
       _items._buffer =
           (string *) SOMMalloc(sizeof(string) * dog_maxSize);
   }
/* Add next item.
   -------------- */
   if(_items._length >= _items._maximum) return;
   _items._length++;
   next = (string) SOMMalloc(strlen(newItems)+1);
   strcpy(next, newItems);
   _items._buffer[_items._length] = next;
}
```

```
void print(dog somSelf, Environment *ev)
{
   dogData *somThis = dogGetData(somSelf);
   long n;
   for (n=0; n<=_items._length; n++) {
     printf("%s\n", _items._buffer[n]);
   }
}
```

The code for add_item first makes sure the sequence has been initialized. It then makes sure there is enough room left for the next item, and if not, returns. It might also choose to raise an exception (see Section 4.10 on page 68) or reallocate the buffer, making more space for new items.

The client code, in this case, is oblivious to the sequence.

```
#include <dog.h>
void main()
{
  dog snoopy;
  Environment *ev;
  snoopy = dogNew();

  _set_item(snoopy, ev, "Name = Snoopy");
  _set_item(snoopy, ev, "Bark = Woof Woof");

  _print(snoopy, ev);
  _somFree(snoopy);
}
```

The output from this program is:

```
Name = Snoopy
Bark = Woof Woof
```

4.11.6   array

Arrays can be declared and map into C arrays. Sequences are much more common, and we will not discuss arrays in any depth.

4.11.7   any

An any is a type that can be declared to contain any possible valid IDL type. Its use is complicated, and we will not explore it here.

4.11.8   typedef

Typedefs work as they do in C. Any type can be typedef'ed. It is less common in IDL than in C because the constructed types end up being typedef'ed automatically.

4.12 Inheritance and Method Resolution

We have already roughly described the concept of inheritance and method resolution in SOM back in Section 1.1 on page 11. Here we will fill in the pseudocode
with real code and show the IDLs once more.

The animal.idl defines an animal with a name attribute and a print
method.

```
#include <somobj.idl>
interface animal : SOMObject {
  void set_name(in string newName);
  string get_name();
  void print();
  implementation {
    string name;
    releaseorder: set_name, get_name, print;
  };
};
```

The animal implementation is:

```
#define animal_Class_Source
#include <animal.ih>

void set_name(animal somSelf, Environment *ev, string newName)
{
  animalData *somThis = animalGetData(somSelf);
  if(_name)SOMFree(_name);
  _name = (string) SOMMalloc (strlen(newName)+1);
  strcpy(_name, newName);
}

string get_name(animal somSelf, Environment *ev)
{
  animalData *somThis = animalGetData(somSelf);
  string newName;
  newName = (string) SOMMalloc(strlen(_name)+1);
  strcpy(newName, _name);
  return newName;
}

void print(animal somSelf, Environment *ev)
{
  animalData *somThis = animalGetData(somSelf);
  printf("\nMy name is: %s\n", _name);
}
```

Next is dog, a class derived from animal, that adds a new operation, bark, and
overrides an existing operation, print. We use the keyword *override* in the implementation section to indicate an override.

Object Persistence

```
#include <animal.idl>
interface dog : animal {
  void bark();
  implementation {
    releaseorder: bark;
    override: print;
  };
};
```

The implementation of dog is:

```
#define dog_Class_Source
#include <dog.ih>
#include <stdio.h>
void bark(dog somSelf, Environment *ev)
{
  printf("unknown dog noise\n");
}


void print(dog somSelf,  Environment *ev)
{
    dog_parent_animal_print(somSelf, ev);
  _bark(somSelf, ev);
}
```

Notice that the override of print invokes the animal print before doing its own thing. Next is littleDog, which overrides bark. This is very similar to code we have already examined in Section 4.5 on page 54.

```
#include <dog.idl>
interface littleDog : dog {
  implementation {
    override: bark;
  };
};
```

Next is littleDog's implementation.

```
#define littleDog_Class_Source
#include <ldog.ih>
#include <stdio.h>

void bark(littleDog somSelf,  Environment *ev)
{
  printf("woof woof\n");
}
```

Next is bigDog, who has a different idea on how to bark:

```
#include <dog.idl>
interface bigDog : dog {
  implementation {
    override: bark;
  };
};
```

And the bigDog implementation:

```
#define bigDog_Class_Source
#include <bdog.ih>
#include <stdio.h>

void bark(bigDog somSelf,  Environment *ev)
{
  printf("WOOF WOOF\n");
  printf("WOOF WOOF\n");
}
```

The client code demonstrates how the dog print method invokes both the animal print method and the dog bark method, the latter of which is overridden by little-Dog's bark, in the case of toto, or by bigDog's bark, in the case of lassie.

```
#include <bdog.h>
#include <ldog.h>
#include <dog.h>
#include <animal.h>

main()
{
  animal pooh;
  dog snoopy;
  littleDog toto;
  bigDog lassie;
  Environment *ev;

  pooh = animalNew();
  snoopy = dogNew();
  toto = littleDogNew();
  lassie = bigDogNew();

  _set_name(pooh, ev, "Pooh");
  _set_name(snoopy, ev, "Snoopy");
  _set_name(toto, ev, "Toto");
  _set_name(lassie, ev, "Lassie");
```

```
  _print(pooh, ev);
  _print(snoopy, ev);
  _print(toto, ev);
  _print(lassie, ev);

  _somFree(pooh);
  _somFree(snoopy);
  _somFree(toto);
  _somFree(lassie);
}
```

The output from this program is:

```
My name is: Pooh

My name is: Snoopy
unknown dog noise

My name is: Toto
woof woof

My name is: Lassie
WOOF WOOF
WOOF WOOF
```

4.13 Protecting Interfaces

The CORBA specification says that interfaces cannot be defined more than once. This might not seem like a problem. After all, why would anybody want to define an interface more than once? But it actually turns out to be easy to unintentionally define interfaces multiple times.

Consider the following set of definitions. We have cat and dog both derived from animal, and a person with attributes of type cat and dog. The interfaces are each put in a separate file, as follows.

animal.idl:

```
#include <somobj.idl>

interface animal : SOMObject {
  attribute string name;
  implementation {
    releaseorder: _get_name, _set_name;
  };
};
```

cat.idl:

```
#include <animal.idl>

interface cat : animal {
  attribute string meow;
  implementation {
    releaseorder: _set_meow, _get_meow;
  };
};
```

dog.idl:

```
#include <animal.idl>

interface dog : animal {
  attribute string bark;
  implementation {
    releaseorder: _set_bark, _get_bark;
  };
};
```

person.idl:

```
#include <somobj.idl>
#include <dog.idl>
#include <cat.idl>

interface person : SOMObject {
  attribute dog myDog;
  attribute cat myCat;
  implementation {
    releaseorder: _set_myDog, _get_myDog,
                  _set_myCat, _get_myCat;
  };
};
```

The animal, cat, and dog definitions will compile without problem. However, person has a problem. When the IDL compiler encounters the line

```
#include <dog.idl>
```

it reads in the dog definition. Inside the dog definition is the line

```
#include <animal.idl>
```

Thus, by the time the second line in the animal definition has been processed (the line that includes the dog.idl), the following interfaces have been fully defined:

- SOMObject (from the first include).
- animal (from the indirect include within dog.idl).
- dog (from the include of dog.idl).

The next line of the person definition includes the cat definition, which also includes the animal definition.

Now the compiler has a problem. This is the second time the animal interface has been defined, and this is not legal. So the compiler does the only thing it can do in this kind of situation: It complains.

There are two possible solutions to this problem. The first is to enclose all definitions in protecting #ifdefs. The second is to use a forward reference. We will look at both.

The #ifdef compiler directive works exactly like the C preprocessor counterpart. It is usually used in this type of construction:

```
#ifndef something
#define something
compilable line 1
compilable line 2
...
#endif
```

If "something" is not defined, then everything else is processed up to the #endif. The only way "something" can be undefined is if this body of code has never before been encountered. If this segment of code has been already encountered, say, by being multiply included, then "something" will have already been defined, and the block of code will be skipped.

We commonly enclose interfaces within an #indef protection block. By putting the animal code in this block, we can eliminate any possible problem if the interface file happens to be multiply included, as in this example. The protected animal looks like:

```
#ifndef animal_idl
#define animal_idl
#include <somobj.idl>

interface animal : SOMObject {
  attribute string name;
  implementation {
    releaseorder: _get_name, _set_name;
  };
};

#endif
```

It is hard to predict when a given definition will be multiply included. It is, therefore, good practice to enclose all definitions in such protective blocks. In this book, it would add significantly to the code examples to use this construct in every interface. We will therefore only use it where necessary. However, in professional coding, this should always be used.

The other technique to avoid multiple definitions is *forward referencing*. Forward referencing is a way to declare to the compiler that you will eventually declare an interface but aren't doing so at this time. When the compiler sees a reference to an interface that has been forward referenced, it accepts the reference even though the interface has not yet been defined. The following rewrite of person shows this technique:

```
#include <somobj.idl>

interface dog;   /* Forward reference */
interface cat;   /* Forward reference */

interface person : SOMObject {
  attribute dog myDog;
  attribute cat myCat;
  implementation {
    releaseorder: _set_myDog, _get_myDog,
                  _set_myCat, _get_myCat;
  };
};
```

A good rule of thumb is to use forward references for all interface references except those used as base classes. This eliminates the need for many #includes and will also avoid the bulk of the multiple definitions. Then, always use protecting #ifdefs to guard against any remaining problems.

4.14 Modules

Interfaces, type declarations, compound variables, and exceptions can be grouped together in modules. The main purpose of a module is to give an added level of scoped name space. The following shows the dog.idl placed inside a module:

```
#include <somobj.idl>
module animals {

  interface dog : SOMObject {
    void bark();
    void print();
    implementation {
      releaseorder: bark, print;
    };
  };
};
```

Next is the dog implementation. Notice that all of the procedure names are prefixed by the module name.

```
#define SOM_Module_dog_Source
#include <dog.ih>

void animals_dogbark(animals_dog somSelf,
Environment *ev)
{
  printf("unknown dog noise\n");
}

void animals_dogprint(animals_dog somSelf, Environment *ev)
{
  printf("\ndog says...\n");
  _bark(somSelf, ev);
}
```

The client code now needs to be modified. All uses of the name dog must be pre-fixed by animal. Method names must either be fully qualified with module and interface name (the official CORBA standard) or use the SOM shorthand of _methodName. Both forms of the method invocation are shown here.

```
#include <dog.h>
void main()
{
  animals_dog snoopy;
  Environment *ev;
  snoopy = animals_dogNew();
  _print(snoopy, ev);
  animals_dog_print(snoopy, ev);
  _somFree(snoopy);
   }
```

The output from this program is:

```
dog says...
unknown dog noise

dog says...
unknown dog noise
```

The C++ bindings work slightly differently in this case. Even with the module construction, method names are invoked by using only the method name, as shown in this C++ client code.

```
#include <dog.xh>
void main()
{
  animals_dog *snoopy;
  Environment *ev;
  snoopy = new animals_dog();
  snoopy->print(ev);
//snoopy->dog_print(ev);            invalid
//snoopy->animals_dog_print(ev);    invalid
//snoopy->animals_print(ev);        invalid

  delete snoopy;
}
```

4.15 Object Initialization and Deinitialization

Objects often have data that needs to be initialized when the object is created. Objects often have allocated resources that need to be deallocated when the object is freed. SOM provides two hooks for this purpose: somDefaultInit and somDestruct. Both are defined in SOMObject. Since all objects are derived from SOMObject, either directly or indirectly, all objects support these methods. The SOMObject implementation doesn't actually do anything. The assumption is that you will override these in any interface that needs to initialize or deinitialize data. SOM automatically invokes somDefaultInit when the object is created and somDestruct when the object is freed.

The following dog.idl demonstrates how these methods are overridden. We start with the dog.idl, which overrides somDefaultInit and somDestruct:

```
#include <somobj.idl>
interface dog : SOMObject {

  attribute string noise;
  void print();

  implementation {
    noise: noset, noget;
    override: somDefaultInit, somDestruct;
    releaseorder: _get_noise, _set_noise,
                  print;
  };
};
```

The implementation of dog now includes the overridden initialization and deinitialization methods. The initialization method, somDefaultInit, now creates a default string for the noise. The deinitialization method, somDestruct, now frees the dog's noise when the dog is freed. In both of these methods, there is quite a bit of overhead. This is code that is automatically generated by the emitter. The code we added is shown in bold.

```
#ifndef SOM_Module_dog_Source
#define SOM_Module_dog_Source
#endif
#define dog_Class_Source

#include "dog.ih
void somDefaultInit(dog somSelf, somInitCtrl* ctrl)
{
    dogData *somThis; /* set in BeginInitializer */
    somInitCtrl globalCtrl;
    somBooleanVector myMask;
    Environment ev;
    dogMethodDebug("dog","somDefaultInit");
    dog_BeginInitializer_somDefaultInit;

    dog_Init_SOMObject_somDefaultInit(somSelf, ctrl);
/*
    local dog initialization code added by programmer
    -------------------------------------------------- */
    _noise = NULL;
    _set_noise(somSelf, &ev, "Unknown dog noise");
}

void somDestruct(dog somSelf, octet doFree, somDestructCtrl* ctrl)
{
    dogData *somThis; /* set in BeginDestructor */
    somDestructCtrl globalCtrl;
    somBooleanVector myMask;
    dogMethodDebug("dog","somDestruct");
    dog_BeginDestructor;
/*
    local dog deinitialization code added by programmer
    --------------------------------------------------- */
    printf("About to free: %s\n", _noise);
    SOMFree(_noise);

    dog_EndDestructor;
}
```

SOM adds special code to these two methods to ensure they are called once and only once, and in the proper order in the case of multiple inheritance. This is a less than ideal solution to the problem of "diamond inheritance," where a class may find itself represented more than once in the derivation graph. Consider, for example, the following:

```
interface namedThings      : SOMObject           { /* ... */ };
interface animal           : namedThings         { /* ... */ };
interface performer        : namedThings         { /* ... */ };
interface performingAnimal : animal, performer { /* ... */ };
```

This situation is called diamond inheritance, because if one were to graph the derivation diagram, it would have a diamond appearance, as shown in Figure 13.

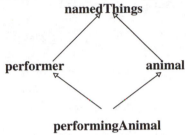

Figure 13. Derivation Pattern of Diamond Inheritance

Assume all four of these interfaces override somDefaultInit, and each implementation of somDefaultInit invokes the somDefaultInit of each of its base classes (which would be expected). Then when we instantiate a performingAnimal, we would invoke the following somDefaultInits:

- performingAnimal::somDefaultInit, from the instantiation of performingAnimal.
- animal::somDefaultInit, from the performingAnimal::somDefaultInit.
- performer::somDefaultInit, also from the performingAnimal::somDefaultInit.
- namedThings::somDefaultInit, from animal::somDefaultInit.
- namedThings::somDefaultInit, from performer::somDefaultInit.

In most implementations of namedThings::somDefaultInit, it would make little difference that the method had been invoked twice. However, when the method invocation has side effects, such as maintaining a count of the total number of objects instantiated, this double invocation will cause problems.

To avoid this problem, SOM adds extra code in somDefaultInit and somDestruct. The major purpose of this code is to ensure that double invocations are not made. I consider this an imperfect solution to the issue of diamond inheritance because it treats somDefaultInit and somDestruct as special cases, whereas in fact this is a much more general problem. But this is the best solution we currently have available.

The remainder of the dog methods are:

```
string _get_noise(dog somSelf,  Environment *ev)
{
   dogData *somThis = dogGetData(somSelf);
   string noise;
   long length;

   length = strlen(_noise) + 1;
   noise = (string)SOMMalloc(length);
   strcpy(noise, _noise);
   return noise;
}
```

```
void _set_noise(dog somSelf,  Environment *ev, string noise)
{
    dogData *somThis = dogGetData(somSelf);
    long length;
    length = strlen(noise) + 1;
    _noise = (string) SOMMalloc(length);
    strcpy(_noise, noise);

}
void print(dog somSelf,  Environment *ev)
{
    dogData *somThis = dogGetData(somSelf);
    printf("\ndog says...\n%s\n", _get_noise(somSelf, ev));
}
```

Our client program is

```
#include <dog.h>
#include <stdio.h>
void main()
{
  dog snoopy, lassie;
  Environment *ev;

  snoopy = dogNew();
  lassie = dogNew();

  __set_noise(lassie, ev, "Woof Woof");

  _print(snoopy, ev);
  _print(lassie, ev);

  _somFree(snoopy);
  _somFree(lassie);
}
```

Our program output is:

```
dog says...
Unknown dog noise

dog says...
Woof Woof
About to free: Unknown dog noise
About to free: Woof Woof
```

Notice the first two lines of output, from snoopy, which show the result of running somDefaultInit, and the last two lines, which show the deinitialization in
somDestruct.

IBM recommends that somDefaultInit and somDestruct always be overridden, even when the class implementor has no code to add. This ensures that the proper ordering of base class versions of these methods is maintained. However, this will significantly complicate the simple examples we are showing. Therefore, for pedagogical reasons we will, in this book, not follow this recommendation.

4.16 Dynamic Loading

The CORBA object model requires the ability to dynamically load objects whose type is not known until run time. This important capability is not possessed by some of the more common object models, for example, C++. In this section, we will examine how SOM satisfies this need. Later (in Section 4.19 on page 112) we will see how this folds into the CORBA concept of factories and factory finders.

We will use a modified dog example to demonstrate dynamic loading. Let's consider the following problem. The company Dog, Inc., is selling binary classes that implement a dog class. They have set up their binary code into a dynamically linked library, abbreviated DLL. A DLL can be loaded at run time.

Dog, Inc., (DI) also packages a dog application. However, they want third parties to be able to derive new classes from dog. These new classes (e.g., littleDog and bigDog) use most of the dog code but specialize some behaviors by overriding specific methods. The dog application is designed to work with either the original dog or any class derived from dog, even if that class if created by a completely independent third party, say Other Dogs, Inc. (ODI). The DI application must be able to run with ODI dog derivations, even though it has no knowledge of where these derivations came from, how they are derived, or what methods they override.

DI uses the following dog definition:

```
#include <somobj.idl>

  interface dog : SOMObject {
    void bark();
    implementation {
      dllname = "dog.dll";
      releaseorder: bark;
    };
  };
```

The implementation of the DI dog is:

```
#ifndef SOM_Module_dog_Source
#define SOM_Module_dog_Source
#endif
#define dog_Class_Source

#include <dog.ih>
#include <stdio.h>

SOM_Scope void SOMLINK bark(dog somSelf,  Environment *ev)
{
  printf("Generic dog noise\n");
}
```

The DI dog application will start by asking the user what kind of a dog is wanted. The answer can either be dog or some type derived from dog (for example, one of the ODI dog types.) The system will then dynamically load the appropriate dog type and ask that dog to bark. If the dog type was the original DI-supplied dog, the bark will be the generic dog noise. If the dog type is a derivation of dog, then the bark will either be the generic dog noise if the new dog type does not override bark, or some new dog noise if the new dog type does override.

The part that makes this problem interesting is the requirement that the dog application itself has no idea of these new dog types. They were not available when the application was written, compiled, or linked. The application doesn't get to find out about these new types until the application is actually run.

Let's consider first how this application would be written if dog was not meant to be overridden. We have seen this code already several times:

```
#include <dog.h>
#include <som.h>
#include <stdio.h>

void main()
{
  dog snoopy;
  Environment *ev;
  snoopy = dogNew();

  printf("Snoopy says:\n");
  _bark(snoopy, ev);
  _somFree(snoopy);
}
```

Of course this code only works if snoopy will always be a dog, which violates our requirements. The line

```
snoopy = dogNew();
```

always instantiates snoopy as a dog. The following modified version allows the user to specify the type of the dog and instantiates the correct type. It works regardless of whether the application knew about the type (as in the case of DI

dog) or whether the application did not know about the type (as in the case of
ODI littleDog or bigDog.)

```c
#include <dog.h>
#include <som.h>
#include <stdio.h>
void main()
{
/* Local declarations.
   ------------------ */
    dog snoopy;
    SOMClass classObject;
    Environment *ev;
    somId nameId;
    char dogType [100];

/* Initialize system.
   ----------------- */
    somEnvironmentNew();

/* Find out what type to create.
   ---------------------------- */
    printf("Snoopy's Type: ");
    fflush(stdout);
    scanf("%s", dogType);
    printf("Snoopy instantiated as %s\n\n", dogType);

/* Do a dynamic lookup on the type.
   ------------------------------- */
    nameId = somIdFromString(&dogType[0]);
    classObject = SOMClassMgr_somFindClass
                  (SOMClassMgrObject, nameId, 0, 0);

/* Let 'em know if the dynamic lookup failed.
   ----------------------------------------- */
    if (!classObject) {
        printf ("--->  %s could not be loaded\n", dogType);
        exit(0);
    }
/* Instantiate object as the dynamic type.
   -------------------------------------- */
    snoopy = _somNew(classObject);

/* Have snoopy do his thing.
   ------------------------ */
    printf("Snoopy says:\n");
    _bark(snoopy, ev);

/* Close up.
   --------- */
    _somFree(snoopy);
}
```

The significant difference between the original program and this new version is that the lines that in the former were

```
snoopy = dogNew();
```
have changed to
```
nameId = somIdFromString(&dogType[0]);
classObject = SOMClassMgr_somFindClass
              (SOMClassMgrObject, nameId, 0, 0);
snoopy = _somNew(classObject);
```

The first of these new lines converts a string to a token of some type. The second takes this token and finds an object that knows how to instantiate a new object of the requested type. In SOM, an object that knows how to instantiate an object of a given type is usually referred to as a *class object*, although class objects can have other functions as well. The third line asks the class object to instantiate an object and stores the reference to the newly instantiated object in snoopy.

Although one can tell by looking at the code that there are no references to dogs other than the DI-created dog class, it is more difficult to prove we did not sneak in some knowledge of the ODI dog types at either compile or link time. In order to prove that the dog application executable is completely innocent of any knowledge of derived types, we need to look at the commands used to build the executable. We will not describe the syntax of the commands. They are specific to SOM running on OS/2®. The important point here is what they don't contain, rather than what they do contain, namely, information about the ODI derivations.

The following components are used in building our application:

- dog.obj is the compiled object code for dog. This is created by using the following compiler commands:

  ```
  icc $(DLLOPTS) $(INCLUDES) dog.c
  ```

  The variables DLLOPTS and INCLUDE are environment variables, not relevant to this discussion.

- A linker-readable dog.lib, which contains definitions of dynamic links. This is created by using the following librarian command:

  ```
  implib /NOI dog.lib dog.def
  ```

- A human-readable dog.def, which contains human-readable definitions of the dynamic links. The contents of this file are:

  ```
  LIBRARY dog INITINSTANCE
  DESCRIPTION 'dog Class Library'
  PROTMODE
  DATA MULTIPLE NONSHARED LOADONCALL
  EXPORTS
     dogCClassData
     dogClassData
     dogNewClass
     SOMInitModule
  ```

- A doginit.c, which contains code used to initialize the dog DLL. We won't go into details, except to point out that this, too, is uncontaminated by references to ODI dogs:

```
#include <dog.h>
#include <stdio.h>
#pragma linkage (SOMInitModule, system)

void SOMEXTERN SOMInitModule
(integer4 majorVersion, integer4 minorVersion,
 string ignore)
{
   dogNewClass(0,0);
}
```

- The compiled version of doginit.c, compiled with the command

```
icc $(DLLOPTS) $(INCLUDES) doginit.c
```

- A dog.dll, which contains the dynamically linked library with the dog binaries. This file is created with the following command:

```
icc $(DLL_LINK_OPTS)  -Fe dog.dll dog.obj doginit.obj
somtk.lib dog.def
```

  Again, the environment variable DLL_LINK_OPTS is not relevant. The somtk.lib is the library containing the SOM runtime code. The other components are ones we have already discussed.

- An executable, test1.exe, which is the runnable application. This is created from the following command from previously discussed components:

```
icc $(EXOPTS) -Fe test1.exe somtk.lib dog.lib test.c
```

Many of these components are intermediary components and are not distributed to clients. The components that are distributed to clients are:

- The executable, test1.exe, which is what the end user will run.
- The dog DLL, dog.dll, to which the end user will dynamically link at run time.
- The dog interface definition, dog.idl, from which a class developer, such as ODI, can derive new classes.
- The dog library, dog.lib, which the class developers can use in building their DLLs.

The application can be run as distributed by DI. One such run is shown here, with user input shown in bold.

```
test1
```
Snoopy's Type: **dog**
Snoopy instantiated as dog

Snoopy says:
Generic dog noise

Now this is not particularly interesting, since this could have been accomplished without dynamic loading. Indeed, if we ask for any type other than dog, we get an error message:

```
test1
```
Snoopy's Type: **littleDog**
Snoopy instantiated as littleDog

---> littleDog could not be loaded

But now let's assume we have purchased a DLL from ODI containing binaries for both littleDog and bigDog. The littleDog definition and implementation are

```
#include <dog.idl>
interface littleDog : dog {
  implementation {
    dllname = "others.dll";
    override: bark;
    releaseorder: bark;
  };
};
```

and

```
#ifndef SOM_Module_ldog_Source
#define SOM_Module_ldog_Source
#endif
#define littleDog_Class_Source
#include "ldog.ih"
#include <stdio.h>

SOM_Scope void  SOMLINK bark(littleDog somSelf,  Environment *ev)
{
  printf("woof woof\n");
}
```

The bigDog definition and implementation are

```
#include <dog.idl>
interface bigDog : dog {
  implementation {
    dllname = "others.dll";
    override: bark;
  };
};
```

and

```
#ifndef SOM_Module_bdog_Source
#define SOM_Module_bdog_Source
#endif
#define bigDog_Class_Source

#include "bdog.ih"
#include <stdio.h>

SOM_Scope void  SOMLINK bark(bigDog somSelf,  Environment *ev)
{
  printf("WOOF WOOF\n");
  printf("WOOF WOOF\n");
}
```

The process used to create this new DLL (we will call it others.dll) is analogous to the steps used to create the original dog.dll. If this DLL is incorporated into the run time (a process that can be done by the end user through steps we will describe shortly), the user can now specify any of the newly available ODI dog types, as shown in these program runs:

test1
Snoopy's Type: **littleDog**
Snoopy instantiated as littleDog

Snoopy says:
woof woof

test1
Snoopy's Type: bigDog
Snoopy instantiated as bigDog

Snoopy says:
WOOF WOOF
WOOF WOOF

Of course, we are still limited to available types. Should we attempt to give Snoopy an unimplemented type, we again get an error message:

```
test1
Snoopy's Type: cat
Snoopy instantiated as cat

--->  cat could not be loaded
```

There are a series of steps that must be done to integrate the ODI classes into our runtime environment. On OS/2, these steps are as follows.

1. Purchase the ODI class library. This seems rather obvious, but the enabling of such class developers is one of the driving forces behind SOM. The purchase will include other.dll, bdog.idl, and ldog.idl.
2. Place other.dll in one of the directories in which OS/2 looks for DLLs at run time. These are the set of directories specified in the environment variable LIBPATH.
3. Make known to SOM the mappings between classes and DLLs. This is done by updating the so-called *interface repository* (IR). The interface repository is a database containing information about classes; it can be queried by the SOM kernel or, in fact, by any other code. The IR is updated by issuing the following commands:

```
sc -u bdog
sc -u ldog
```

There are a few possible variants on this theme which we will not bother to discuss here. The extent of information contained in the IR can be gleaned by using the IR dump utility, irdump. If we invoke irdump with the line

```
irdump littleDog
```

we get the following output:

```
"littleDog": 1 entry found

1 InterfaceDef "littleDog"
   id:      ::littleDog
   4 modifiers:
     dllname = others.dll
     override = bark
     releaseorder = bark
     filestem = ldog
   1 base interface:
     "::dog"
   instanceData: TypeCodeNew (tk_null)
```

Most of the information shown is not of immediate interest. However, we note one line which says which dll needs to be dynamically loaded to access code for this class:

```
dllname = others.dll
```

Like all IR information, this particular piece of information came from the original definition file, ldog.idl. The line in ldog.idl that contained this information is shown here in bold:

```
#include <dog.idl>
interface littleDog : dog {
  implementation {
    dllname = "others.dll";
    override: bark;
    releaseorder: bark;
  };
};
```

The ability to dynamically load new classes is a powerful feature of SOM and other CORBA implementations and is the basis for third-party class derivations and open framework architectures. Of course, the details will differ from operating system to operating system, and from CORBA implementation to CORBA implementation, but most will provide this capability in some form.

4.17 Class Objects

SOM extends the CORBA object model by encapsulating classes of objects as objects in their own right. This has three benefits for SOM programmers.

1. Classes are objects. As objects, they support methods, and these methods can be used by programmers.
2. The class of an object can be changed by changing the class of its class object.
3. It is possible to create frameworks for class objects, making it possible to develop sophisticated capabilities.

We aren't going to cover this issue in a lot of detail, since it goes quite a bit beyond the basic object model defined by CORBA. But we need to cover at least enough detail to show how we can implement the basic requirements of the Life Cycle Service and to set the groundwork for describing the mechanisms used to coordinate persistence and transactions, which we look at in Section 6.2 on page 155.

One way to get a reference to a class object is to use the method somGet-Class, a method defined on SOMObject. The following code uses somGetClass to get the class object for dog. It then uses another SOMObject method, somGet-ClassName, to print the class of the class object for dog. First, a simple dog definition:

```
#include <somobj.idl>
interface dog : SOMObject {
  void bark();
  implementation {
    releaseorder: bark;
  };
};
```

By now you should be able to imagine the implementation, so we will go right to the test program:

```
#include <dog.h>
void main()
{
  dog snoopy;
  SOMClass dogClass;

  Environment *ev;

  snoopy = dogNew();

  dogClass = _somGetClass(snoopy);
  printf("Snoopy's class is a %s\n",
    _somGetClassName(snoopy));
  printf("dogClass's class is a %s\n",
    _somGetClassName(dogClass));

}
```

The output from this program is:

```
Snoopy's class is a dog
dogClass's class is a SOMClass
```

We often use a shorthand terminology for describing the class of an object's class object. In the above code, we can see that the class of snoopy's class object is SOMClass. The terminology we use for this is saying that snoopy's *metaclass* is SOMClass. When we read the metaclass of an object is a particular class, we are just saying that the class of the object's class object is that particular class.

One of the useful methods that SOMClass objects support is somNew. This method instantiates objects. A given class object can only instantiate objects of one type. In the class of dogClass, the objects will be dogs. This is demonstrated in the following test program:

```
#include <dog.h>
void main()
{
  dog snoopy, lassie;
  SOMClass dogClass;
  Environment *ev;
  snoopy = dogNew();
  dogClass = _somGetClass(snoopy);
  lassie = _somNew(dogClass);

  printf("Snoopy's class is a %s\n",
    _somGetClassName(snoopy));
  printf("Lassie's class is a %s\n",
    _somGetClassName(lassie));
}
```

This program gives the following output:

```
Snoopy's class is a dog
Lassie's class is a dog
```

The metaclass of all objects is either SOMClass or some class derived from SOM-Class. SOM provides several classes derived from SOMClass, which can be used either directly as metaclasses or as base classes for metaclasses.

One of the most important of these, at least as far as persistence is concerned, is the SOMMBeforeAfter class. This class, like all metaclasses, is derived from SOMClass. This class introduces two new methods, sommBefore and sommAfter. The default implementation of these methods does nothing.

Classes derived from SOMMBeforeAfter are expected to override sommBefore and/or sommAfter. The overridden sommBefore will be invoked before each method invoked on any object, using the derived class as its metaclass. Similarly, the overridden sommAfter will be invoked after any method invoked on any object, using the derived class as its metaclass.

The following demonstrates this. We will write a metaclass that uses before and after methods to trace the flow of execution of methods within the class. Our dogClass is such a metaclass. It is derived from SOMMBeforeAfter (and therefore indirectly from SOMClass). The definition of dogClass is

```
#include <sombacls.idl>

interface dogClass : SOMMBeforeAfter {
  implementation {
    override : sommBeforeMethod, sommAfterMethod;
  };
};
```

The implementation of dogClass is as follows. The file is fairly ugly, but the ugly code is all emitted by the precompiler. The only code the dogClass implementor must add is shown in bold.

```
#ifndef SOM_Module_dogcls_Source
#define SOM_Module_dogcls_Source
#endif
#define dogClass_Class_Source

#include "dogcls.ih"
#include <stdio.h>

boolean sommBeforeMethod(dogClass somSelf, Environment *ev,
SOMObject object, somId methodId, va_list ap)
{
    printf("Before Method\n");
    return (dogClass_parent_SOMMBeforeAfter_sommBeforeMethod
      (somSelf, ev, object, methodId, ap));
}
```

```
void sommAfterMethod(dogClass somSelf,  Environment *ev,
SOMObject object, somId methodId, somToken returnedvalue,
va_list ap)
{
   printf("After Method\n");
   dogClass_parent_SOMMBeforeAfter_sommAfterMethod(
      somSelf, ev, object, methodId, returnedvalue, ap);
}
```

Now that we have a valid metaclass, we can use it in any class we desire. In this case, we will make this the metaclass for dogs. The following interface is exactly the same as before, with two changes shown in bold. These lines change the metaclass of dog from the default of SOMClass to the newly created dogClass.

```
#include <somobj.idl>
#include <dogcls.idl>
interface dog : SOMObject {
  void bark();
  implementation {
    releaseorder: bark;
    metaclass = dogClass;
  };
};
```

The test program is unchanged:

```
#include <dog.h>
void main()
{
  dog snoopy;
  Environment *ev;

  snoopy = dogNew();
  _bark(snoopy, ev);
  _somFree(snoopy);
}
```

The output of this program, with lines numbered for reference, is:

```
1. Before Method
2. After Method
3. Before Method

4. woof woof

5. After Method
6. Before Method
7. Before Method
8. After Method
9. After Method
```

Lines 1 and 2 are the before and after method surrounding somDefaultInit, which is defined in SOMObject and which we have not overridden. Lines 3 and 5 are the before and after method surrounding _bark. Line 6 is the before method preceding _somFree. Line 7 is the before method preceding _somDestruct. Lines 8 and 9 are the after methods following _somDestruct and _somFree, respectively. The methods somFree and somDestruct, like somDefaultInit, are all defined in SOMObject.

4.18 Distributed Objects

If all SOM and CORBA had to offer was what we have already mentioned, both would be uninteresting side notes to software history. It is true that SOM offers language neutrality, as discussed in Section 4.5 on page 54. It is true that SOM offers the upward binary compatibility, as discussed in Section 4.2 on page 49. It is true that SOM offers advanced object modeling capability such as metaclasses, as discussed in Section 4.17 on page 103.

But these are all relatively uninteresting. The language neutrality story is marred by the lack of non-IBM compiler vendors supporting SOM. At press time, the only non-IBM compiler with SOM language bindings is Metaware's C++ compiler. The upward binary compatibility is an issue that impacts only C++ programmers. And the fact that C++ has survived and thrived despite having the weakest of all the object models is good evidence that object models are not a major issue outside the theoretical confines of academia.

So if these three "major" capabilities of SOM are dismissed, what is left? The fact is that the most important capability of SOM is the one most often ignored. This is the ability to distribute objects. This capability, and this alone, will ensure SOM and CORBA a major place in the history of software. We will be studying the implications of distributed objects long after we have forgotten all of the other supposedly state-of-the-art SOM capabilities.

It is beyond the scope of this book to provide a full thesis on distributed object technology. But we will use this section to give a basic introduction to the important ideas.

If a few basic object implementation rules are followed, it becomes relatively easy to distribute objects without any changes to the objects themselves. These rules include the following:

- Objects should not make assumptions about what process they are in. In particular, they should not assume their process owns any input/output devices.
- Objects should not update memory buffers they did not allocate.
- Don't use any nonstandard types.

Assuming these rules have been followed, the only code that needs to be changed to allow objects to be distributed is the client code that deals with instantiating and deinstantiating objects, and much of this can be managed by the use of factories, which are described in the next section.

Instantiating distributed objects can get quite complicated in SOM. We will give only a single example of how this can be accomplished and leave fuller explanations for books specifically about SOM.

We are going to use our basic dog example, with a few complexities thrown in to demonstrate some distributed object capabilities. The major changes are:

- We will add derived dog types, similar to those in Section 4.12 on page 83.
- We will modify our implementation to take into account the distributed object rules.
- We will add the ability for two dogs to interact with each other, to show how distributed objects can work together.

Let's start by looking at a new dog definition.

```
#include <somobj.idl>
interface dog : SOMObject {
  string getBark();
  string bark();
  string converse(in dog partner);
  implementation {
    releaseorder: getBark, bark, converse;
    dllname = "dog.dll";
  };
};
```

Our bark method has been changed to return a string. Our earlier versions actually printed out a message. But this only works when the dog process is the process that "owns" the user's terminal. This assumption is not valid in a distributed environment. We have also added a new method, getBark, to simplify further derivations. We will discuss the relationship between getBark and bark when we look at the code implementation.

We have added the converse method, which causes two dogs to have a conversation. The purpose of this method is to demonstrate distributed objects interacting with each other.

In the implementation section of the idl, we see a newly added section describing the dllname. This is used to identify the dynamically loadable module that contains the binary libraries for dog.

Next, let's look at the dog code. The file starts with standard include directives:

```
#ifndef SOM_Module_dog_Source
#define SOM_Module_dog_Source
#endif
#define dog_Class_Source

#include "dog.ih"
```

The first method is bark. Unlike earlier versions, we want this distributed version to return a string, so that it works properly when not located in the process that has access to the user's terminal. The bark method manages all of the details of allocating and returning this string and leaves it to the method get-Bark to decide which bark string should be returned.

```
string bark(dog somSelf,  Environment *ev)
{
    string myBarkString;
    string myBark;

    myBarkString = _getBark(somSelf, ev);
    myBark = (string) SOMMalloc(strlen(myBarkString) + 1);
    strcpy(myBark, myBarkString);
    return myBark;
}
```

The method getBark is purposely kept very simple, so that programmers special-izing the dog class only have to implement a few lines of code.

```
string getBark(dog somSelf,  Environment *ev)
{
    static string myBarkString = "Unknown Dog Noise\n";
    return myBarkString;
}
```

The converse method interacts with some other dog to create a string containing both dogs' bark string.

```
string converse(dog somSelf,  Environment *ev, dog partner)
{
    string myBark, partnerBark, newString;

    myBark = _bark(somSelf, ev);
    partnerBark = _bark(partner, ev);

    newString = (string) SOMMalloc(strlen(myBark) +
                    strlen(partnerBark) + 1);
    strcpy(newString, myBark);
    strcat(newString, partnerBark);

    return;
}
```

The littleDog definition is shown next. Since we have set up getBark to be the standard overridden method, the IDL shows this specialization.

```
#include <dog.idl>
interface littleDog : dog {
  implementation {
    override: getBark;
    dllname = "dog.dll";
  };
};
```

The implementation of littleDog is:

```
#ifndef SOM_Module_ldog_Source
#define SOM_Module_ldog_Source
#endif
#define littleDog_Class_Source

#include "ldog.ih"

string getBark(littleDog somSelf,  Environment *ev)
{
    static string myBarkString =
        "littleDog says\nwoof woof\n";
    return myBarkString;
}
```

The definition of bigDog follows the same pattern as littleDog:

```
#include <dog.idl>
interface bigDog : dog {
  implementation {
    override: getBark;
    dllname = "dog.dll";
  };
};
```

And the implementation of bigDog just changes the barkString:

```
#ifndef SOM_Module_bdog_Source
#define SOM_Module_bdog_Source
#endif
#define bigDog_Class_Source

#include "bdog.ih"

string getBark(bigDog somSelf,  Environment *ev)
{
    static string myBarkString =
        "bigDog says \nWoof Woof\nWoof Woof\n\n";
    return myBarkString;
}
```

Our test program shows the modifications necessary to instantiate different types of dogs remotely. The significant changes are shown in bold.

```
#include <somd.h>
#include <ldog.h>
#include <bdog.h>
#include <stdio.h>
void main()
{
  littleDog toto;
  bigDog lassie;
  string barkString;
  Environment *ev = SOM_CreateLocalEnvironment();

  SOMD_Init(ev);

  toto = _somdNewObject(SOMD_ObjectMgr, ev, "littleDog", "");
  lassie = _somdNewObject(SOMD_ObjectMgr, ev, "bigDog", "");

  barkString = _converse(toto, ev, lassie);
  printf("%s", barkString);

  _somdDestroyObject(SOMD_ObjectMgr, ev, toto);
  _somdDestroyObject(SOMD_ObjectMgr, ev, lassie);

  SOMD_Uninit(ev);
  SOM_DestroyLocalEnvironment(ev);
}
```

The output of this program, showing toto and lassie conversing with each other, is:

```
woof woof
Woof Woof
Woof Woof
```

The changes in the program should be easy to follow. We have added a new header file that includes the various distributed definitions. We have added a line to initialize the distributed system. We have changed the object instantiations to instantiate remotely. And we have changed the deinstantiations to deinstantiate remotely.

With these relatively small changes in our program, we have made some major changes in our system. Our two dogs are now running in remote processes. They are no longer in the same address space as the rest of the program. They may be in another process on the same machine. They may be on a different machine. They may be running on a networked machine in orbit around the earth.

It should be pointed out that DSOM offers several other ways of instantiating objects. The one shown here is probably the most common and, for the purposes of this book, representative.

The distribution of objects and processes is shown in Figure 14. As shown in this figure, the client code appears to be interacting with toto and then requesting that toto interact with lassie. In fact, the client is interacting with a proxy object that forwards the communications request to the actual remote object running in some server process.

That remote object then interacts with an object it thinks is remote (lassie), but is also a local proxy that forwards its request to the remote object on whose behalf the proxy is running. That request is returned from lassie to toto's lassie proxy, which returns its information to the client's toto proxy and then back to the client. And all this with no object code changes at all, and very few changes to the client code. This is all based on the CORBA distributed architecture described in Section 3.1 on page 37.

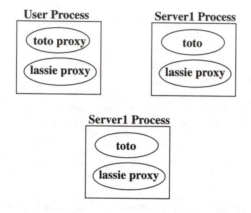

Figure 14. Distribution of Objects

There is a registration process that clients must use to define which objects will live in which processes. The process is very straightforward, but operating system dependent, and we will therefore not describe it here.

4.19 Factories and Factory Finders

The last section described the changes necessary to make objects distributed. There are two problems with our methodology. First, the client has to use significantly different code to instantiate and deinstantiate objects, depending on whether those objects are local or remote. Second, the methodology does not conform to the OMG specification for how objects are instantiated.

In this section, we will show how we can modify our system to eliminate both of these problems.

The OMG Life Cycle specification says that objects are instantiated by means of special objects called factories. It should be clear that OMG factories look very much like the SOM class objects described in Section 4.17 on page 103. If we create a factory metaclass and encapsulate within it the logic for deciding whether objects should be created locally or remotely, we will both remove this responsibility from the client and make our code OMG compliant.

In this section we will show how this might be done. It is expected that the next release of SOM will offer mechanisms along these lines, probably implemented much as we are showing here.

First, let's look at the Factory class. This will be a class derived from SOM-Class; it will add a new method, create, that we will start using for our objects.

```
interface Factory : SOMClass {

  SOMObject create();

  implementation {
     releaseorder: create;
     dllname = "sample.dll";
  };
};
```

Next is the implementation of the Factory class. Notice that the create method is implemented as a pass-through to the _somNew method, which this class inherits from its base, SOMClass.

```
SOM_Scope SOMObject SOMLINK create(
Factory          somSelf,
Environment*     ev)
{
   return _somNew(somSelf);
}
```

Next we have a FactoryCreated class, which will serve as a base class for all classes and which will offer local/remote transparency. The metaclass of this class is Factory. Since all classes have, by default, the metaclass of their base class (or at least a metaclass derived from the metaclass of their base class), all classes derived from FactoryCreated will have a metaclass derived from Factory. The definition of FactoryCreated is:

```
interface FactoryCreated : SOMObject {
  implementation {
    dllname = "sample.dll";
    metaclass = Factory;
  };
};
```

Since we declare no methods or attributes for FactoryCreated, we have no significant code in the implementation file.

The next file contains the IDL for the FactoryFinder. The interface also defines an enumeration constant (such constants are described in Section 4.11.3 on page 77.) This enumerator will be used to specify to the factoryFinder whether the factory is intended for local or remote objects.

```
interface FactoryFinder : SOMObject {

   enum location {local, remote, dont_care};

   Factory find_factory(in string className,
                        in location where);
   void     free_object (in SOMObject obj);
   void     free_factory(in Factory fact);

   implementation {
     releaseorder: find_factory, free_object, free_factory;
     dllname = "sample.dll";
   };
};
```

Next we will show the method code for FactoryFinder. The code in these methods is relatively advanced and is included for those readers who might want to understand this technique. Rest assured that it is not necessary to understand these implementations to be able to understand the rest of this book.

The file starts out by declaring a static variable to keep track of how many remote factories have been instantiated.

```
static long totalRemoteFactories = 0;
```

The first method is free_object. It makes use of a SOMObject method, _somIsA, to see if the object in question is derived from _SOMDClientProxy, a base class for all distributed objects. Most programmers are unaware of this derivation, but it is basically the class that defines the proxy described in Section 4.18 on page 107.

```
SOM_Scope void SOMLINK free_object(
FactoryFinder    somSelf,
Environment*     ev,
SOMObject        obj)
{
/* Free remote object.
   ------------------ */
   if(_somIsA(obj, _SOMDClientProxy)){
      _somdDestroyObject(SOMD_ObjectMgr, ev, obj);
   }
/* Free local object.
   ----------------- */
   else {
      _somFree(obj);
   }
}
```

Next comes a standard procedure for freeing Factories, very similar to freeObject. The main difference is that this also includes code for deinitializing DSOM when the total count of remote factories goes down to zero.

```
SOM_Scope void SOMLINK free_factory(
FactoryFinder    somSelf,
Environment*     ev,
Factory          fact)
{
/* Free remote Factory.
   ------------------- */
   if(_somIsA(fact, _SOMDClientProxy)){
      _somdReleaseObject(SOMD_ObjectMgr, ev, fact);

/*    If this is the last remote factory, close up DSOM.
      --------------------------------------------------- */
      totalRemoteFactories--;
      if (totalRemoteFactories == 0) {
           SOMD_Uninit(ev);
      }
   }
/* Free local Factory.
   ------------------- */
   else {
      _somFree(fact);
   }
}
```

The next method is find_factory. This procedure will take three parameters. The first will be className of the class we want the factory to instantiate. The second is the environment variable, used potentially to return error information. The third is an enumeration variable defined in the FactoryFinder definition.This gives the client code the possibility of deciding whether objects will be local or remote by manipulating a single switch. This method returns a Factory that knows how to create objects of a particular type (className) and in a particular process. Notice that if the request is made for a remote instantiation, standard DSOM mechanisms are used to locate the process in which the object will live.

```
SOM_Scope Factory SOMLINK find_factory(
FactoryFinder    somSelf,
Environment*     ev,
string           className,
location         where)
{
/* Declarations.
   ------------- */
   somId nameId;
   SOMClass classObject;
   SOMDServer server;
   static boolean firstTime = TRUE;
```

```
/* Process local case.
   ------------------- */
   if (where == FactoryFinder_local) {
     nameId = somIdFromString(className);
     classObject = SOMClassMgr_somFindClass
       (SOMClassMgrObject, nameId, 0, 0);

     if (!classObject) {
      somPrintf("%s could not be instantiated\n", className);
      return (NULL);
     }
     return classObject;
   }

/* If this is the first remote factory, initialize DSOM.
   --------------------------------------------------- */
   if (firstTime) {
     SOMD_Init(ev);
     firstTime = FALSE;
   }
/* Process remote case.
   ------------------- */
   totalRemoteFactories++;
   server = _somdFindAnyServerByClass(SOMD_ObjectMgr, ev,
           className);
   classObject = _somdGetClassObj(server, ev, className);
   if (!classObject) {
     somPrintf("%s could not be instantiated\n", className);
     exit(1);
   }
   return classObject;

/* Return statement to be customized: */
   return;
}
```

Now let's see how all this is used. First, the definition of a local/remote transparent object. Notice that dog is now derived from FactoryCreated, but otherwise there is nothing special here. The fact that dog is derived from FactoryCreated does not make the dog either a local or remote object, but rather an object whose location can be easily determined.

```
interface dog : FactoryCreated {
  attribute string bark;
  implementation {
    releaseorder: _get_bark, _set_bark;
    bark: noset, noget;
    override: somDefaultInit, somDestruct;
    dllname = "sample.dll";
  };
};
```

There is nothing special in the dog implementation, so we will not show that here.

Now we can look at the client code. Notice snoopy1 is created from one factory (localDogFactory) and snoopy2 another (remoteDogFactory). However, the real decision as to whether these factories will be creating their object locally or remotely is made at find_factory time, through use of the switch on the third parameter. This is a huge improvement over the type of code we had to write in Section 4.18 on page 107.

```c
#include <stdio.h>
#include <fact.h>
#include <dog.h>

main(){

    dog snoopy1, snoopy2;
    Factory localDogFactory;
    Factory remoteDogFactory;
    FactoryFinder ff;
    Environment *ev;
    FILE *output = stdout;

    somEnvironmentNew();

    ev = SOM_CreateLocalEnvironment();
    ff = FactoryFinderNew();

    localDogFactory = _find_factory (ff, ev, "dog",
                    FactoryFinder_local);
    remoteDogFactory = _find_factory (ff, ev, "dog",
                    FactoryFinder_remote);

    snoopy1 = _create(localDogFactory, ev);
    snoopy2 = _create(remoteDogFactory, ev);

    __set_bark(snoopy1, ev, "Woof Woof");
    __set_bark(snoopy2, ev, "woof woof");

    fprintf(output, "%s\n", __get_bark(snoopy1, ev));
    fprintf(output, "%s\n", __get_bark(snoopy2, ev));

    _free_object(ff, ev, snoopy1);
    _free_object(ff, ev, snoopy2);

    _free_factory(ff, ev, localDogFactory);
    _free_factory(ff, ev, remoteDogFactory);
}
```

The output from this program is:

```
Woof Woof
woof woof
```

Notice that a given factory creates a particular object in a particular process. The localDogFactory is specialized not only in the objects it will create (dogs), but in which process it will create them (the local process of the client program.)

At press time for this book, SOM 3.0 had not yet gone to Beta, so it is not clear what mechanism (if any) will be used to implement local/remote transparency. If such a mechanism is included, it will most likely look (and be implemented) much like the code in this section.

4.20 Review of Instantiation

We have seen a variety of possible techniques for instantiating objects. At this point, it is probably one of the more confusing aspects of writing client code. In this section we briefly review each of the possible techniques.

It is not important for the purpose of this book how clients choose to instantiate objects. We assume most clients will be using a system that is more or less consistent with the OMG Life Cycle specification. The technique that is most similar to OMG Life Cycle is the use of factories and FactoryFinders, as described in Section 4.20.4. However, in our examples, we will use the simplest possible mechanism consistent with whatever point we are illustrating, and this will often be <className>New technique, as described in Section 4.20.1.

4.20.1   <className>New

As we have seen (e.g., in Section 4.3 on page 51), SOM automatically provides a macro of the form <className>New, which can be used to instantiate objects. This macro is defined, in the C language bindings, in the client header file (the ".h" file). This macro will always instantiate a local object, that is, in the same process as the code instantiating the object.

4.20.2   _somNew on the Class Object

As discussed in Section 4.17 on page 103, classes are represented as class objects. Class objects are objects whose type is derived from SOMClass. One of the methods defined on SOMClass is somNew. When somNew is invoked on a class object, a new object of the appropriate class will be instantiated. This object will always be located in the same process as the process in which the class object resides. From the client's perspective, there is no way to tell if the instantiated object is local or remote without knowing whether the class object is local or remote.

4.20.3   DSOM Instantiators

One can use one of the various flavors of DSOM instantiators, one of which is shown in Section 4.18 on page 107. Using these instantiators, one is assured that the object will be instantiated in some server process.

4.20.4   Specialized Factories

One can use factories to unify the code used to instantiate local and remote objects. One possible way of doing this is demonstrated in Section 4.19 on page 112. There are many other techniques one could use for implementing factories, for telling factories in which process an object should be created, and for finding or creating the factories themselves.

In this book, we demonstrated the use of "FactoryFinders" as a way of locating a particular factory that is able to create a particular type of object in a particular process. One can also imagine using a naming service to keep track of factories and then using that service to locate appropriate factories.

4.21   The Interface Repository

The OMG CORBA specification defines a database called the Interface Repository. This database contains all of the available interface information about each available object. It is basically a runtime queryable representation of the Interface Definition Files. We are not going to describe how to make use of the Interface Repository, except to note that it exists. It is used extensively by the SOM distribution mechanism.

In SOM, one adds the contents of an IDL file to the Interface Repository by using a special switch on the SOM precompiler. The exact command for this is operating system dependent and can be determined from the system documentation.

4.22   Summary

This book is not intended to be a complete reference on using SOM. But we do need to look at SOM in enough detail so that you can follow the description of the Persistence Specification. There are many important features of SOM that are not covered here, but you have seen enough to understand this is a very flexible system for creating distributed objects.

The Interfaces of Persistence

The Persistent Object Service (POS) describes over 25 interfaces, 16 attributes, and 75 operations. This seems like a rather large number for a service that is responsible for nothing more than storing and restoring objects. Fortunately, most of these interfaces and operations are optional, meant to serve as examples.

There are only 7 required interfaces in the POS. Between them, these interfaces have only 17 operations and 2 attributes. Most of these are in the form of a family of 5 related I/O operations. This family of I/O operations includes connect, disconnect, store, restore, and delete. These operations are supported at three different interfaces, the persistent object (PO), the persistent object manager (POM), and the persistent data service (PDS).

The persistent object (PO) and persistent data service (PDS) represent two opposite extremes of the service. The PO is the highest-level interface, the one clients call to ask objects to perform I/O operations. The PDS is the lowest-level interface, the one that actually knows how to write bytes out to a datastore. There will be many specialized implementations of PDS around, at least one for each datastore being supported by the Persistent Object Service.

Since an I/O request to an object might potentially end up at one of many PDSs, someone needs to act as a router between object requests and low-level storage objects. This router is the persistent object manager (POM). In effect, the passage of requests from the persistent object and the persistent data service ensures that client code remains unchanged as object datastores are changed.

Similarly, the persistent data service interface serves as a contract between the POS and a datastore vendor.

The interfaces generally have names of the form <ServiceName><Module-Name>::<InterfaceName>, where <ServiceName> can be either "CosPersistence" or "somPersistence", <ModuleName> is the special module containing this interface, and <InterfaceName> is the name of the interface. The prefix "Cos" is defined by OMG and stands for one of the modules associated with the Common Object Service. The keyword "Persistence" is also assigned by OMG and means this module is part of the Persistence Service. An example of a name analysis is shown in Figure 15.

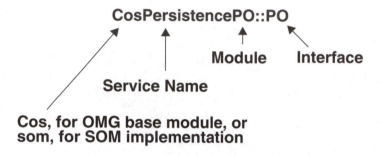

Figure 15. Name Composition of Persistence

The SOM implementation of the POS interfaces defines a series of modules starting with the word "CosPersistence" for each of the modules defined in POS. These interfaces are abstract, in that they have no real implementation. Some of these are never implemented, such as CosPersistencePO::SO. For those interfaces that require an implementation, SOM defines a parallel set of interfaces starting with word "somPersistence." The overall derivation relationship is shown in Figure 16.

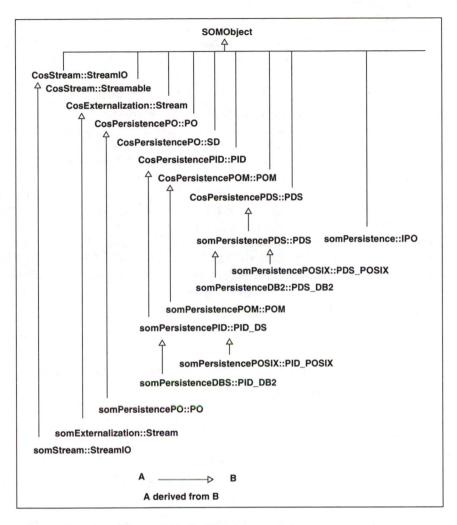

Figure 16. Interface Relationships of Persistence

5.1   PID (Persistent Identifier) Modules

```
module CosPersistencePID {

  interface PID : SOMObject {
    attribute string datastore_type;
    string get_PIDString();
  };
```

The CosPersistencePID module contains the OMG-defined interfaces for the generic PID.

```
module somPersistencePID {
  interface PID_DS :
    CosPersistencePID::PID,
    somStream::StringStreamIO {
      void set_PIDString(in string buffer);
  };
};
```

The somPersistencePID module contains the SOM extensions.

The OMG-defined Persistent Identifier (PID) is an object that identifies where the persistent state for an object is stored. It needs to contain all of the information needed to locate data in some datastore. As you can see, there is very little information in a generic PID. The assumption is that different datastore providers will include in their products specializations of this PID. The SOM-extended PID (the PID_DS, where DS stands for datastore) is still datastore neutral, but extends the OMG concept slightly.

Datastore providers are expected to implement versions of the PID_DS that are specialized for their own datastores. These PIDs will contain additional attributes specific for their datastores. For example, a PID specialized to support POSIX files might look like:

```
interface PID_POSIX : somPersistencePID::PID_DS {
  attribute string pathName;
};
```

while a PID specialized to support a relational database might look like

```
interface PID_DB2 : somPersistencePID::PID_DS {
  attribute string dbalias;
};
```

5.1.1   attribute string datastore_type

The POS specification gives the following definition of the attribute datastore_type:

> This identifies the interface of a Datastore. Example datastore_types might be "DB2," "StreamFS" and "ObjectStore". The PDS hides the Datastore's interface from the client, the persistent object and the POM, but PDS implementations are dependent on the Datastore's interface.

After working with several datastores, I believe that each datastore will have its own specialized PID. This means that the datastore type is available from the PID in two forms: first, from the attribute datastore_type; second, from the type of the PID. One might conclude from this that the attribute datastore_type is superfluous. In fact, this appears to be true.

The datastore type is present for historical reasons. In the original SOM architecture, the PID was not subclassable. It contained three attributes, the first of which was essentially a datastore type. In the architecture that Dan Chang and I presented to the OMG, this was the PID we showed.

George Copeland had been suggesting for some time that the PID should be subclassable and that its type should be a reflection of the type of the object's datastore. This change in the PID was one of George's important contributions to the overall architecture.

However, in the last minute rush to come up with an acceptable proposal, it was not clear that the datastore_type was redundant. Given more time, I believe this would have been obvious. In later versions of specification, it might be well to revisit the need for this attribute.

Client code using this attribute might look like:

```
CosPersistencePID_PID myPID;
string datastoreType;
Environment *ev;
/* ... */
datastoreType = __get_datastore_type(myPID, ev);
printf("Datastore Type: %s\n", datastoreType);
```

Since the datastore_type is an attribute, one can set as well as get its value. However, it's not clear this is a meaningful action, since a change in datastore type is almost certainly going to require a new type of PID. This would imply the attribute should have been defined read-only. Perhaps future versions of the POS specification will see this change.

5.1.2   string get_PIDString()

The POS description of the get_PIDString operation is:

> This operation returns a string version of the PID called the PIDString. The PIDString is the stored representation for a reference to persistent data. A client should only obtain the PIDString using the get_PIDString operation. This allows the PID implementation to decide the form of the PIDstring.

The operation get_PIDString is defined as returning a string. This string must contain all of the essential information of the PID object. For a generic PID object (if there was really such a thing), this string would contain just the datastore_type. For more specialized types, this string would contain any additional information added by the specialization.

Client code using this operation might look like:

```
CosPersistencePID_PID myPid;
string pidString;
Environment *ev;
/* .. */
pidString = _get_PIDString(myPid, ev);
```

Once you have the string returned by get_PIDString, there is really only one thing you can do with it, and that is to pass it into set_PIDString, which we will discuss next.

5.1.3   set_PIDString

The set_PIDString operation is used to initialize a PID given a PID_string returned by get_PIDString (see Section 5.1.2) . This is not part of the OMG standard, but one of the SOM enhancements of somPersistencePID::PPID. It is difficult to imagine not having this method, since it is a logical counterpart to set_PIDString.

The PIDString is assumed to contain all of the information necessary to initialize this new PID. The following code demonstrates the relationship between this operation and PID::get_PIDString:

```
string pidString;
somPersistence_PID_PID_DS myPID1, myPID2;
/* ... */
pidString = _get_PIDString(myPID1, ev);
myPID2 = _set_PIDString(myPID2, ev, pidString);
```

At the end of this code segment, myPID1 and myPID2 should contain the same information.

5.2   PO (Persistent Object) Modules

```
module CosPersistencePO {

    interface PO : SOMObject {
      attribute CosPersistencePID::PID p;
      CosPersistencePDS::PDS connect (
          in CosPersistencePID::PID pid);
      void disconnect (in CosPersistencePID::PID pid);
      void store (in CosPersistencePID::PID pid);
      void restore (in CosPersistencePID::PID pid);
      void Delete (in CosPersistencePID::PID pid);
    };

    interface SD : SOMObject {
      void pre_store();
      void post_restore();
    };
};
```

The CosPersistencePO module contains the OMG-defined interfaces.

```
  1.  module somPersistencePO {
  interface PO : CosPersistencePO::PO {
  };
};
```

The somPersistencePO module is the definition of the SOM implementation. As you can see, it adds no methods beyond those inherited from CosPersistence.

Because the SD interface is an abstract interface and has no SOM implementation, there is no SOM-derived counterpart to the OMG definition.

The Persistent Object (PO) interface is the optional interface that persistent objects can support if they choose to make their persistence controllable by clients. The five persistence operations (connect, disconnect, store, restore, and delete) are echoed through the three interface layers (Persistent Object, Persistent Object Manager, and Persistent Data Service).

This interface was added at the bequest of Mike Powell, of SunSoft. The IBM architecture would have had clients storing objects by making requests of the Persistent Object Manager (POM). Dan and I believed that going through the POM allowed even existing objects to be made persistent.

The debate over the need for the PO interface centered around the heavyweight/lightweight object controversy. Proponents of lightweight objects believed that objects should not be required to carry the baggage of services. Proponents of heavyweight objects believed that only an object can know how a particular service should be implemented for that object.

Lightweight object proponents believe that objects should only know about their direct behaviors. Since an object has no idea how it will be used, it can't know in advance what service specific interfaces it should support.

Heavyweight objects also seem to imply an explosion of object types. Imagine if we have a Persistent Object (PO) interface and a Transactional Object (TO) interface. Now if we want a dog object, we need a dog, a PO_dog, and TO_dog, and a PO_TO_dog. If we start to add other services, such as Lockable, this situation quickly gets out of hand.

Heavyweight object proponents believe only an object knows what services it will support and how it will support them. Lightweight object proponents believe that the implementation of common object services should be outside of the object.

There was also a major technical problem with not requiring that objects support a PO-like interface. This is due to quirk in a completely unrelated service specification, that of Life Cycle.

The oddity of the Life Cycle Service had to do with object identity. Everybody had assumed that one of the purposes of the Life Cycle Service was to tell if two object references were referring to the same object. In fact, the OMG Request for Proposals on the Life Cycle specification specifically required object equivalence.

The Life Cycle Service, as championed by SunSoft, omitted this critical feature. This was done consciously; in fact, a white paper written by Mike Powell and widely distributed within the OMG argued that object identity is a very difficult operation to support. There was considerable discussion over this omission, and SunSoft was able to convince OMG that this operation should be left out.

Not having object identity, however, makes it very difficult to implement any algorithm that is based on collections of objects. Consider trying to implement a software black box with the following interface.

```
interface blackBox {
   addNewObject(in object obj)raises (ObjectAlreadyInBox);
   sequence<objects> getObjects();
};
```

The operation addNewObject takes an object and adds it into the blackBox. If the object is already in the blackBox, it is supposed to raise an ObjectAlreadyInBox exception and presumably reject the object. In order to see if the object is already in the box, the program must check the new object against each of the objects in the box. In order to check two objects to see if they are the same, one must depend on object identity.

Our original architecture would have implemented the Persistent Object Manager (POM) as such a blackBox. Rather than having the object keep track of its Persistent ID, as implied by the PID attribute on the PO interface, the POM would have kept track of object/PID relationships or at least could have been implemented this way. This means, though, that when an object is assigned a PID, the POM must make sure the object hasn't already been assigned one. This would require the POM to go through each of its known object/PID mappings to see if the object was already mapped. And this, or course, requires object identity.

When it was clear that the Life Cycle Service was going to pass without object identity, we decided to reevaluate our architecture. The PO interface did provide a convenient place to store object/PID relationships, and in any case it was presented as a non-negotiable item by SunSoft.

Although the POS specification presents the PO interface as the required path for client persistence requests, it is not clear that this can be enforced. Since all object persistence requests must eventually route through the POM, there seems to be nothing stopping clients from requesting persistence operations directly on the POM. Thus, we may have been giving up less than we thought at the time. In fact, our standard programming model has objects supporting an ImplicitPO interface, which is a layer built on top of the OMG architecture.

The ImplicitPO interface is described in Section 6.2 on page 155. It provides a coordinated effort between the Persistence and Transaction Services, and the most logical implementation completely bypasses the PO interface in favor of directly using the POM. Although this POM does not support the black box collection characteristics (and can't, because of lack of object identity), it does have the remainder of our original POM architectural elements, namely the ability to store objects not supporting the PO interface.

5.2.1   PID Attribute

The main purpose of the PID attribute is to provide a convenient holding place for the PersistentID (PID). The implication of storing the PID in a single attribute is that a given object can have no more than one PID at a time.

Notice that all of the persistence operations take a PID as an optional argument. Any object whose persistence is being managed *must* have an associated PID, but there are two ways the PID can become associated. One is via the PID attribute on PO. The other is through a PID being explicitly passed to the operation. As discussed in Section 4.20 on page 118, there are many ways to instantiate an object, and we will use one of the simplest here. The following code snippet shows the use of a PID attribute:

```
company ABC;
Environment *ev;
CosPersistencePOSIX_PID_POSIX pidCompany;

pidCompany = CosPersistencePOSIX_PID_POSIXNew();
__set_datastore_type(pidCompany, ev, "File1");
__set_pathName(pidCompany, ev, "abc.dat");

abc = companyNew(companyFact, ev, pidCompany);
__set_p(abc, ev, pidCompany);
_restore(abc, ev, NULL);
```

Notice the last three lines, shown in bold. The first instantiates a company. The second associates a pid (not just any PID, but a PID specialized for POSIX files.) The third restores the company object. The PID contains the information saying where the data is located. Since the restore has no third parameter, the persistence framework uses the PID associated through the attribute set method.

By removing the attribute set method and making a minor change in the last lines, we can pass in a PID. The new lines are:

```
abc = companyNew(companyFact, ev, pidCompany);
_restore(abc, ev, pidCompany);
```

In general, it's more convenient to pass in the PID when software is reusing the same PID for many stores. But as we are moving more toward an implicit storage story, as exemplified by the ImplicitPO interface, this becomes more of a moot point anyway, since we generally assume the PID has been associated at creation time.

5.2.2 General Discussion on PO behaviors

The PO operations are all really pass-through to the corresponding Persistent Object Manger (POM) operations. The behaviors that are described here are the client-visible behaviors, but the implementation of the behavior requires passing through the different layers of the POS interfaces.

5.2.3 PDS connect (in PID pid)

According to POS (section 4.3.1),

This begins a connection between the data in the PO and the Datastore location indicated by the PID. The persistent state may be updated as operations are performed on the object. This operation returns the PDS that handles persistence for use by those Protocols that require the PO to call the PDS.

This operation has been the subject of more arguments than probably all other POS operations combined. There are two hotly contested issues involved with this operation. The first is the semantics of the operation. The second is the return value.

This operation did not appear in the original IBM specification. SunSoft, however, considered itself to be the champion of the object-oriented databases. The most successful OODB, and the one that formed the basis of the ODMG specification, is Object Store™ by Object Design Incorporated (ODI).

ODI's product is an example of a so-called *single-level* store datastore. Single-level store datastores are characterized by a virtual tight coupling of memory to disk, so tight that for all intents and purposes, memory and disk are one and the same. There is a moment in time when this coupling is defined by the client, usually the time at which the object is instantiated. SunSoft felt that the connect operation would be useful when implementing single-level stores as object stores, believing that the connect operation would serve to couple the memory to the disk.Therefore, they insisted it be added in the last-minute negotiations between George Copeland and Mike Powell.

It is far from clear that the connect operation has any value. A great deal of time has been spent trying to understand how best to support single-level datastores within the POS architecture, and there is little indication this operation will be useful.

One of the problems in trying to interpret connect as a mapping between memory and disk is that, by virtue of being part of the PO interface, it must necessarily be invoked on an already instantiated object. Single-level datastores typically do this mapping at the time of instantiation. It is not surprising, therefore, that the most promising work involving POS support for single-level datastores centers around the Life Cycle creation operations.

The semantics of connect are vague at best. According to POS, the operation "begins a connection between the data in the PO and the Datastore location," but the semantics of this connection are unspecified. The object's "persistent state may be updated as operations are performed on the object." Some people believe this *allows* automatic updates to the persistent state; others believe this *requires* automatic updates. Based on the history of the POS proposal, a strict interpretation of the language, and many discussions with George Copeland about what he and Mike Powell meant by this operation, I have concluded that *allows* is the only reasonable interpretation. But the arguments are not over on this topic.

This might seem like an academic argument, but the semantics of connect are of major significance for datastore vendors. In the unlikely event that connect is interpreted as *requiring* that updates to the object be automatically reflected in updates to the persistent store, multi-level datastore vendors will find this operation very expensive, or even impossible, to support. And since the operation occurs after instantiation, even the single-level datastore vendors, for whom this operation was intended, might have trouble implementing this efficiently.

The other problem with connect is in its return value. It is defined as returning a Persistent Data Service (PDS). A PDS is the object that knows how to interact with a datastore, the object that would receive the routing request from the Persistent Object Manager (POM).

The POS specification says that the PDS is returned "for use by those Protocols that require the PO to call the PDS"; however, this seems illogical in view of the fact that POs are not the initiators of this call, they are the targets of the call. The fact that connect returns a PDS implies the client, not the Persistent Object, is intended to access the PDS. Why would a client want access to a PDS?

The only reason a client might want access to a PDS is to directly invoke operations on the PDS rather than go through the Persistent Object Manager (POM). All standard PDS operations can and should be invoked through the POM. So the only operations that logically should be invoked directly through the PDS are nongeneral PDS operations, but operations added to specific PDS specializations.

The concept of specialized PDS operations opens a philosophical can of worms. One of the great values of POS is that it provides a datastore-independent coding model. Most datastore vendors claim to support datastore independence but also believe their particular datastore offers unique and/or critical operations and want clients to be able to access these operations. These specialized operations, they say, still provide datastore independence with any other datastore that also provides these operations.

I see a danger in any assumptions that clients will invoke methods directly on the PDS. This will encourage datastore vendors to add all kinds of extraneous methods to their PDS specialization. This rapidly defeats the purpose of POS and limits the ability of their customers to take advantage of higher-level programming models (such as Implicit Persistence) that don't recognize such datastore-specific operations.

So we are left with two problems with the PO connect operation. Vague semantics and a return value that encourages disrespect for datastore independence. It is difficult to believe this operation will survive many more revisions of the architecture.

Given that the semantics of connects are so vague, implementors are left pretty much to their own devices to decide on what, exactly, the operation does. One logical implementation is to have the connect operation open the datastore and then restore the object. Operations on the persistent object are not automatically synchronized with the datastore until the disconnect. Another possible "implementation" is simply to raise a NOT_IMPLEMENTED exception.

Since the whole concept of connect/disconnect is of questionable value, it doesn't seem to matter much how the actual implementation is done. I would simply recommend that clients not use it.

5.2.4   void disconnect (in PID pid)

According to POS,

> This ends a connection between the data in the PO and the Datastore location indicated by the PID. It is undefined whether or not the object is usable if not connected to persistent state. The PID can be nil.

The disconnect operation is the reverse of connect. Since I do not recommend using connect, it should come as no surprise that I do not recommend using disconnect. Regardless of implementation, the use of a connect without a corresponding disconnect is considered an error, and the result is undefined.

One of our first interpretations of connect/disconnect was that connect would "open" a datastore and disconnect would "close" the datastore, using a reference count algorithm. In pseudocode, the algorithms for these two methods would be as follows:

```
po::connect()
{
  find underlying datastore;
  if (datastore is not open) open datastore;
  increment open count for this datastore;
}
po::disconnect()
{
  find underlying datastore;
  decrement open count for this datastore;
  if (open count for this datastore == 0)
    close datastore;
}
```

This seemed like a reasonable interpretation, until we started thinking how connect/disconnect would be used in real programs. Consider the following code fragment:

```
/* Declare variables.
   ------------------ */
  Account account;
  somPersistencePID_PID_DB2 accountPID;
  Environment *ev;
  string accountID;
  account = AccountNew();

/* Set up account PID.
   ------------------- */
  accountPID = somPersistencePID_PID_DB2New();
  __set_DBAlias(accountPID, ev, "ACCOUNTS");
```

```
/* Start looping through account records.
   ------------------------------------- */
   done = FALSE;
   for (;;) {
     accountNumber = getAccountNumberFromUser();
     __set_ID(accountPID, ev, accountNumber);
     if (accountNumber = NULL) break;
     _connect(account, ev, accountPID);
     _getAccountChangesFromUser(account, ev);
     _disconnect(accound, ev, accountPID);
   }
}
```

This code has a serious performance problem. This code results in a series of objects all being written to the same datastore. Each time a connection is made, the datastore will be open, and with each disconnection, the datastore will be closed. If one hundred objects are stored, we will have one hundred open and closes of the datastore. Typically, opens of a datastore are slow, much slower than I/O operations that use the datastore. For this reason, code is always written to minimize the number of times the datastore must be opened.

Associating the connect/disconnect on the PersistentObject with the open/close of the underlying datastore virtually guarantees that the datastore has no way of optimizing opens. Since the datastore has no way of knowing another object is about to be sent its way, it doesn't know that it should optimize itself by staying open.

So, I am left with the conclusion that connect/disconnect have little meaning, and my recommendation to customers is that connect/disconnect not be used.

This leaves a little problem of opening and closing the datastore. If the only obvious interface for opening and closing is in connect/disconnect and we recommend against the use of this interface, what can we offer as an alternative?

Originally we considered adding methods to the PID to open and close datastores. Some of our early implementations did just that. This mapped well to POSIX files, and even to some IBM relational databases. As we tried to map this to various other products, such as IBM's IMS™, we soon found this to be a non-general approach.

George Copeland finally came up with the solution. He suggested leaving the responsibility for opening and closing datastores to the specialized PDS. This is an elegant solution and one that appears heading for product stability. We discuss this further in Section 8.5.3 on page 215.

5.2.5   void store (in PID pid)

According to POS,

> This gets the persistent data out of the object in memory and puts it in the Datastore location indicated by the PID. The PID can be nil.

The store operation transfers the persistent data from the object to the datastore. If the datastore was not already opened, then this presumably results in the datastore being opened, although this is up to the PDS implementation.

5.2.6   void restore (in PID pid)

According to POS,

> This gets the object's persistent data from the Datastore location indicated by the PID and inserts it into the object in memory. The PID can be nil.

This operation is the reverse of the store operation. The persistent data is transferred from the datastore to the object. Again, if the datastore was not already opened, this will presumably result in a datastore open; but again, this is up to the PDS.

5.2.7   void Delete (in PID pid)

According to POS,

> This deletes the object's persistent data from the Datastore location indicated by the PID. The PID can be nil.

The Delete operation is a request to the underlying datastore to delete the persistent data associated with this object. This operation does not delete the object itself. This is a function of the Life Cycle Service and/or the ORB.

The original OMG specification defines delete as starting with a lowercase "d." However, we have found that this generally conflicts with the C++ keyword "delete." Until this is resolved by the OMG, we have changed all of the "delete" methods to "Delete."

There is an odd discrepancy between the description of disconnect and delete. The description of disconnect specifically says that after the operation is invoked, "It is undefined whether or not the object is usable." No such caveat is included with the delete operation, even though for both operations it is clear that the data and the object must be disassociated.

This lends further credence that connect/disconnect were meant to provide functionality for the single-level datastores. The POS specification does not say what happens if one does a connect followed by a delete. Is the object usable? This is further evidence of the last-minute insertion of connect/disconnect without adequate time for reflection.

5.2.8   SD (Synchronized Data) Interface

```
interface SD : SOMObject{
  void pre_store();
  void post_restore();
};
```

The Synchronized Data (SD) interface is an optional interface that can be supported by objects that have both persistent and transient data and a need to keep these two data partitions synchronized.

As an example of an SD object, consider a Word Processing Object (WPO). The WPO might be implemented by having a large virtual address space in which a document is maintained (the docStoreBuffer) and a small address space in which the most recently accessed portions are kept (the docCache). All updates to the document are made to the docCache and then moved out to the docStoreBuffer, using a least recently accessed algorithm.

WPO has two distinct partitions of its data, a transient partition and a persistent partition. The transient partition is the docCache, and the persistent partition is the docStoreBuffer. When a request is made to store the object, only the docStoreBuffer will be stored; however, the WPO might have recent updates in the docCache that have not been reflected in the docStoreBuffer.

The SD interface provides a mechanism to synchronize these two data partitions at the time the store or restore occurs. The synchronization will take place between the docCache and the docStoreBuffer. When the WPO is about to be stored, the docCache will be flushed out to the docStoreBuffer. When the WPO has just been restored, the docCache will be updated with some portion of the docStoreBuffer.

Support for the SD interface does not imply support for the PO interface, and support for PO does not imply support for SD. These two interfaces are orthogonal to each other. The PO interface says that clients will control when the object is stored/restored, regardless of whether the object's persistent state is synchronized with its transient state. The SD interface says the object's state will be kept synchronized on store/restore, regardless of whether the store/restore requests are made by the client of the object or the object itself.

The SD interface is an abstract interface, in the sense that no default implementation is expected. The object implementation should override both SD operations with operations that make sense from that particular object's perspective. In the implementation of pre_store, we would expect WPO to flush its docCache updates to the docStoreBuffer. In the implementation of post_restore, we would expect WPO to initialize its docCache from the newly read-in docStoreBuffer.

An example of simple WPO definition using the SD and PO interfaces is:

```
interface WordProcessor : CosPersistencePO::PO,
                          CosPersistencePO::SD {
  attribute string docCache;
  attribute string docStorageBuffer;
  /* ... */
  implementation {
    override: pre_store;
    override: post_restore;
  };
};
```

The example shown uses SOM syntax to show the overriding of pre_store and post_restore, since standard IDL does not define how to override.

5.2.9   void pre_store()

According to POS,

> This ensures that the persistent data is synchronized with the transient data. It can be invoked either by the object, the POM or the PDS.

The pre_store operation is invoked on the object just before the object is stored. As discussed, this operation should be overridden by the object implementation if synchronization before store is desired.

The POS specification is in error when it says the operation "can be invoked either by the object, the POM or the PDS." It is very important that the system guarantee this operation is invoked once and only once. This guarantee cannot be met if the operation can be invoked by any object that so desires. The proper place for this operation to be invoked is in the POM.

5.2.10   void post_restore()

According to POS,

> This ensures that the transient data is synchronized with the persistent data. It can be invoked either by the object, the POM or the PDS.

The post_restore operation is invoked on the object just after the object is restored. As discussed, this operation should be overridden by the object implementation if synchronization after restore is desired. The same arguments that dictate pre_store be called by and only by the POM also apply to post_restore.

The idea for the SD interface came directly out of the original persistence framework for the first release of SOM. Given what we now know about persistence, I am not sure if this interface is still useful.

Arguing against continued support for SD is the fact that we now believe persistence is closely tied into the Externalization Service. This relationship is described more fully in Section 7.2 on page 173. For now, we just point out that if we assume objects use externalization protocols for moving data in and out of themselves, then objects already have a natural way to know when they have been stored. Objects will always have externalize_to_stream called once and only once during a store, and this is a reasonable place to synchronize persistent and transient data. Similarly, objects can use internalize_from_stream to take whatever measures are necessary as part of the restore stage.

Arguing in favor of continued support for SD is that objects never know why they have been externalized_to_stream or internalized_from_stream. The supposition that they were stored or restored is only one of several possible reasons for these methods being invoked. Although this is certainly true, it is not clear if there is any significant difference between these methods being invoked as part of store/restore and within the course of one of the algorithms in which they are used. We need more experience with designing serious objects before we can make a definitive call on this issue.

5.3 POM (Persistent Object Manager) Module

```
module CosPersistencePOM {
  interface POM {
    PDS connect (in Object obj, in PID pid);
    void disconnect (in Object obj, in PID pid);
    void store (in Object obj, in PID pid);
    void restore (in Object obj, in PID pid);
    void Delete (in Object obj, in PID pid);
  };
};
```

The somPersistencePOM module defines the SOM implementation of a POM, which, for the purposes of this discussion, adds nothing to the OMG definition.

The POM is primarily a router object. Its main purpose is to find the appropriate Persistent Data Service (PDS) for this object and forward the operation onward. The POS specification does not specify how this routing is to be done or how PDS routing information is expressed to the POM.

The POM always routes to one of possibly many PDSs. Each PDS knows about some subset of datastores and some subset of protocols for getting persistent data in and out of an object. Therefore, the POM must route to a PDS based on both the protocol(s) the object supports and the datastore(s) in which the object's persistent data resides.

By *protocol* we mean some mechanism for moving data in and out of an object.

The POM needs information from both the object and the PersistentID (PID) to determine which PDS will receive the request. The object contains the knowledge about supported protocols. The PID contains the knowledge about the datastore. That knowledge is both explicitly through its attribute datastore_type (described in Section 5.1.1 on page 124) and implicitly through its type.

There are many ways the POM might determine the protocol(s) supported by an object, none of which are specified by the POS specification. Possible ways the POM might determine the protocol include the following:

- The POM might check for a given protocol by seeing if the object supports some interface that is identified with a protocol. An example of this is the externalization service protocol.We can assume objects support the externalization service protocol if they are derived from CosStream::Streamable, an interface described in Section 7.2.4 on page 180.

- A POM might read the Interface Repository (IR) (see Section 4.21 on page 119) to get information on protocols associated with particular object types.
- The POM might offer a set of operations allowing the registration of relationships between object types and protocols.
- The POM might ask the object which protocol it would like to use, assuming the object supported some such informational operation. This cannot be the only mechanism, since the POM cannot depend on operations that are not part of the POS specification.

Once the POM knows both the intended protocol and target datastore, it must choose an appropriate PDS. There are many ways the appropriate PDS can be determined, similar to the determination about object protocols, and this is also undefined by the POS specification. Some options include the following:

- The POM might read the Interface Repository (IR) to get information on which datastores are associated with which PDSs.
- The POM might offer a set of operations allowing the registration of relationships between PDSs and datastores.
- The POM might ask the PDSs which datastores they support, assuming the PDSs supported some such informational operation. This could not be the only mechanism, since the POM cannot require that the PDSs support operations other than those identified in the POS specification.

In the prototype, we used an easily implemented file registration mechanism for mapping between objects, datastores, and PDSs. At POM instantiation time, the POM reads a file with the following format:

```
object_type_1        datastore_type_1      PDS_type_1

object_type_2        datastore_type_2      PDS_type_2
object_type_3        datastore_type_3      PDS_type_3
etc.
```

An example of this file might look like:

```
dog          IBM_POSIX         somPersistencePOSIX::PDS_POSIX
cat          IBM_POSIX         somPersistencePOSIX::PDS_POSIX
account      IBM_BTREE         somPersistenceBTREE::PDS_BTREE
account      IBM_DB2           somPersistenceDB2::PDS_DB2
```

This file would be interpreted as saying the dogs stored to POSIX files use the PDS specialized for POSIX files, as do cats stored to POSIX files. However, accounts stored to DB2 use the DB2 specialization, and accounts stored to Btrees use the BTREE specialization.

    We allow default routings to be specified according to object hierarchies. Thus, if a routing is not found for a particular object type, the POM checks to see if there is a routing for the base type. For example, if dog and cat are both derived from animal, the above file can be simplified to:

```
animal      IBM_POSIX      somPersistencePOSIX::PDS_POSIX
account     IBM_BTREE      somPersistenceBTREE::PDS_BTREE
account     IBM_DB2        somPersistenceDB2::PDS_DB2
```

The externalization protocol, if used, is reflected in the interface hierarchy. Therefore, the type of object using this protocol will typically be listed as "CosStream::Streamable."

The POM operations are intended to be called by the persistent object. If the persistent object is a Persistent Object (PO), then the implementation of each of the PO I/O operations will pass through to the POM associated with the address space.

The only behavior that is described by POS is the actual routing behavior. However, one could imagine other behaviors the POM might engage in as well. The POM might check for error conditions, synchronize the object via the Synchronized Data interface (see Section 5.2.8 on page 134), or perform optimizations for storage.

The POM methods are all used pretty much the same, so we can demonstrate the use of any of the methods as being representative of the lot. We will show the use of the store method. There are two logical places from which to call the POM store.

The first possibility is from inside the PO implementation of store. This sample pseudocode demonstrates a possible implementation:

```
void PO::store (in CosPersistencePID_PID pid)
{
  If (pid) pidToUse = pid;
  else pidToUse = get_pid();
  check for errors;
  Invoke POM::store();
}
```

The second likely place to see a POM store method invoked is inside the code that does implicit storage in conjunction with the Transaction Service. This type of storage is described in Section 6.2 on page 155.

5.3.1   PDS connect (in Object obj, in PID pid)

According to POS,

> This begins a connection between data in the object and the Datastore location indicated by the PID. The persistent state may be updated as operations are performed on the object. This operation returns the PDS that is assigned the object's PID for use by those Protocols that require the PO to call the PDS.

The POM connect operation must first find the appropriate PDS for this object and datastore and then pass through the connect invocation to the PDS connect.

Notice that this operation, like the Persistent Object's connect, returns a Persistent Data Service (PDS). In Section 5.2.3 on page 129, we described why returning a PDS from the PO connect was at best debatable. At the POM level, however, returning a PDS is more logical, because the PO connect is called by the object's client, who has no business making direct calls to the PDS. The POM connect is called by the persistent object. Giving the persistent object access to the PDS allows the flexibility of the persistent object taking control of the protocol.

In practice, it is not clear that the connect operation here is any more useful than the PO connect. Only time will tell if any reasonable implementations are created which make good use of connect.

5.3.2   void disconnect (in Object obj, in PID pid)

According to POS,

> This ends a connection between the data in the object and the Datastore location indicated by the PID. It is undefined whether or not the object is usable if not connected to persistent state. The PID can be nil.

The POM disconnect operation must first find the appropriate PDS for this object and datastore and then pass through the disconnect invocation to the PDS disconnect.

This operation is the inverse of the connect operation. If history decides the connect operation is not useful (see discussion in Section 5.3.1 on page 139), then this operation's fate will also be in question.

5.3.3   void store (in Object obj, in PID pid)

According to POS,

> This gets the persistent data out of the object in memory and puts it in the Datastore location indicated by the PID. The PID can be nil.

The POM store operation must first find the appropriate PDS for this object and datastore and then pass through the store invocation to the PDS store.

The POM store is associated with the synchronized data pre_store operation. Persistent objects that support synchronized data operations do so because they want the opportunity to synchronize their persistent and transient data at store and restore time. The POM store will invoke the synchronized data pre_store before actually storing data for the object. If the persistent (and synchronized) object has overridden pre_store, it should have done so with an implementation that brings its persistent data up to date with its transient data in preparation for storage. The pre_store operation is described in Section 5.2.8 on page 134.

The simplest possible implementation of a POM store might look like:

```
void store(POM somSelf,Environment *ev, Object obj, PID pid)
{
    CosPersistence_PDS_PDS pds;
    pds = _get_appropriate_pds(somSelf, ev, obj, pid);
    if (is_a(obj, ""SD")) _pre_store(obj, ev);
    CosPersistence_PDS_PDS_store(pds, ev, obj, pid);
}
```

5.3.4   void restore (in Object obj, in PID pid)

According to POS,

> This gets the object's persistent data from the Datastore location indicated by the PID and inserts it into the object in memory. The PID can be nil.

The POM restore operation must first find the appropriate PDS for this object and datastore and then pass through the restore invocation to the PDS restore.

Similar to the relationship between POM store and SD pre_store is the relationship between POM restore and SD post_restore. The POM restore is associated with the synchronized data post_restore operation. The POM restore will invoke the synchronized_data post_restore just after restoring the persistent data for the object. If the synchronized object has overridden post_restore, it should have done so with an implementation that brings its transient data up to date with its persistent data in preparation for further client usage. The post_restore operation is described in Section 5.2.8 on page 134.

The simplest possible implementation of a POM restore might look like:

```
void restore(POM somSelf,Environment *ev, Object obj, PID pid)
{
    CosPersistencePDS_PDS pds;
    pds = _get_appropriate_pds(somSelf, ev, obj, pid);
    CosPersistence_PDS_PDS_store(pds, ev, obj, pid);
    if (is_a(obj, ""SD")) _post_restore(obj, ev);
}
```

5.3.5   void Delete (in Object obj, in PID pid)

According to POS,

> This deletes the object's persistent data from the Datastore location indicated by the PID. The PID can be nil.

The POM delete operation must first find the appropriate PDS for this object and datastore and then pass through the delete invocation to the PDS delete. The actual delete must be done by the PDS, since, like the other POM I/O operations, the POM doesn't know how to find, much less delete, actual data from a datastore.

5.4   PDS (Persistent Data Service) Module

```
module CosPersistencePDS {
  interface PDS {
    void connect (in Object obj, in PID pid);
    void disconnect (in Object obj, in PID pid);
    void store (in Object obj, in PID pid);
    void restore (in Object obj, in PID pid);
    void Delete (in Object obj, in PID pid);
  };
};
```

According to POS,

> Some Protocols may require specialization of the PDS interface. However, no matter what Protocol and Datastore is used, a PDS always supports at least the following interface.

There are many possible specializations of the PDS, one for each protocol/datastore pair. Hopefully, people will agree to limit the number of protocols to one (externalization).

The PDS interface represents the contract between a POM and a datastore provider. The interface is intended to be an abstract base class, in that it defines behavior but does not necessarily provide an implementation. The actual implementations are provided by the datastore vendors. The decisions that must be made in creating these implementations are discussed when we look at the datastore provider's perspective.

It is possible for datastore vendors to add new operations to a particular implementation of the PDS; however, new operations should be added only to support particular protocols. New operations should not be added as a way of giving clients new operations on the datastore. Any operations designed for client usage would violate the principle of datastore independence, as we discussed earlier.

The value of adding new operations is somewhat questionable in any case. The only time anybody can access the PDS directly is when using either the PO or the POM connect operation. If a client was using either the PO or POM store or restore operations, the client would have no access to the underlying PDS, since neither of these operations returns the PDS. Since, as we have already discussed, connect is of no or limited value, it is not clear how one would access any operations added to specializations of the PDS, even if it was desirable.

Although adding new operations to the PDS interface is of limited value, specializing the existing operations is of supreme importance and is at the heart of the plug-and-play philosophy. These standard PDS operations represent the expectations of the POM on the underlying datastore. The POM will interact with a given PDS, knowing nothing about the underlying datastore the PDS supports or the protocols with which the PDS works. If there were any new operations added to the PDS, the POM would have no way of knowing about them. The only assumptions the POM can make is that the PDS supports five methods — connect, disconnect, store, restore, and delete.

In a typical POS running system, there will be many implementations of the PDS interface, each supporting some datastore. The routing of the POM method invocation to PDS implementation is taken care of by standard runtime method resolution. Consider this possible implementation of the POM restore method:

```
void restore(POM somSelf,Environment *ev, Object obj, PID pid)
{
    PDS pds;
    pds = _get_appropriate_pds(somSelf, ev, obj, pid);
    PDS_restore(pds, ev, obj, pid);
    if (is_a(obj, ""SD")) _post_restore(obj, ev);
}
```

Notice how the method declares an object reference to a PDS without knowing which PDS implementation will eventually be used. The method then invokes restore on that PDS without knowing which of many possible PDS restore implementations will be invoked.

These PDS restore implementations are dramatically different from each other. In fact, other than sharing a common signature and a common semantics, they may have nothing in common. A PDS restoring from a relational database, such as DB2, might use a static SQL interface, whereas a PDS restoring from a POSIX file might use a stream-like interface. They might not even agree on how to get data in and out of the persistent object. But the fact that they all restore through a defined restore operation, with defined parameters, means that although the POM may not know how they do the restore, the POM does know how to invoke the restore operation and how to interpret the results.

5.4.1   void connect (in Object obj, in PID pid)

According to POS,

> This connects the object to its persistent state, after disconnecting any previous persistent state. The persistent state may be updated as operations are performed on the object.

As with the rest of the connect family, the PDS connect is vague and poorly defined. In addition to the usual connect vagaries, we have the issue of how the connect disconnects any previous persistent state, since most likely any previous persistent state would be in some other datastore.

Although the POS specification says that the "persistent state may be updated as operations are performed on the object," it doesn't say what happens to the object if the datastore is updated in a way that changes the underlying persistent state.

5.4.2   void disconnect (in Object obj, in PID pid)

According to POS,

> This disconnects the object from the persistent state. It is undefined whether or not the object is usable if not connected to persistent state.

The usual discussions about disconnect apply here as well.

5.4.3   void store (in Object obj, in PID pid)

According to POS,

> This saves the object's persistent state.

The PDS store method is the bottom-level store, as far as the POS specification is concerned. The PDS store may be implemented by use of lower-level classes. The official OMG specification gives several examples of how a PDS might be implemented, but none of these example architectures are required.

The store method is responsible for getting the persistent data out of the object, using some mutually agreed on protocol, and putting that persistent data into some datastore location identified by the PID.

According to POS, once the data transfer has been completed, the datastore will not be updated until the next store request. In general, this is difficult to guarantee. Should the datastore be updated through a non-POS path (such as a standard database update), the PDS will not be involved.

5.4.4   void restore (in Object obj, in PID pid)

According to POS,

> This loads the object's persistent state. The persistent state will not be modified unless a store_object or other mutating operation is performed on the persistent state.

The restore method is the inverse of the PDS store method. It is responsible for getting the persistent data out of some datastore location identified by the PID and moving it into the object.

5.4.5   void Delete (in Object obj, in PID pid)

According to POS,

> This deletes the object's persistent data from the Datastore location indicated by the PID.

This is the lowest-level delete method. It is responsible for finding the data in some datastore as identified by the PID and deleting it.

5.5   Summary

As you can see, although the POS documents a large number of interfaces and operations, only a few are actually required. As long as you can remember that the PID contains the data location information, the PO contains the optional client interface, the POM is a router, and the PDS is ultimately responsible for moving data between objects and datastores, you basically understand OMG Persistence.

In the next three chapter we will look in detail at three different perspectives of POS. These are:

- POS from the client's perspective.
- POS from the object implementor's perspective.
- POS from the datastore provider's perspective.

One of the nice features of POS is that each of these three needs understand only a piece of the overall POS framework.

The Application Developer Perspective

In this chapter, we will describe the client programming model inherent in POS. The POS specification itself describes only a low-level interface to storing and restoring objects, basically describing the actual commands to transfer data in a datastore-independent manner. At the time we designed the architecture, it was difficult to know how clients would use these interfaces for two reasons:

- The Persistence specification was completed before many related services, in particular, the Transaction Service, had even started.
- Although the final proposal with SunSoft encompassed all our key architectural features unchanged, some minor interface changes were made, and one significant interface, the Persistent Object interface, was added. These changes were strictly paper designs; neither company had actually implemented any of the modifications.

The OMG process was originally designed to ensure that specifications are based on actual products. This is to ensure that specifications are based on real technology, not vaporware. In the past, this has been taken with a large grain of salt.

The reality is that the commitment to real technology is at odds with another important OMG principle: consensus. Companies are encouraged to make joint submissions. It was not considered desirable for the OMG to be forced to vote between competing proposals. In fact, at the time the Persistence Proposal was being prepared, the OMG had never successfully adopted a specification by vote. Many of us were skeptical that a decision by vote was even possible.

Since OMG consensus dictates that disparate companies submit joint proposals, it is almost impossible to have a final proposal based on actual running
technology. At best, proposals are based on bits of pieces of technology from different companies, some of which have never been implemented, and none of
which have been put together in a running product.

This is not a criticism, only a description of reality. In my experience, the
decision to favor consensus rather than preexisting technology is correct. In
areas of core technology, standards can only work if they are widely accepted.

Since the formal adoption of POS, several things have changed. In particular,

- I have prototyped the entire Persistence specification and written dozens of
  test cases that have helped clarify the client model.
- George Copeland has worked with Single-Level Datastore providers, understanding how their products can seamlessly fit into a unifying programming model.
- The Transaction specification has been completed and has gone through the
  initial round of approvals, allowing us to work out how these two closely
  related services will work together.
- Guylaine Cantin and I have presented the Persistence prototype to thousands of customers and have received valuable feedback.

This chapter describes the original, low-level persistence interface as defined in
the OMG specification, called here the Explicit Persistence Model, and a much
easier to use, higher-level client programming model, called here the Implicit
Persistence Model.

6.1   The Explicit Persistence Model

POS defines a straightforward client programming model. It describes an interface called PO for Persistent Object. This interface supports the client-level operation for the underlying datastore. Any objects that are to be stored must be
derived from the PO interface. Thus, if you purchase a dog type object and you
are told it is a POS persistent object, you can reasonably assume it supports the
operations defined in PO.

There are only three useful operations defined in PO. These are store,
restore, and delete. Since your dog object is derived from PO, you can tell some
instance of dog, say, lassie, to store, restore, or delete herself.

Most datastore products differentiate between storing existing and storing
new data. Files, for example, are opened differently depending on whether they
are going to be created from scratch or already contain data. SQL datastores distinguish between insert, for new data, and update, for existing data.

Unlike these underlying datastores, POS chose not to make this distinction.
The same operation, store, is used regardless of whether the object data is brand-
new or is overwriting existing data.

The decision not to distinguish between store_new and store_existing has been controversial. When first designing the specification, we believed the distinction between these two was largely a result of how datastores are implemented, rather than how programmers want to interact with the datastores. We believed that code segments such as the following were all too common:

```
in_store=is_data_already_in_store(data);
if(in_store)store_existing(data);
else store_new(data);
```

Our belief was that the vast bulk of this could be written much more simply as:

```
store(data)
```

if the underlying datastore did not make this distinction.

I still believe that in the majority of cases, this unified view of store is easier to deal with. However, I have heard a number of complaints about this from customers who say they need to distinguish between these two store cases. I have not yet seen a convincing scenario where this distinction actually seems useful. I am still not sure if these customers are correct or if they are just habituated into thinking this way.

The truth may turn out to be someplace in between. Many applications distinguish between store_new and store_existing only because they think they must, and some because they have a genuine need.

A true need to know if data already exists can still be accommodated within POS by preceding the store by restore, such as:

```
restore(lassie)
if(exception showing no data found)
  existing = TRUE;
else
  existing = FALSE
..
```

Given the controversy over this, one might expect further discussion and possible evolution of the POS specification and/or vendor adaptations to accommodate real or perceived needs.

In addition to the three useful operations defined by PO, we have two operations which have little, if any, value. These are connect and disconnect. As discussed in Section 5.2.3 on page 129, these were added as one of several political compromises in an effort to achieve peace between IBM and SunSoft. Speaking as one who has spent many weeks in a search for some meaningful interpretation of these operations, I have come to the conclusion that this search is and will be in vain. In the current version of the IBM implementation, these methods raise an exception indicating they are not implemented.

In addition to the three PO operations, there is one more concept important to the application-level interface. This is the concept of a PersistentID, or a PID. The PO operations describe an action taken on an object. The PID describes

where the underlying data for that object lives. Every invocation of a PO operation is associated with some PID.

PIDs should not be confused with the CORBA concept of an object reference. An object reference leads to some specific instantiation of an object, say,
lassie, an instance of a dog. A PID leads to some location in some datastore, say,
the row whose primary key is "lassie" in the dog table in the database named
"animal."

The information in a PID can be quite datastore specific. Consider the differences we might expect to encounter between storing lassie's data in a POSIX
file and in a relational database. For the POSIX file, we might need nothing
more than a filename, assuming we are storing one object per file. For the relational database, on the other hand, we might need a database name, table name,
and information for an SQL statement identifying a particular row.

This leads to the conclusion that not only is the information in the PID different for different datastores, but the type of the information contained is different. This is exactly how the PIDs are set up. POS defines a generic PID. This
PID is then used by the datastore providers as a base type for further derivations. The base PID type is described in detail in Section 5.1 on page 123. Its IDL
definition is:

```
module somPersistencePID {
   interface PID : SOMObject {
     attribute string datastore_type;
     string get_PIDString();
   };
   ...
};
```

As you can see, it contains one attribute and one method. The attribute is
datastore_type, which is used to specify the type of the datastore to which the
object data is being stored. Valid values might include "POSIX" and "DB2." The
method, get_PIDString, returns a string representation of the PID. We will discuss the use of this string later.

Those of us working on the prototype have found that the base PID type
defined by POS is overly generalized. We provide a generic PID type derived
from CosPersistencePID::PID, which, in our Beta version, we are calling
PID_DS, for PID Datastore. It mainly supplements the POS PID functionality by
adding an inverse operation to the get_PIDString defined by POS and some operations designed to simplify the handling of PID strings in derived classes. We
discuss these operations when we examine POS from the datastore provider's
perspective.

In general, we expect each datastore provider to define an appropriate PID.
This effectively defines a PID hierarchy, rooted in somPersistencePID::PID_DS,
as shown in Figure 17. This figure shows a PID_DB2, PID_POSIX, and

PID_BTREE, all derivations from PID_DS, and provided by vendors for DB2, POSIX files, and a BTree product, respectively.

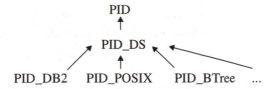

Figure 17. PID Hierarchy

The first issue applications developers have to deal with is instantiation. Instantiation is a Life Cycle issue, and the mechanism used by the OMG Life Cycle Service for instantiating objects is Factories and FactoryFinders, as described in Section 4.19 on page 112. However, as we pointed out in Section 4.20 on page 118, there are many ways to instantiate objects. Because using the Life Cycle Service interfaces for instantiation would add considerable irrelevant code to our sample programs, we will generally use a much simpler instantiation mechanism. We will use the <class>New macro, described in Section 4.20.1 on page 118.

We choose the type of PID to instantiate by choosing an appropriate <class>New macro. The following code instantiates a PID, defined in somPersistencePOSIX::PID_POSIX, which is specialized for POSIX:

```
somPersistencePOSIX_PID_POSIX pid;
pid = somPersistencePOSIX_PID_POSIXNew();
```

Because we are in a C program, we use the C language bindings to refer to a class. A class that would be referred to as moduleName::className becomes, in the C bindings, moduleName_className.

Having created the PID, we can now fill it in with datastore-specific information:

```
__set_pathName(pid, ev "lassie.dat");
```

Notice we are using SOM-provided name shortcuts, as described in Section 4.14 on page 89. The official CORBA specification for this code is:

```
somPersistencePOSIX_PID_POSIX_set_pathName
  (pid, ev "lassie.dat");
```

Next, we instantiate the persistent object and associate it with newly created pid. The code for this is:

```
lassie = dogNew();
__set_p(lassie, ev, pid);
```

The PO interface includes a PID attribute called p. As discussed in Section 4.9 on page 64, the associated set method for this would be _set_p and would be invoked as __set_p.

We can also associate PIDs with objects at method invocation time by passing in a PID as a third parameter to the PO methods. This is described in Section 5.2 on page 126. From the perspective of the PO methods, it doesn't matter which technique we choose.

We now have an instantiated dog, which is derived from PO. It has an associated PID that has been filled in with information tying our dog object to specific space in some datastore. We can now invoke PO methods on lassie.

Before we move off into PO methods, let's consider the other mechanism for creating a PID, which is based on a PIDstring. All PID types are derived from CosPersistencePID::PID. One of the methods defined in POS for CosPersistencePID::PID is get_PIDString. POS defines nothing about this string; however, the assumption is that this string can be used to recreate a new PID of the same type as the one that returned the string, and containing the same information. This is superficially similar to the ability of the Object Request Broker to create a string form of an object reference and then recreate a functionally equivalent object reference given that string.

If a PID string can be used to repopulate the PID with data, one might assume that the PID would support a set_PIDString method that would do the inverse of the get_PIDString method. The reason this did not make it into the specification is that the setting of the PID string was considered to be the private business of the PID Factory. In real life, however, we have found that the factory mechanism is cumbersome, and we need to allow for the possibility of other forms of instantiation.

Since other forms of instantiation will most likely require the set_PIDString, we have added it to the class. However, to keep the CosPersistencePID::PID interface as close as possible to the OMG specification, we have added the method to the somPersistencePID::PID_DS interface, as shown in Section 5.1 on page 123. The use of this method is shown here:

```
somPersistenceDB2_PID_DB2 pid;
string pid_string;

pid = somPersistenceDB2_PID_DB2New();
pid_string = get_pid_string_from_somewhere();
_set_PIDString(pid, ev, pid_string);
```

It turns out that the most confusing part of using POS is instantiating objects, because of the large number of available techniques. This has little to do with POS.

Having instantiated a persistent object, that is, an object of some type derived from PO, one can call any of the three recommended PO operations, that is, store, restore, and delete, and even the two nonrecommended operations—connect and disconnect.

Let's put all this together in a sample program. First, let's look at the IDL for a persistent person:

```
interface person : somPersistencePO::PO {

  attribute string name;
  attribute short age;

  void print(in void *output);

  implementation {

    dllname = "testlib.dll";
    releaseorder : _get_name, _set_name, _set_age,
                   _get_age, print;
    name: noset, noget;
    override: somInit;

  };
};
```

We won't look at the implementation for person, because that is the subject of the next chapter.

We are an application developer, and we have acquired person from some source. The issue we are addressing here is how we use our person objects. The following program demonstrates instantiation, adding data to, and storing person objects. Notice that the derivation of person from Persistent Object is a standard use of inheritance. We can read the line

```
interface person : somPersistencePO::PO {
```

as saying that a person object supports all the operations defined in person plus all of the operations defined in Persistent Object. We will simplify our program by using standard SOM shortcuts for method invocation. Here is the program:

```
#include <person.h>
#include <utils.h>

main()
{
/* Set up.
   ------- */
   person John, Sally;
   Environment *ev;
   somPersistencePOSIX_PID_POSIX pidJohn, pidSally;
   ev = SOM_CreateLocalEnvironment();

/* Prepare John pid.
   ----------------- */
   pidJohn = somPersistencePOSIX_PID_POSIXNew();
   __set_pathName(pidJohn, ev, "john.d1");
```

```
/* Prepare Sally pid.
   ----------------- */
   pidSally = somPersistencePOSIX_PID_POSIXNew();
   __set_pathName(pidSally, ev, "sally.d1");

/* Create people.
   -------------- */
   John = personNew();
   Sally = personNew();

/* Set up John.
   ------------ */
   __set_name(John, ev, "John");
   __set_age(John, ev, 22);

/* Set up Sally.
   ------------- */
   __set_name(Sally, ev, "Sally");
   __set_age(Sally, ev, 24);

/* Store objects.
   -------------- */
   _store(John, ev, pidJohn);
   _store(Sally, ev, pidSally);
}
```

The restore side looks like similar, but with store replaced by restore, and a few print statements added to verify the code:

```
#include <person.h>
#include <utils.h>

main()
{
/* Set up.
   ------- */
   person John, Sally;
   Environment *ev;
   somPersistencePOSIX_PID_POSIX pidJohn, pidSally;
   ev = SOM_CreateLocalEnvironment();

/* Prepare John pid.
   ----------------- */
   pidJohn = somPersistencePOSIX_PID_POSIXNew();
   __set_pathName(pidJohn, ev, "john.d1");

/* Prepare Sally pid.
   ------------------ */
   pidSally = somPersistencePOSIX_PID_POSIXNew();
   __set_pathName(pidSally, ev, "sally.d1");
```

```
/* Create people.
   -------------- */
   John = personNew();
   Sally = personNew();

/* Restore objects.
   ---------------- */
   _restore(John, ev, pidJohn);
   _restore(Sally, ev, pidSally);

/* Print original objects.
   ----------------------- */
   _print(John, ev, stdout);
   _print(Sally, ev, stdout);
}
```

The output from this program is:

```
        Name: John
         Age: 22

        Name: Sally
         Age: 24
```

This program associated PIDs with objects at PO method invocation time. It could have used the __set_p technique. If neither had been done, the PO methods will raise an exception. If both had been done, the PID parameter will take priority over the PID associated with the object. Thus, if we wanted to instantiate a person associated with data in a relational database, but, as an aside, store that data in a POSIX file, we could invoke a second store operation by using a POSIX PID.

6.2   Implicit Persistence Model

One of the problems with POS is that it favors a two-level store model at the expense of a single-level store model. A two-level store model is one that pictures memory and persistent storage as being distinct. The store command is thought of as moving data from memory to permanent storage, and the restore command as moving data from persistent storage to memory. The POSIX file system is an example of a two-level store. Most relational databases are another example.

In contrast, single-level stores see memory and permanent storage as being the same thing. In these systems, when you update memory, you automatically update the underlying storage. There is no need to issue store or restore commands, because from the perspective of the application, there is no difference between memory and storage. ODI's object-oriented database, IBM's AS/400™ system, and most implementations of virtual memory are all examples of single-level stores.

POS is meant to be a datastore-independent way of storing objects. This should mean that the application developer model should be the same regardless of whether the object lives in a single- or two-level store. How can we achieve this in a model based on store/restore, which is obviously a two-level store view of the universe?

This is a question that many of us have spent a great deal of time considering. This section contains ideas contributed by myself, George Copeland, Guy-laine Cantin, and Steve Munroe. This group contains representatives from Object Technology, DB2, AS/400, and Transaction Specialists. We have started to put together a model that unifies the two-level POS view with the single-level storage models. We have done this by defining a relationship between Persistence and the Transaction Service.

It's easy enough to think of single-level stores as being made up of memory tightly coupled with a datastore. However, this breaks down when one considers transactions. Applications are not made up of random updates of memory. They are usually memory updates within the context of a transaction. The application code would look like:

```
begin transaction;
  update memory;
commit transaction;
```

From the application's perspective, the datastore is not actually updated until the transaction is committed. If the commit is replaced by a rollback (also called an abort) the datastore is never updated. Thus, we can see that while the single-level stores present themselves as tightly coupled memory/datastore systems, actually the datastore update takes place only when, and if, the application requests a commit.

This view of single-level stores starts looking more and more like two-level stores. A single-level store is really a two-level store where the store request comes from the transaction manager, rather than the application.

A similar issue involves restore. The transaction manager in a single-level restore needs to synchronize the memory with the datastore the first time the memory is accessed. This is effectively a "restore" operation.

This gives us a clue as to how we can unify the two datastore types. We need to move responsibility for store and restore from the application to the Transaction Service. The application, then, is responsible for indicating when the transaction begins and when it commits (or rolls back).The Transaction Service then decides when to issue store and restore requests.

Before we show how the Transaction Service can take on this responsibility, let's examine some basic transaction algorithms.

The simplest possible transaction algorithm is the single-phase commit. When the application issues a commit request to a datastore, the datastore is allowed to make either of two possible responses. It may either refuse or agree to commit.

If the datastore refuses the commit, it is responsible for returning the datastore to its state just before the transaction started and for returning some error code indicating why the commit was refused.

If the datastore accepts the commit, it is responsible for updating the data-store. This update must be "durable," in the sense that the update will appear, regardless of what happens next, even if what happens next is a catastrophic system failure.

Transactions are said to be all-or-nothing, meaning that either *all* of the updates contained within the transaction occur or *none* occur. This is fairly easy to ensure when only one datastore is involved in the transaction. In this case, the datastore either refuses or accepts the commit. In the first case, none of the updates commit. In the second, all of the updates commit. In either case, the all or nothing requirement is fulfilled.

A more interesting case occurs when more than one datastore is involved. Let's consider a bank application that handles money transfers between check-ing and savings accounts. The application looks like:

```
declare savings data;
declare checking data;
begin transaction;
  get_transfer_ammount;
  savings = savings - transfer_amount;
  checking = checking + transer_amount;
commit transaction;
```

Now let's assume that the savings accounts are stored in Datastore1 and the checking accounts are stored in Datastore2. Let's also assume that the two datastores are both transactional and are independent of each other. When the commit occurs, we now have two different datastores that must participate in the commit. Since they are independent of each other, neither knows the other is involved in the transaction.

This might work out fine. If both datastores accept the commit, then both the savings and the checking account will be properly updated. This is obviously the best possible outcome. It is also possible both datastores will reject the com-mit. This is not as good as both accepting the commit, but it is an acceptable out-come and one that fulfills the all-or-nothing criterion.

But suppose Datastore1 accepts the commit and Datastore2 rejects it. This means the savings account is debited, but the checking account is never credited. This makes for a very unhappy customer, one who is much unhappier than the one whose transaction was simply lost *in toto*.

Keep in mind that there is nothing the higher-level Transaction Service can do to salvage the situation. Datastore1 has committed the update. It is too late to roll it back. When a transaction is committed, it is *committed*.

In order to solve this problem, the two-phase commit algorithm was invented. In the two-phase commit, the transaction manager makes two passes of the datastores. In pass one, the datastores are warned that a commit has been requested by the application and asked if they can do the commit. Each datastore in turn either agrees it will do the commit or says it cannot do the commit. An agreement to commit is an absolute promise to the transaction manager, a commitment to commit, so to speak.

Once the transaction manager finishes the first pass, either one of two situations has occurred. Either every datastore has agreed to go through with the commit, or at least one datastore has declined the commit. The transaction manager is now ready for the second pass.

If all datastores agreed to commit, then in the second pass, the datastores are all told to commit. Since they have all promised to commit, they are not allowed to back out now. In the second pass, each datastore in turn irrevocably writes out its data.

If at least one datastore declined the commit, then in the second pass, all datastores are told to roll back, and an appropriate error message is returned to the application. Thus, the all-or-nothing requirement is again fulfilled.

These are the two basic algorithms used by transactional systems: single-phase commit, for systems that support only a single transactional datastore, and two-phase commit, for those that support multiple transactional datastores.

Let's extend this discussion to see how this relates to the OMG Object Transaction Service (OTS). The most important new concept OTS brings to the table is the idea that datastores are not the only thing that can participate in transactions. Objects can also participate. This means that all of the traditional operations one normally associates with transactional datastores, that is, begin transaction, commit, and rollback, can also be applied to objects.

This requires us to extend our preconceived notion about commit and rollback. We normally think of commit as moving data irrevocably to a datastore. But objects are not datastores, and transactional objects may or may not be persistent. The commit operation, when it involves objects, means making all changes that occurred during the scope of the transaction permanent and visible to the outside world. The rollback operation means to return the object to the state it was in before the beginning of the transaction.

One point that immediately becomes clear is that at least some superset of the two-phase commit protocol is a requirement for the Object Transaction Service (OTS). Anything less than this would limit the system to managing only a single transactional resource, clearly an unacceptable limitation.

Now that we have looked at the basic algorithms of transactional systems and have seen how they apply to the OTS, let's return to the original question: How can we use OTS to coordinate the store/restore of persistent objects?

One solution that almost works is to assume that persistent objects are regular transactional resources, that is, that they are part of the two-phase protocol and are included in both phases of the two-phase protocol. In this scenario, the persistent object would be warned of the commit in phase one and would write out its data. Then, the datastore would get phase-one notification as usual. If the datastore declines the commit on phase one, then on the following pass, everybody, including the persistent object, will be told to roll back.

This almost works, except for one problem. Once a datastore has voted on a prepare, it will not accept any more stores until receiving either a commit or a rollback. Let's see where this causes problems.

Consider our banking example again, but this time, instead of two datastores, we will have two objects both being written to one datastore. The two objects are the savings account and checking account objects. We can rewrite our banking application as:

```
savings_accnt = instantiate_savings_account;
checking_account = instantiate_checking_account;
begin_transaction;
  get_transfer_amount
  withdraw(savings_accnt, transfer_amount);
  deposit(check_accnt, transfer_amount);
commit_transaction;
```

The commit will trigger a prepare message to the savings_accnt. This forces a store to the datastore. The store results in the datastore being registered as a resource that should be included in the prepare pass. The Transaction Service then tells the datastore to prepare. Let's say it votes "yes, ok to commit."

So far, no problem. The data from the savings_accnt has been written and the datastore has agreed to commit the change. The problem occurs as we continue the prepare pass, which next encounters the checking_accnt object.

The checking_accnt object is told to prepare. It now stores its data to the datastore. Unfortunately, the datastore has already accepted a prepare and can't take any more stores until it finishes processing the commit with either a commit or a rollback.

What we need is a mechanism to ensure that all of the persistent objects are given the signal to store themselves before any of the datastores are asked if they can handle the commit. One mechanism that has been proposed for this is a preliminary pass that is only recognized by persistent objects. Some of us have been calling this pass the "preprepare" pass, in honor of the warning pass usually being called the "prepare" pass.

I have implemented one prototype of such a transaction manager. It works as follows. An Implicit PO class (IPO) is defined as having special characteristics as to how methods are invoked. Whenever a method is invoked on an IPO, another method is invoked first. This method is called a *before* method, so called because it is automatically invoked before the invoked method starts up. The purpose of the before method is to check to see if the receiving object is already registered with the Transaction Service as a resource manager that should be included in the transaction passes. If the object is not registered, it does a restore on the object and registers it. Then, when the application issues the commit, each of the registered IPO objects is included in a preprepare pass. During this pass, all the IPO objects are stored.

We add these before/after methods by changing the metaclass of the IPO objects. The new metaclass is one that is derived from the SOM-provided SOMMBeforeAfter class and that overrides the two SOMMBeforeAfter methods, sommBeforeMethod and sommAfterMethod. This general process is described in Section 4.17 on page 103.

If all this seems complicated, don't worry about it. These are just implementation details, probably of more interest to implementors of POS. From the application's perspective, developers can now write code that requires neither explicit restores nor explicit stores. We can see how this works by looking at how the following class is used:

```
#include <sompipo.idl>

interface person : somPersistenceIPO::IPO {

  attribute string name;
  attribute short age;

  void print(in void *output);

  implementation {

    dllname = "testlib.dll";
    releaseorder : _get_name, _set_name, _set_age,
                   _get_age, print;
    name: noset, noget;
    override: somDefaultInit;

  };
};
```

There is nothing special about this class, except that it is derived from IPO, similarly to how the last person was derived from PO. However, this derivation is quite different from the PO derivation. The PO derivation added new operations. The IPO derivations allow the object to act as a single-level store object, adding no new operations from the client perspective, but instead setting up a coordination between the object and the Transaction Service. Let's look at the following code, which instantiates and stores this new object.

```
#include <person.h>
#include <utils.h>
main()
{
/* Set up.
   ------- */
   person John, Sally;
   Environment *ev;

   somPersistencePOSIX_PID_POSIX pidJohn, pidSally;
   somTransaction_TransMgr transMgr;
   ev = SOM_CreateLocalEnvironment();

   transMgr = somTransaction_TransMgrNew();
```

```
/* Prepare John pid.
   ----------------- */
   pidJohn = somPersistencePOSIX_PID_POSIXNew();
   __set_pathName(pidJohn, ev, "john.d1");

/* Prepare Sally pid.
   ----------------- */
   pidSally = somPersistencePOSIX_PID_POSIXNew();
   __set_pathName(pidSally, ev, "sally.d1");

/* Create people.
   -------------- */
   John = personNew();
   __set_p(John, ev, pidJohn);
   Sally = personNew();
   __set_p(Sally, ev, pidSally);

/* Start transaction.
   ----------------- */
   _startTrans(transMgr, ev);

/* Set up John.
   ------------ */
   __set_name(John, ev, "John");
   __set_age(John, ev, 22);

/* Set up Sally.
   ------------- */
   __set_name(Sally, ev, "Sally");
   __set_age(Sally, ev, 24);

/* End transaction.
   ---------------- */
   _commitTrans(transMgr, ev);
}
```

Most of this code is standard setup code. The interesting code is what does not appear, namely, any invocation of the store method, which we might otherwise have expected just before, or perhaps instead of, the transaction commit.

The IPO interface, unlike the PO interface, does not include any client-callable methods. It does, however, have a PID attribute, which must be set before the object can be used within a transaction. The technique for associating PIDs and IPO objects is under evaluation and may still change. Most likely, the association will be made through a factory interface.

When dealing with existing data, we let the Transaction Service handle restore as well, as seen in the following program.

```
#include <person.h>
#include <utils.h>

main()
{
/* Set up.
   ------- */
   person John, Sally;
   Environment *ev;

   somPersistencePOSIX_PID_POSIX pidJohn, pidSally;
   somTransaction_TransMgr transMgr;
   ev = SOM_CreateLocalEnvironment();

   transMgr = somTransaction_TransMgrNew();

/* Prepare John pid.
   ----------------- */
   pidJohn = somPersistencePOSIX_PID_POSIXNew();
   __set_pathName(pidJohn, ev, "john.d1");

/* Prepare Sally pid.
   ------------------ */
   pidSally = somPersistencePOSIX_PID_POSIXNew();
   __set_pathName(pidSally, ev, "sally.d1");

/* Create people.
   -------------- */
   John = personNew();
   __set_p(John, ev, pidJohn);
   Sally = personNew();
   __set_p(Sally, ev, pidSally);

/* Start transaction.
   ------------------ */
   _startTrans(transMgr, ev);

/* Print original objects.
   ----------------------- */
   _print(John, ev, stdout);
   _print(Sally, ev, stdout);

/* End transaction.
   ---------------- */
   _commitTrans(transMgr, ev);
}
```

The output from this program is:

```
Name: John
 Age: 22


Name: Sally
 Age: 24
```

The biggest problem with the preprepare algorithm is that we have added yet another pass to the commit. We started with a single pass when we had only a single datastore. We added a second prepare pass to accommodate multiple datastores. Now we have added a third prepare pass to accommodate multiple objects being written to the same datastore.

Since most applications are likely to have many times more persistent objects than datastores, we can assume that this preprepare pass will be quite lengthy. In the next section, we will consider another algorithm that does not require three passes.

6.3   The RePrepare Transactional Algorithm

Section 6.2 described the Preprepare algorithm for the Transactional Service. The purpose of this algorithm was to ensure all Implicit Persistent Objects (IPO) have a chance to store their data before any of the datastores are asked to prepare for a commit. As we discussed, datastores can only vote yes or no on a commit based on what they know, not on data they haven't yet been asked to store.

In this section, I describe another algorithm that I call the Reprepare (as opposed to the Preprepare) Algorithm. This algorithm is the result of collaboration between John Freund and Simon Holdsworth, of the IBM Hursley Transactional Group, and others.

Let's briefly review the problems of the standard two-phase commit algorithm. The algorithm falls apart when a second object attempts to propagate its store and prepare to a datastore that has already accepted a prepare. The standard datastore response is to reject the second prepare.

The simple solution is to modify the requirements of prepare to say datastores must accept multiple requests to prepare. If they vote "no commit" on any one of their prepares, then the Transaction Service will roll back the transaction. Because the datastore must be prepared to accept multiple prepare requests, I call this algorithm the Reprepare Algorithm.

The Reprepare Algorithm has two advantages over the Preprepare Algorithm. First, it eliminates one extra pass. Transaction processing systems are always hypersensitive to performance, and eliminating one full pass is bound to help in this area. Second, the Reprepare Algorithm is a simpler algorithm. There are no extra methods on objects, and it requires nothing more than minor modification to the expected semantics of existing operations.

For all the charm of the Reprepare Algorithm, it has one unfortunate drawback that will likely prohibit its use for at least the next five years: It requires significant changes to two existing standards (the OMG Transaction Service and the X/Open XA Specification) and most of the datastore products on the market today.

Despite the likely widespread adoption of the Preprepare Algorithm, I can't resist including this description of Reprepare. It provides a glimpse of a future where datastore products will have to rethink many basic algorithms as they learn to accommodate a world where programming with distributed objects, using well-defined plug-and-play services, is the prevailing paradigm.

6.4   Embedded Objects

The POS specification is vague about how to deal with objects that have references to other objects. There are two main reasons for this vagueness. One is that POS intentionally did not describe how a POS implementation would move data in and out of objects, an area it described as Protocol. Dealing with object references is one of the trickiest parts of designing a Protocol. We discuss Protocol in depth in the next chapter, since it is primarily of interest to object implementors.

The other reason embedded objects were shortchanged is because of SunSoft's view that this was an issue for the Relationship Service to manage. Indeed, the specification for the Relationship Service describes how one goes about describing how objects are related to each other, what the nature of those relationships is, and how to follow those relationships from object to object.

The Relationship Service is indeed complete, and its use could eliminate the need for objects to contain references to other objects. The specification has one major problem. It is difficult to understand. It is unlikely to be used in situations requiring only the equivalent to C++ object pointers.

We believe that it is up to the application to specifically handle restore and store of any object it has created, even when those objects are embedded in another PO (Persistent Object). The easiest way for the application to handle the embedded restore/store is to make use of the Transaction Service. The major advantage of making use of the Transaction Service is that the restores/stores closely resemble those in single-level datastores, as described starting in Section 6.2 on page 155.

Single-level datastores are easier to use even when objects are not embedded. But they really shine when they are managing complex and unpredictable webs of object relationships. Restoring is much simpler because they automatically read in objects on demand. Storing is easier because they store only those objects that have actually been updated.

To show how much simpler persistence is when coupled with Transaction, let's compare two programs. Both have a company object that can have embedded people. The first does not use OTS, using instead the explicit model for persistence (as described in Section 6.1 on page 148). The second does use OTS, using the implicit model for persistence (as described in Section 6.2 on page 155). The company and person definition for the explicit persistent objects are:

```
#include <somppo.idl>

interface person : somPersistencePO::PO {
  attribute string name;
  attribute short age;
  void print(in void *output);
  implementation {
    name: noset, noget;
  };
};
```

```
#include <somppo.idl>
interface person;
interface company : somPersistencePO::PO {
  const long MaxPeople = 20;
  void add_person(in person newPerson);
  person get_person(in long n);
  long total_people();
  void print_company(in void *output);
  implementation {
    sequence <person, MaxPeople> people;
  };
};
```

The explicit store program must manage not only the embedding of objects, but also the storing of the embedded objects:

```
/* ... */
/* Set up John.
   ------------ */
   __set_name(John, ev, "John");
   __set_age(John, ev, 22);
   _add_person(objectWatch, ev, John);

/* Set up Sally.
   ------------- */
   __set_name(Sally, ev, "Sally");
   __set_age(Sally, ev, 24);
   _add_person(objectWatch, ev, Sally);

/* Store all the objects.
   --------------------- */
   _store(John, ev, NULL);
   _store(Sally, ev, NULL);
   _store(objectWatch, ev, NULL);
```

The difference between the explicit and implicit programming styles shows up in the store segment. In the explicit code, the application is responsible for knowing which objects need storing. In the implicit style, the application just commits the transaction and lets the transaction manager figure out which objects need to be stored:

```
/* ... */
/* Start transaction.
   ----------------- */
   _startTrans(transMgr, ev);

/* Set up John.
   ----------- */
   __set_name(John, ev, "John");
   __set_age(John, ev, 22);
   _add_person(objectWatch, ev, John);

/* Set up Sally.
   ------------ */
   __set_name(Sally, ev, "Sally");
   __set_age(Sally, ev, 24);
   _add_person(objectWatch, ev, Sally);

/* End transaction.
   --------------- */
   _commitTrans(transMgr, ev);
```

Having the application track which objects need storing doesn't look so bad in this simple example. But imagine an application with objects embedded in objects embedded in yet other objects, and where a human being decides which object to update by pointing and clicking an object-oriented user interface tool. Turning over this responsibility to the Transaction Service can significantly simplify the code.

The restore story is a little different, because in either implicit or explicit persistence, we don't have to worry about PIDs for embedded objects. These will be managed by the POS framework. Even the instantiation of embedded objects can be managed, although this is all undefined by the official OMG specification. In our prototype, although PIDs and object instantiation are automatically managed, restoration still is the responsibility of the application. This is illustrated in the following code segment:

```
/* Prepare company PID.
   -------------------- */
   pidCompany = somPersistencePOSIX_PID_POSIXNew();
   __set_pathName(pidCompany, ev, "comp.d1");

/* Create company.
   --------------- */
   objectWatch = companyNew();
   __set_p(objectWatch, ev, pidCompany);
```

```
/* Restore company.
   --------------- */
   _restore(objectWatch, ev, NULL);
   total = _total_people(objectWatch, ev);
   for (n=1; n<=total; n++) {
       person = _get_person(objectWatch, ev, n);
       _restore(objectWatch, ev, NULL);
   }
/* Print original objects.
   ---------------------- */
   _print_company(objectWatch, ev, stdout);
}
```

Notice how much simpler this becomes when we use the Transaction Service:

```
/* Prepare company PID.
   ------------------- */
   pidCompany = somPersistencePOSIX_PID_POSIXNew();
   __set_pathName(pidCompany, ev, "comp.d1");

/* Create company.
   --------------- */
   objectWatch = companyNew();
   __set_p(objectWatch, ev, pidCompany);

/* Start transaction.
   ----------------- */
   _startTrans(transMgr, ev);

/* Print original objects.
   ---------------------- */
   _print_company(objectWatch, ev, stdout);

/* End transaction.
   --------------- */
   _commitTrans(transMgr, ev);
}
```

Keep in mind the different responsibilities here. The POS framework, at least the prototype implementation, is responsible for instantiating each of the embedded objects and assigning their PIDs, all of which was stored as part of the stream information within the write_object implementation. The Transaction Service is responsible for reading in the embedded objects on an as-needed basis, as methods are invoked on the objects. Although we don't see any methods invoked on the embedded objects, this is presumed to happen within the print invocation of the company, when the company will ask each of its embedded objects to print itself.

6.5   Persistent IDs and Object References

Persistent IDs look a lot like Object References, and they are often confused with each other. After all, both identify things related to objects, both can be turned into strings, and both can be reconstituted from strings.

However, Persistent IDs are not Object References. A Persistent ID identifies a location within a datastore in which an object's data will be stored. An Object Reference identifies an object.

The following program segment creates two different object references; however, both object references refer to the same object. We will use a hypothetical instantiation method to avoid having to go through the formal factory mechanism. We use the DSOM global object, _SOMD_ObjectMgr, for managing the relationship between object references and strings. A picture of the resulting object relationships is shown in Figure 18.

```
somPersistencePOSIX_PID_POSIX pid;
company myCompany, yourCompany;
string obj_string;
pid = instantiate_PID_POSIX();
__set_pathname(pid, ev, "code.dat");
myCompany = instantiate_company()
__set_p(myCompany, ev, pid);

obj_string = _somdGetIdFromObject(
            SOMD_ObjectMgr, ev, myCompany);
yourCompany = _somdGetObjectFromId(
            SOMD_ObjectMgr, ev, obj_string);
```

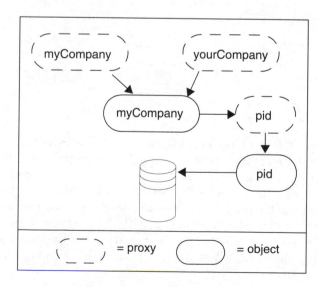

Figure 18. Copying Object References

The next program creates two different objects with different PIDs; however, the two PIDs both refer to the same persistent location. The diagram for the resulting objects is shown in Figure 19.

```
somPersistencePOSIX_PID_POSIX myPid, yourPid;
company myCompany, yourCompany;
string pid_string;

myPid   = instantiate_PID_POSIX();
yourPid = instantiate_PID_POSIX();

__set_pathname(myPid, ev, "code.dat");

pid_string = _get_PIDString(myPid, ev);
_set_PIDString(yourPid, ev, pid_string);

myCompany = instantiate_company()
__set_p(myCompany, ev, myPid);

yourCompany = instantiate_company()
__set_p(yourCompany, ev, yourPid);
```

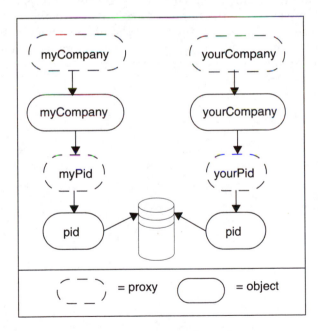

Figure 19. Copying Object References

As we can see from these two diagrams, there is a great difference between having object references point to the same object and having PIDs point to the same persistent storage.

In the former case, the object reference to myCompany and yourCompany both refer to the same object. If these references are in different processes, both processes can share information via the actual myCompany object.

In the latter case, the object references to myCompany and yourCompany refer to different objects. If these references are in different processes, any updates made to myCompany will be made to a different object than those made to yourCompany. The two processes have no ability to share information via the company objects.

6.6   Summary

From the Applications Developer's perspective, POS boils down to two issues. The first issue is PID management. The Application Developer must instantiate pids, fill them in, and associate them with objects. The second issue is the persistence programming model.

When the persistence programming model is the Explicit Model, the Application Developer must be responsible not only for storing the primary object, but also for storing any embedded objects and any objects they embed.

Because managing embedded objects can get very complicated, my recommendation is that people use the Implicit Model. When using the Implicit Model, the Transaction Service coordinates with the Persistence Service to manage both the reading and writing of objects. Reading is done on an as-needed basis, allowing single-level datastore semantics to be used with either single- or multilevel datastores.

The Object Implementor Perspective

A PDS (Persistent Data Service) is ultimately the object that will move data between the object being stored/restored and the datastore being stored/restored to. All of the other objects are conduits to the PDS. In some sense, it is the PDS that is the heart (or more accurately, hearts) of the Persistence Framework.

Once the PDS gets control, it has basically two tasks. First, it must get data in or out of the object, and second, it must get data in or out of the datastore. Getting data in or out of the datastore is a problem that is local to the PDS. However, getting data in or out of the object requires some agreement between the object implementor and the PDS implementor. The agreement between the object and PDS implementors is what we call the *object protocol*.

The major responsibility of the object implementor is making sure the object supports whatever protocol is expected by the PDS implementation that will ultimately be storing and restoring its data.

The usage of the word "protocol" has an interesting history which goes back to the days when IBM and SunSoft were competing with each other in the OMG Persistence arena. The SunSoft proposal was based on an OODB architecture, where memory associated with the object's data was directly mapped onto a file. Therefore, there was no need to get data in or out of the object; the memory was virtually mapped directly to the datastore. The IBM proposal was based on support for traditional datastores and, as such, needed a mechanism to move data in and out of the object.

Dan Chang and I believed the mechanism should not be specified in the architecture. We believed this was an area that needed time to evolve. Rick Cattell, of SunSoft, hit us hard on this point. He called this the "magic" required to make our proposal work and described this mechanism as a "conspiracy" between the PDS and the object.

Although the word "conspiracy" was meant in a derogatory way, Dan and I in time became quite attached to it. In our second round of proposal, we ourselves used this term to describe the process of moving data to and from the object. I liked it because it seemed to capture the idea that the process was not necessarily understood by anyone other than the object and the PDS.

When George Copeland, of IBM, and Mike Powell, of SunSoft, prepared the final proposal, the term "conspiracy" disappeared and was replaced by the term "protocol." Apparently, SunSoft could never get over the negative connotation of the world "conspiracy" and requested the use of the more neutral, but in my view less colorful, term "protocol."

7.1   Concept of Protocol

The word "protocol" describes a technique for moving data in and out of objects. The OMG proposal gave several possible protocols. None were required, and none have, in my opinion, turned out to be technically viable.

One might assume that the protocol section of the POS specification would be without conflict, since it is straightforward and consists only of examples on how protocols *might* be constructed, not rules on how they *must* be constructed. In fact, this area has been the source of some conflict even within IBM. The problem is that although the specification doesn't dictate protocol, without a common agreement on protocol it becomes impossible to present a unified programming model to the clients.

Although Dan and I had taken the position that the details of how to move data in and out of persistent objects should not yet be architected, after Rick Cattell's attacks on this issue, we finally decided to show one sample mechanism.

The mechanism we came up with was one "borrowed" from the SunSoft proposal, with improvements based on some X/Open CLI work. We did this part of the proposal in a short time and never subjected it to outside review. At the time, I did not take this work too seriously, since I considered it only an example. We dubbed this mechanism The Dynamic Data Object (DDO), and it survived the Mike Powell/George Copeland final POS editing.

The DDO is essentially a mechanism for implementing a fully self-describing data object. I believe it served its purpose as a sample protocol, but as a working protocol, it has several deficiencies. First, it is complex. Second, it is slow. Third, it is out of line with the Externalization Service. At the time we wrote the DDO, the Externalization Service was still being negotiated. It has now been accepted as a standard. Because I now believe there are better protocols available for illustration, I will not discuss the DDO further.

7.2   The Streamable Protocol

The only protocol I will describe in any depth is the Streamable protocol. There are three reasons I will discuss this exclusively.

The first is that I like this protocol. I first started working with it in a very early prototype of persistence. I tried to come up with an easily implemented protocol that could work with any object type. What I came up with was an early version of the Streamable protocol. I originally considered this to be throwaway code. However, as I worked with the protocol and implemented it with many test objects, I quickly became enamored with its potential.

The second is that this protocol is similar to the C++ concept of streams. The C++ stream operators are replaced by CORBA operations, but other than this, the two concepts are remarkably similar. This similarity will help C++ programmers identify with this concept.

The third is that this protocol is consistent with the Externalization Service. The Externalization Service is defined by OMG as the service that specifies how objects externalize and internalize their data. This service is the basis for many basic object capabilities, including object copying and passing objects by value as parameters to methods. I use the terms Streamable Protocol and Externalization Protocol interchangeably.

The streamable protocol is built around two interfaces. The first is the Streamable interface. This is the interface supported by an object that is going to be stored by the persistence framework. The second is the StreamIO protocol. This is supported by an object that knows how to contain data. The Streamable interface is used by a client to tell an object to store itself to a stream. The StreamIO interface is used by the object to store its data to some stream implementation.

In trying to explain the streamable protocol, we run into a chicken and egg problem. It's hard to explain the Streamable interface without understanding the StreamIO interface. And it's hard to explain the value of the StreamIO interface without knowing how it will be used within the implementation of the Streamable interface. So, bear with this for a few sections. Once we have examined the trees in enough detail, we will step back and look at the forest.

7.2.1   strcpy2

Before we get into Stream and Streamable, let's briefly look at a procedure we will start using to simplify our code examples. When working with strings in objects, we frequently find ourselves having to copy a string into a newly allocated segment of memory. This code looks something like the following.

```
length = strlen(strToCopy);
newCopy = SOMMalloc(length + 1);
strcpy(newCopy, strToCopy);
```

We have already seen many examples of this code (see, for example, set_bark in Section 4.8 on page 61.) We will now encapsulate this code into a simple procedure called strcpy2. The code for strcpy2 is:

```
char *strcpy2(char *source);

#include <string.h>
#include <som.h>
string strcpy2(string source)
{
  long length;
  string copy;
  length = strlen(source);
  copy = SOMMalloc(length +1);
  strcpy(copy, source);
  return copy;
}
```

We will use this procedure from now on.

7.2.2   StreamIO Interface

There are two types of operations you can do on any StreamIO object. Later we will look at specializations of this basic StreamIO that provide additional functionality, but for now we will discuss the generic StreamIO. The first type of operation you can do with a stream is to put data into it. The second type of operation you can do is to get data out of the stream.

All StreamIO objects will support other operations. For example, the OMG Externalization specification also describes a Stream interface, and it is assumed that most implementations of streams will be derived from both the StreamIO and the Stream interfaces, but this is not required and is not relevant from the perspective of the object implementor.

It's difficult to conceptualize a "StreamIO" object. We generally think of "Stream" objects that support, among other things, the StreamIO interface. From now on, when we are discussing instances of a StreamIO object, we will describe it as a stream.

A stream can be thought of as a data holding area and an associated cursor. The cursor moves forward in the holding area as data is either added to or retrieved from the holding area. Most implementations of a stream will also include some sort of reset method, which will be used to reset the pointer.

When data is moved to or from the stream, three pieces of information are presented to the stream. The first is either the starting address of the data being moved in, when data is moving into the stream, or the address to which the data should be moved, when data is moving out of the stream. The second is the number of bytes that are going to be moved. The third, which is somewhat optional, is the type of the data being moved.

One might imagine a stream interface that looks like this:

```
interface Stream : SOMObject {
   enum dataType {shortInt, longInt, String, ...}
   write_data(
      in void *buffer,
      in long nBytes,
      in dataType type);
   read_data(
      in void *buffer,
      in long nBytes,
      in dataType type);
   reset();
};
```

Often streams are implemented with read and write methods for each basic data type. Since for a given system, a given type always consists either of a specific number of bytes (in the case of basic types like long ints) or of a determinable number of bytes (in the case of strings), one can always calculate the length of the data item given the type. Therefore, given a type, the length is optional.

There are two primary ways we could associate a type with a get/set method. One is by having a parameter that identifies the type of the data. This is used by the C file mechanism, where the fwrite procedure serves as a data put and the fread procedure serves as a data get. Consider the statement

```
fwrite(fout, "%d %s", data1, data2);
```

This says "write" two data items, the first of which is an integer and the second of which is a pointer to the beginning of a string.

The other way to associate types is by having a series of write/read methods, one for each of the possible data types. This is the mechanism used by the Externalization StreamIO interface.

The following interface describes the Externalization StreamIO interface. Rather than show every possible data type, we show short ints, long ints, and strings. One can deduce the rest.

```
module CosStream {
   interface StreamIO : SOMObject {
      short read_short();
      void write_short(in short item);

      long read_long();
      void write_long(in long item);

      string read_string();
      void write_string(in string item);

      /* ... */
   };
};
```

7.2.3   Memory-Based Streams

Let's consider one possible implementation of the StreamIO interface shown in
the previous section. Let's look at a memory-based stream, one which stores its
data in a memory buffer. The simplest possible implementation of this would be
to have the stream allocate a block of memory when first instantiated, then use
this block to store data items. It will use a data member, buff, to store the beginning address of the storage buffer, and the data member, length, to indicate
where in the buffer we are currently storing or retrieving data elements.

```
interface MemoryStream : CosStream::StreamIO {
  const long buffLength = 1000;
  void reset();
  implementation {
    string buff;
    long length;
    override: read_short, write_short,
             read_long, write_long,
             read_string, write_string,
             /* ... */,
             somDefaultInit;
  };
};
```

The implementation of this class is as follows. The put methods all work by doing
a memory copy of the stored item into the next location of the memory buffer,
then incrementing the length variable to prepare for the next data item store.

```
#define MemoryStream_Class_Source
#include <memstrm.ih>
#include <utils.h>

short read_short(MemoryStream somSelf, Environment *ev)
{
    short value;
    MemoryStreamData *somThis = MemoryStreamGetData(somSelf);
    memcpy((void *) &value,
        (void *) &_buff[_length], sizeof(short));
    _length += sizeof(short);
    return value;
 }

void write_short(MemoryStream somSelf, Environment *ev, short item)
{
    MemoryStreamData *somThis = MemoryStreamGetData(somSelf);
    memcpy((void *) &_buff[_length],
        (void *) &item, sizeof(short));
    _length += sizeof(short);
}
```

```
long read_long(MemoryStream somSelf, Environment *ev)
{
    long value;
    MemoryStreamData *somThis = MemoryStreamGetData(somSelf);
    memcpy((void *) &value,
        (void *) &_buff[_length], sizeof(long));
    _length += sizeof(long);
    return value;
}

void write_long(MemoryStream somSelf,
    Environment *ev, long item)
{
    MemoryStreamData *somThis = MemoryStreamGetData(somSelf);
    memcpy((void *) &_buff[_length],
        (void *) &item, sizeof(long));
    _length += sizeof(long);
}

string read_string(MemoryStream somSelf, Environment *ev)
{
    string value;
    long length;
    MemoryStreamData *somThis = MemoryStreamGetData(somSelf);
    value = strcpy2(&_buff[_length]);
    length = strlen(value) + 1;
    _length += length;
    return value;
}

void write_string(MemoryStream somSelf, Environment *ev, string item)
{
    long length;
    MemoryStreamData *somThis = MemoryStreamGetData(somSelf);
    length = strlen(item) + 1;
    memcpy((void *) &_buff[_length], (void *) item, length);
    _length += length;
}
```

The reset sets the buffer location offset back to zero, so that the next get invocation will pull in the first stored data item.

```
void reset(MemoryStream somSelf,  Environment *ev)
{
    MemoryStreamData *somThis = MemoryStreamGetData(somSelf);
    _length = 0;
}
```

The initialization method is used to initialize memory. The general idea of memory management is described in Section 4.15 on page 91. The version here initializes the buffer that will be used for storing data.

```
void somDefaultInit(MemoryStream somSelf, somInitCtrl* ctrl)
{
   MemoryStreamData *somThis; /* set in BeginInitializer */
   somInitCtrl globalCtrl;
   somBooleanVector myMask;
   Environment ev;
   MemoryStream_BeginInitializer_somDefaultInit;

   MemoryStream_Init_StreamIO_somDefaultInit(somSelf, ctrl);
/*
   Local initialization code added by programmer
   -------------------------------------------- */
   _buff = SOMMalloc(MemoryStream_buffLength);
   _length = 0;
}
```

This is a very rudimentary implementation of a stream. For example, it is very inefficient when small numbers of items are stored, since it allocates a large block of memory, most of which may never be used. It also fails when large numbers of items are stored, since it never checks to see if it is out of memory. A better implementation would check with each memory copy to see if there is room left in the buffer, then allocate more buffer space as needed. But we are focusing on the behavior of streams here, not studying implementation strategies.

Now that we know what streams are, let's see how they are used. A client using a stream places a series of data items in the stream, each of whose type is known. The client then resets the stream and gets another series of data items from the stream. The code that gets the items must be a mirror image of the code that put the data items into the stream. Some sample client codes looks like this:

```
#include <memstrm.h>

void getCustomerInfo(Stream stream, Environment *ev);
void printCustomerInfo(Stream stream, Environment *ev);

main()
{
   MemoryStream stream;
   Environment *ev;

   ev = SOM_CreateLocalEnvironment();
   stream = MemoryStreamNew();

   getCustomerInfo(stream, ev);
   _reset(stream, ev);
   printCustomerInfo(stream, ev);

   _somFree(stream);
}
```

```
void getCustomerInfo(Stream stream, Environment *ev)
{
    char *name = "Charlie Brown";
    long creditLimit = 100;

    _write_string(stream, ev, name);
    _write_long(stream, ev, creditLimit);
}
void printCustomerInfo(Stream stream, Environment *ev)
{
    char *customerName;
    long customerCreditLimit;

    customerName = _read_string(stream, ev);
    customerCreditLimit = _read_long(stream, ev);

    printf("        Name: %s\n", customerName);
    printf("Credit Limit: %d\n", customerCreditLimit);
}
```

Of course, this code isn't very interesting. But have patience. Soon we will see the value to streams. In the meantime, let's notice a few important points about streams that this program illustrates.

The code that puts data into the stream (the *donor* code) is a mirror image of the code that receives data from the stream (the *recipient* code.) The donor inserts a name as a string, followed by a creditLimit as a long. The recipient receives the name as a string, followed by a creditLimit as a long.

The recipient code is written by someone with intimate knowledge of the usage of the stream by the donor code, and vice versa. The recipient knows that there are two things in the stream. It knows the first item is a string and the second is a long. The recipient knows that the first item is one which represents the data for a name and that the second item is one which represents a creditLimit.

The recipient and donor do *not* need to agree on the name of the variables that are used for storing that data. The donor uses name as a variable, the recipient customerName. In fact, they need not understand anything about each other, other than how each uses the stream.

The donor and recipient do not need to know what type of stream they are using. They use very generic stream functions. The read/write methods represent their contract with stream object. Therefore, they are able to declare the stream as the most generic stream type. The fact that the actual implementation of the stream is memory based is relevant only to code outside the donor and recipient regions, namely, the code that instantiates the stream and the code that initializes (if necessary) the stream. We could completely replace the memory-based stream by a file-based stream, and neither donor nor recipient would require any changes.

This concludes a basic introduction to streams. Now let's see how they can be used.

7.2.4   Streamable Interface

The StreamIO interface is used by an object to transfer its data into a stream. The interface is the contract all streams guarantee to support regardless of how they are internally implemented and regardless of what other methods they add to the basic set.

The Streamable interface is also defined by the Externalization specification. This interface is supported by objects that want to allow the outside world to request they transfer the data into or out of a stream. The Streamable interface contains only two methods: externalize_to_stream and internalize_from_stream. Both take a stream parameter that should be used for writing to or reading from. The internalize_from_stream method also takes a FactoryFinder, which is not needed by persistence. We will use NULL for the FactoryFinder when invoking this method. The definition of Streamable is:

```
module CosStream {
  interface Streamable : SOMObject {
     void externalize_to_stream(in StreamIO stream);
     void internalize_from_stream(
       in StreamIO stream,
       in CosLifeCycle::FactoryFinder);
  };
};
```

One can imagine default implementations of Streamable. One possible default implementation of externalize_to_stream, which follows closely the logic of the SOM 2.1 Persistence, is to go through each of the attributes of the object and, one by one, add them into the stream. Pseudocode for this implementation of externalize_to_stream would look like:

```
Streamable::externalize_to_stream(Streamable self, Stream s)
{
  find out what my class is;
  look up that class in the interface repository;
  get list of attributes supported by this class;
  for (each attribute) {
     get value of attribute;
     place value in stream;
  }
}
```

When I was designing SOM 2.1 Persistence, this seemed like a reasonable idea. After all, we often think of attributes as closely related to data. However, I now believe that there are two faulty assumptions here. The first is that all of the attributes represent persistent data. I now believe that many attributes will typically be transient. But the larger fault lies in the assumption that all persistent data will be available as attributes.

In fact, distributed objects are likely to contain large amounts of complex data, very little of which is likely to be in the form of attributes. An attribute, by definition, includes set and get methods. And very few business objects are going to give direct access to their internal data structures.

For all these reasons, as well as efficiency concerns, I don't see value in a default implementation of Streamable. The best policy seems to be no policy. It should strictly be up to the object implementor to implement the Streamable methods in a way that makes sense for that particular class.

7.3   Examples of Streamable Objects

Let's start with a simple non-Streamable object and then examine the necessary changes to make this object Streamable. The following is a definition of a person object:

```
interface person : SOMObject {
  attribute string name;
  attribute short age;
  void print();
  implementation {
    releaseorder :   _get_name, _set_name,
                     _set_age, _get_age, print;
    name: noset, noget;
  };
};
```

The implementation of person is:

```
#define person_Class_Source
#include <person.ih>
#include <utils.h>

string _get_name(person somSelf, Environment *ev)
{
   personData *somThis = personGetData(somSelf);
   return strcpy2(_name);
}
void _set_name(person somSelf, Environment *ev, string name)
{
   personData *somThis = personGetData(somSelf);
   if(_name) SOMFree(_name);
   _name = strcpy2(name);
}
void print(person somSelf, Environment *ev)
{
   personData *somThis = personGetData(somSelf);
   printf("\n        Name: %s\n", _name);
   printf("        Age: %d\n", _age);
}
```

This code should be easy to understand, comparable to the dog examples shown in the chapter introducing IDL.

To make person Streamable, we need to make several changes. First, we make person derived from Streamable, in addition to any other base classes it used to have. Second, we override the externalize_to_stream and internalize_from_stream methods. Third, we implement externalize_to_stream to write the person data to the stream, making use of the various write stream methods. Fourth, we implement internalize_from_stream to read the person data from the stream, making use of the various read stream methods.

The new person definition, with changes shown in bold, is:

```
interface person : SOMObject, CosStream::Streamable {
  attribute string name;
  attribute short age;
  void print();
  implementation {
    releaseorder :  _get_name, _set_name,
                    _set_age, _get_age, print;
    name: noset, noget;
    override: externalize_to_stream, internalize_from_stream;
  };
};
```

The person implementation needs to have implementations for externalize_to_stream and internalize_from_stream. The rest of the methods are unchanged and are not repeated here. Remember that the FactoryFinder is a formal parameter to the internalize_from_stream, but one that we are not using.

```
void externalize_to_stream(person somSelf, Environment *ev,
CosStream_StreamIO stream)
{
    personData *somThis = personGetData(somSelf);
    _write_string(stream, ev, _name);
    _write_short(stream, ev, _age);
}


void internalize_from_stream(person somSelf,  Environment *ev,
CosStream_StreamIO stream, CosLifeCycle_FactoryFinder ff)
{
    personData *somThis = personGetData(somSelf);
    _name = _read_string(stream, ev);
    _age = _read_short(stream, ev);
}
```

Next, let's consider a slightly more complicated example, a type derived from our Streamable person. In the employee definition, we do not need to explicitly state that employee is derived from Streamable. This is implicit since employee is derived from person, and person is Streamable. The employee definition is:

```
#include <person.idl>
interface employee : person {
  attribute long salary;
  implementation {
    releaseorder: _get_salary, _set_salary;
    override: print;
    override: externalize_to_stream, internalize_from_stream;
  };
};
```

Because employee adds only a long attribute, we can use the default set/get methods (see Section 4.9 on page 64.) The implementation of the employee print method is straightforward:

```
#define employee_Class_Source
#include <emp.ih>
#include <stdio.h>
#include <stream.h>

void print(employee somSelf,  Environment *ev)
{
   employeeData *somThis = employeeGetData(somSelf);
   employee_parent_person_print(somSelf, ev);
   printf("      Salary: %d\n", _salary);
}
```

The externalize_to_stream method first invokes its base class's version of externalize_to_stream, resolving to externalize_to_stream as implemented for the people class. The reason this is invoked is to ensure that any data which is part of the base class will be part of the stream.

```
void externalize_to_stream(employee somSelf, Environment *ev,
CosStream_StreamIO stream)
{
   employeeData *somThis = employeeGetData(somSelf);
   employee_parent_person_externalize_to_stream(somSelf, ev,
     stream);
   _write_long(stream, ev, _salary);
}
```

The internalize_from_stream method is a mirror image of externalize_to_stream, even to the extent of invoking the base class version of internalize_from_stream. Its implementation is as follows.

```
void internalize_from_stream(employee somSelf,
Environment *ev, CosStream_StreamIO stream,
CosLifeCycle_FactoryFinder ff)
{
    employeeData *somThis = employeeGetData(somSelf);
    employee_parent_person_internalize_from_stream(somSelf, ev,
      stream, ff);
    _salary = _read_long(stream, ev);
}
```

Another example of a Streamable object derived from person is the following definition of customer:

```
#include <person.idl>
interface customer : person {
  attribute long creditLimit;
  implementation {
    releaseorder : _set_creditLimit, _get_creditLimit;
    override: print;
    override: externalize_to_stream, internalize_from_stream;
  };
};
```

The implementation of customer is analogous to employee:

```
#define customer_Class_Source
#include <cust.ih>
#include <stdio.h>
#include <stream.h>
void print(customer somSelf, Environment *ev)
{
    customerData *somThis = customerGetData(somSelf);
    customer_parent_person_print(somSelf, ev);
    printf("Credit Limit: %d\n", _creditLimit);
}
void externalize_to_stream(customer somSelf, Environment *ev,
CosStream_StreamIO stream)
{
    customerData *somThis = customerGetData(somSelf);
    customer_parent_person_externalize_to_stream(somSelf, ev,
      stream);
    _write_long(stream, ev, _creditLimit);
}

void internalize_from_stream(customer somSelf,
Environment *ev, CosStream_StreamIO stream)
{
    customerData *somThis = customerGetData(somSelf);
    customer_parent_person_internalize_from_stream(somSelf, ev,
      stream, ff);
    _creditLimit = _read_long(stream, ev);
}
```

7.3.1   Use of Streams in Object Copying

Now that we have an idea about what we mean by Streams and Streamable objects, let's see how these interfaces can be used in interesting ways. One interesting thing we can do with Streamable objects is copy them. The following client code instantiates a person, customer, and employee object, and then makes clones of them. To simplify the code, we will use standard SOM mechanisms for object instantiation and deinstantiation rather than the more complex Life Cycle mechanism.

```
#include <person.h>
#include <cust.h>
#include <emp.h>
#include <memstrm.h>

main()
{
    person John, JohnClone;
    employee Sally, SallyClone;
    customer Anne, AnneClone;
    MemoryStream stream;
    Environment *ev;

    ev = SOM_CreateLocalEnvironment();

    John = personNew();
    Sally = employeeNew();
    Anne = customerNew();

    __set_name(John, ev, "John");
    __set_age(John, ev, 22);

    __set_name(Sally, ev, "Sally");
    __set_age(Sally, ev, 24);
    __set_salary(Sally, ev, 40000);

    __set_name(Anne, ev, "Anne");
    __set_age(Anne, ev, 20);
    __set_creditLimit(Anne, ev, 1000);

    _print(John, ev);
    _print(Sally, ev);
    _print(Anne, ev);

    JohnClone = personNew();
    SallyClone = employeeNew();
    AnneClone = customerNew();
    stream = MemoryStreamNew();
```

```
    _externalize_to_stream(John, ev, stream);
    _reset(stream, ev);
    _internalize_from_stream(JohnClone, ev, stream, NULL);
    _print(JohnClone, ev);

    _reset(stream, ev);
    _externalize_to_stream(Sally, ev, stream);
    _reset(stream, ev);
    _internalize_from_stream(SallyClone, ev, stream, NULL);
    _print(SallyClone, ev);

    _reset(stream, ev);
    _externalize_to_stream(Anne, ev, stream);
    _reset(stream, ev);
    _internalize_from_stream(AnneClone, ev, stream, NULL);
    _print(AnneClone, ev);

    _somFree(stream);
    _somFree(John);
    _somFree(Sally);
    _somFree(Anne);

    _somFree(JohnClone);
    _somFree(SallyClone);
    _somFree(AnneClone);
}
```

The output generated by this program is shown next. Notice that the first set of John, Sally, and Anne printouts come from the "real" John, Sally, and Anne, and the second set come from the clones.

```
          Name: John
           Age: 22

          Name: Sally
           Age: 24
        Salary: 40000

          Name: Anne
           Age: 20
  Credit Limit: 1000

          Name: John
           Age: 22

          Name: Sally
           Age: 24
        Salary: 40000

          Name: Anne
           Age: 20
  Credit Limit: 1000
```

The next few lines of code are an extract of the above program. We will go through them line by line to be sure it's clear how the copying works. In this code segment, first we tell John to write himself to a stream we have created. We know John can write himself to a stream because we know he is a Streamable object and we know Streamable objects support externalize_to_stream. Then we reset the stream, so that future reads from the stream will start from the beginning. We then ask our John clone to read himself from the stream. Again, we know he can do so, because we know he is a Streamable object and that Streamable objects also support internalize_from_stream. Finally, we ask the John clone to print himself, proving that he is indeed the same as our original John. The code extract is:

```
_externalize_to_stream(John, ev, stream);
_reset(stream, ev);
_internalize_from_stream(JohnClone, ev, stream, NULL);
_print(JohnClone, ev);
```

We see that there is an unanticipated result of defining the Streamable and Stream interfaces: Objects that are Streamable are also copyable!

7.3.2 File-Oriented Stream

The last stream was a memory-oriented stream. Now we will define a new stream that is based on storing data items in a file. Notice we are using inheritance to add two new operations to those defined in Stream. The new operations are open and close. The definition for this FileStream is:

```
#include <stream.idl>
interface FileStream : CosStream::StreamIO {
  void open(in string fileName);
  void close();
  void reset();
  implementation {
    void *fileptr;
    override: read_short, write_short,
              read_long, write_long,
              read_string, write_string;
    releaseorder: open, close;
  };
};
```

The data member fileptr is used in the same way as buf was used in the MemoryStream (see Section 7.2.3 on page 176.) We don't need an analog to the MemoryStream data member length, since the file system acts as an automatically self-allocating buffer.

We have used a bit of a trick in declaring the data member fileptr. Rather than declaring a FILE *, which it really is, we have declared it a void *. This eliminates having to define a FILE structure in a way compatible with IDL. Someday, perhaps, all C header files will come with IDL equivalents, and then we won't need tricks like this.

The implementation of FileStream shows a stream that is little more than a front for the file system. This is not surprising, since the file system *is* basically a stream already.

```
#define FileStream_Class_Source
#include <filestrm.ih>
#include <stdio.h>

void open(FileStream somSelf, Environment *ev,
string fileName)
{
   FileStreamData *somThis = FileStreamGetData(somSelf);
   _fileptr = fopen(fileName, "r+");
   if (!_fileptr) _fileptr = fopen(fileName, "a");
}

void close(FileStream somSelf, Environment *ev)
{
   FileStreamData *somThis = FileStreamGetData(somSelf);
   fclose(_fileptr);
}

short read_short(FileStream somSelf, Environment *ev)
{
   short value;
   FileStreamData *somThis = FileStreamGetData(somSelf);
   fread(&value, sizeof(short), 1, _fileptr);
   return value;
 }

void write_short(FileStream somSelf, Environment *ev,
short item)
{
   FileStreamData *somThis = FileStreamGetData(somSelf);
   fwrite(&item, sizeof(short), 1, _fileptr);
}

long read_long(FileStream somSelf, Environment *ev)
{
   long value;
   FileStreamData *somThis = FileStreamGetData(somSelf);
   fread(&value, sizeof(long), 1, _fileptr);
   return value;
}
```

```
void write_long(FileStream somSelf, Environment *ev,
long item)
{
    FileStreamData *somThis = FileStreamGetData(somSelf);
    fwrite(&item, sizeof(long), 1, _fileptr);
}
```

In the FileStream implementation of write_string, we write a string in two parts, first the length, then the actual string bytes. This simplifies the implementation of read_string, which can first read the number of bytes and then the actual bytes without having to scan through looking for a terminating character.

```
void write_string(FileStream somSelf, Environment *ev,
string item)
{
    long length;
    FileStreamData *somThis = FileStreamGetData(somSelf);
    length = strlen(item) + 1;
    _write_long(somSelf, ev, length);
    fwrite(item, length, 1, _fileptr);
}

string read_string(FileStream somSelf, Environment *ev)
{
    string value;
    long length;
    FileStreamData *somThis = FileStreamGetData(somSelf);
    length = _read_long(somSelf, ev);
    value = SOMMalloc(length);
    fread(value, length, 1, _fileptr);
    return value;
}
```

The reset method is most easily implemented as a file rewind:

```
void reset(FileStream somSelf, Environment *ev)
{
    FileStreamData *somThis = FileStreamGetData(somSelf);
    rewind(_fileptr);
}
```

7.3.3   Use of FileStream for Saving Objects

With this new type of stream, we have acquired a new kind of functionality we can apply to Streamable objects: We can save them in permanent storage. The following program creates the same person, customer, and employee objects we saw copied in Section 7.3.1 on page 185, but now saves them. Notice the client code program makes use of the specialized methods open and close.

```
#include <person.h>
#include <cust.h>
#include <emp.h>
#include <filestrm.h>

main()
{
    person John;
    employee Sally;
    customer Anne;
    FileStream stream;
    Environment *ev;

    ev = SOM_CreateLocalEnvironment();

    John = personNew();
    Sally = employeeNew();
    Anne = customerNew();

    __set_name(John, ev, "John");
    __set_age(John, ev, 22);

    __set_name(Sally, ev, "Sally");
    __set_age(Sally, ev, 24);
    __set_salary(Sally, ev, 40000);

    __set_name(Anne, ev, "Anne");
    __set_age(Anne, ev, 20);
    __set_creditLimit(Anne, ev, 1000);

    _print(John, ev);
    _print(Sally, ev);
    _print(Anne, ev);

    stream = FileStreamNew();

    _open(stream, ev, "john.dat");
    _externalize_to_stream(John, ev, stream);
    _close(stream, ev);

    _open(stream, ev, "sally.dat");
    _externalize_to_stream(Sally, ev, stream);
    _close(stream, ev);

    _open(stream, ev, "`anne.dat");
    _externalize_to_stream(Anne, ev, stream);
    _close(stream, ev);
```

```
    _somFree(stream);
    _somFree(John);
    _somFree(Sally);
    _somFree(Anne);
}
```

This program produces the following output:

```
       Name:  John
        Age:  22

       Name:  Sally
        Age:  24
     Salary:  40000

       Name:  Anne
        Age:  20
Credit Limit:  1000
```

So far, this FileStream is not very interesting. After all, the output this program
generates is identical to the copy program shown in Section 7.3.1 on page 185.
The difference in these two programs becomes apparent later, when the following
program runs:

```
#include <person.h>
#include <cust.h>
#include <emp.h>
#include <filestrm.h>

main()
{
    person John;
    employee Sally;
    customer Anne;
    FileStream stream;
    Environment *ev;

    ev = SOM_CreateLocalEnvironment();

    John = personNew();
    Sally = employeeNew();
    Anne = customerNew();

    stream = FileStreamNew();

    _open(stream, ev, "john.dat");
    _internalize_from_stream(John, ev, stream, NULL);
    _close(stream, ev);
```

```
    _open(stream, ev, "sally.dat");
    _internalize_from_stream(Sally, ev, stream, NULL);
    _close(stream, ev);

    _open(stream, ev, "anne.dat");
    _internalize_from_stream(Anne, ev, stream, NULL);
    _close(stream, ev);

    _print(John, ev);
    _print(Sally, ev);
    _print(Anne, ev);


    _somFree(stream);

    _somFree(John);
    _somFree(Sally);
    _somFree(Anne);
}
```

This program uses the internalize_from_stream operations to restore the objects, giving us a rudimentary form of object persistence. The output we get from this program demonstrates that the objects after restoration look identical to the objects before they were stored by the earlier program:

```
        Name:  John
         Age:  22

        Name:  Sally
         Age:  24
      Salary:  40000

        Name:  Anne
         Age:  20
Credit Limit:  1000
```

The most remarkable thing about the use of streams for both copying and storing objects is that from the object's perspective, there is no difference between these two operations. All the object knows is that it was asked to write itself to a stream; it had no idea that in one case the stream was a MemoryStream, which would eventually result in an object copy, whereas in the other case, the stream was a FileStream, which would result in the object being stored.

Streams are quite fascinating because they can be used for so many purposes. Not only can they form the basis for object copying and storing, as we have seen, but they can be used for moving objects, passing objects by value into methods, and synchronizing replicated objects. In fact, our experience with CORBA seems to indicate that streamability is going to be such a ubiquitous requirement that it will be virtually impossible to develop a serious object that does not support the Streamable interface.

This is one of the primary incentives for using streamability as the recommended protocol for object persistence. We can imagine other protocols which would work as well, but there is no purpose in recommending that objects support some new protocol, when they almost certainly already support one that is wholly adequate.

7.4 write/read_object

The StreamIO implementations we looked at supported writes and reads for almost all of the basic data types. Although we looked at only strings, longs and shorts, one can easily extrapolate how they would work for floats, unsigned ints, and most other types. There is one basic type which is not intuitively obvious, and that is the object reference type. It is quite common that objects contain references to other objects. When an object is asked to stream itself, what should it do about the object references?

The answer to this is the same as for all the other types. It should call the write/read for the object reference type. However, the implementation of these write/read methods can get complicated.

The following IDL file shows the StreamIO interface modified to include the official Externalization definitions for write/read_object methods. We see that the write_object follows the standard write pattern; however, the read_object is significantly different.

```
#include <somobj.idl>
module CosStream{
  interface StreamIO : SOMObject {

    short read_short();
    void write_short(in short item);

    long read_long();
    void write_long(in long item);

    string read_string();
    void write_string(in string item);

    /* ... */

    SOMObject read_object(
      in CosLifeCycle::FactoryFinder ff,
      in SOMObject newobj);
    void write_object(in SOMObject item);

    void reset();
```

```
    implementation {
      releaseorder: read_short, write_short,
                    read_long, write_long,
                    read_string, write_string,
                    /* ... */
                    read_object, write_object,
                    reset;
      };
   };
};
```

The read_object method differs from the traditional read method in that it takes two parameters.

The first of these is the FactoryFinder, discussed in Section 4.19 on page 112. The theory here is that when one needs to instantiate a new object, the FactoryFinder will be used to find the correct factory. In fact, this parameter is unwieldy, and there are better ways of getting the FactoryFinder information into the stream, namely, just allowing the stream to store it during write_object. I recommend this parameter not be used, and NULL used instead.

The second of the read_object parameters is an object. The idea here is that an object's internalization_from_stream might want to pass in a reference to the object to be read. This is also a bad idea. It is inconsistent with the general read methods, which all allocate the memory they are returning and none of which give the caller a chance to decide where that memory should live. Again, I recommend this parameter not be used, and NULL passed in instead. In our discussion, we will assume these parameters are not being used.

Since the basic StreamIO interface has been modified, each of the derived Streams will also have to be modified. Their interfaces will be modified to override the new write/read_object operations, and the implementations will have code added to implement these operations. The following shows the modifications to the FileStream definition:

```
#include <stream.idl>
interface FileStream : CosStream::StreamIO {
  void open(in string fileName);
  void close();
  implementation {
    void *fileptr;
    override: read_short, write_short,
             read_long, write_long,
             read_string, write_string,
             /* ... */
             read_object, write_object,
             reset;
    releaseorder: open, close;
  };
};
```

The implementation file has these two method bodies added. As one would expect, they are mirror images of each other.

The write_object we developed for the POSSOM prototype takes four actions. First, it gets the class name of the object that is being written and places it into the stream (itself). Second, it gets the type of the PID and places it in the stream. Third, it gets a stringified PID and places it in the stream. Finally, it externalizes the referenced object to itself. The code for this is:

```
void write_object(FileStream somSelf, Environment *ev,
SOMObject item)
{
    string className;
    string pidString;
    string pidType;
    somPersistencePID_PID_DS pid;
    FileStreamData *somThis = FileStreamGetData(somSelf);

    pid = __get_p(item, ev);
    pidType = _somGetClassName(pid);
    pidString = _get_PIDString(pid, ev);
    className = _somGetClassName(item);

    _write_string(somSelf, ev, className);
    _write_string(somSelf, ev, pidType);
    _write_string(somSelf, ev, pidString);

    _externalize_to_stream(item, ev, somSelf)
}
```

This is the simplest possible implementation of write_object. In most implementations, we would expect to see significant code looking for object cycles and differentiating between persistent and nonpersistent objects.

The read_object takes the mirror image actions. It gets a string from itself containing the class name of the object. Then, it gets a string representing the type of the PID. Then, it gets the stringified PID. Then, it instantiates a PID of the correct type and resets its data. Then, it instantiates an object of the correct type and sets its PID to the newly instantiated PID. Finally, it internalizes the object from itself. As usual, we are hedging here a bit on the object creation so we don't get bogged down in too many Life Cycle details. Assume for this discussion that the object creation methods make use of one of the instantiate techniques described in Section 4.20 on page 118. Also, assume we are ignoring the Factory-Finder and SOMObject parameters, as we discussed earlier. The code for read_object is as follows.

```
SOMObject read_object(FileStream somSelf, Environment *ev,
CosLifeCycle_FactoryFinder ff, SOMObject newobj)
{
    string className;
    string pidType;
    string pidString;
    somPersistencePID_PID_DS pid;

    SOMObject obj;
    FileStreamData *somThis = FileStreamGetData(somSelf);
    className = _read_string(somSelf, ev);
    obj = create_object(className);
    pidType = _read_string(somSelf, ev);
    pidString = _read_string(somSelf, ev);
    _set_PIDString(pid, ev, pidString);

    pid = create_pid(pidType);
    __set_p(obj, ev, pid);
        return obj;
}
```

7.5   Saving Embedded Objects

Now that we have a stream with support for object references, we can save and restore much more interesting types of objects. And, of course, the same streams that will allow saving and restoring will also support copying, pass by value, and the other nice side effects of being a Streamable object.

The following shows a company interface. A company is made up of a sequence of people. The normal rules of inheritance apply, in that any of the people in the sequence can be either a person or some type derived from person. The definition of company is:

```
#include <somobj.idl>
#include <strmable.idl>
interface person;
interface company : SOMObject, CosStream::Streamable {
  const long MaxPeople = 25;
  attribute string companyName;
  void printCompany();
  void addPerson(in person nextPerson);
  implementation {
    sequence <person, MaxPeople> people;
    companyName: noset, noget;
    releaseorder: _get_companyName, _set_companyName,
                  printCompany, addPerson;
    override: externalize_to_stream,
              internalize_from_stream, somDefaultInit;
  };
};
```

The only slightly complicated feature of normal company behavior comes in dealing with the sequence. If you are shaky on sequences, refer to Section 4.11.5 on page 80.

```
#define company_Class_Source
#include <company.ih>
#include <stream.h>
#include <person.h>
#include <utils.h>

string _get_companyName(company somSelf,  Environment *ev)
{
   companyData *somThis = companyGetData(somSelf);
   companyMethodDebug("company","_get_companyName");

   return (strcpy2(_companyName));
}

void _set_companyName(company somSelf,  Environment *ev,
string companyName)
{
   companyData *somThis = companyGetData(somSelf);
   companyMethodDebug("company","_set_companyName");
   _companyName = (strcpy2(companyName));
}

void printCompany(company somSelf, Environment *ev)
{
   long n;
   person next;
   companyData *somThis = companyGetData(somSelf);
   printf("%s\n", _companyName);
   for (n=0; n<_people._length; n++){
        next = sequenceElement(_people, n);
        _print(next, ev);
   }
}
void addPerson(company somSelf, Environment *ev,
person nextPerson)
{
  long last;
  companyData *somThis = companyGetData(somSelf);
  last = sequenceLength(_people);
  sequenceElement(_people, last) = nextPerson;
  sequenceLength(_people) = last + 1;
}
```

```
void somDefaultInit(company somSelf, somInitCtrl* ctrl)
{

   companyData *somThis; /* set in BeginInitializer */
   somInitCtrl globalCtrl;
   somBooleanVector myMask;
   Environment ev;
   company_BeginInitializer_somDefaultInit;

   company_Init_SOMObject_somDefaultInit(somSelf, ctrl);
   company_Init_CosStream_Streamable_somDefaultInit(
     somSelf, ctrl);
/*
   Local initialization code added by programmer
   --------------------------------------------- */
   _people._length = 0;
   _people._maximum = company_MaxPeople;
   _people._buffer = SOMMalloc(
      company_MaxPeople * sizeof(person));
}
```

Beyond these basic company operations, we have to implement the externalize_to_stream and internalize_from_stream, since company is a Streamable object. These are not being implemented only for persistence. As we have discussed in Section 7.3.3 on page 189, streamability is an important requirement for all serious objects, with or without persistence.

The externalize_to_stream method writes out the company name, writes out the number of people in the sequence, and then writes out the people in the sequence, one by one. The internalize_from_stream method does the mirror image of this.

```
void externalize_to_stream(company somSelf,
Environment *ev, CosStream_StreamIO stream)
{
  long n;
  person next;
  companyData *somThis = companyGetData(somSelf);
  company_parent_Streamable_externalize_to_stream(
     somSelf, ev, stream);

  _write_string(stream, ev, _companyName);
  _write_long(stream, ev, _people._length);
  for (n=0; n<sequenceLength(_people); n++) {
      next = sequenceElement(_people, n);
      _write_object(stream, ev, next);
  }
}
```

```
void internalize_from_stream(company somSelf, Environment *ev,
CosStream_StreamIO stream, CosLifeCycle_FactoryFinder ff)
{
    long n;
    person next;
    long nPeople;
    companyData *somThis = companyGetData(somSelf);
    company_parent_Streamable_internalize_from_stream(
        somSelf, ev, stream, ff);

    _companyName = _read_string(stream, ev);
    nPeople = _read_long(stream, ev);
    for (n=0; n<nPeople; n++){
        next = _read_object(stream, ev, NULL, NULL);
        _addPerson(somSelf, ev, next);
    }
    sequenceLength(_people) = nPeople;
}
```

Now let's look at a client program that uses this company to contain person, customer, and employee objects (as defined and implemented in Section 7.3 on page
181) and then stores the whole collection.

```
#include <person.h>
#include <cust.h>
#include <emp.h>
#include <company.h>
#include <filestrm.h>

main()
{
    person John;
    employee Sally;
    customer Anne;
    company myCompany;
    FileStream stream;
    Environment *ev;

    ev = SOM_CreateLocalEnvironment();

    John = personNew();
    Sally = employeeNew();
    Anne = customerNew();
    myCompany = companyNew();

    __set_name(John, ev, "John");
    __set_age(John, ev, 22);
```

```
        __set_name(Sally, ev, "Sally");
        __set_age(Sally, ev, 24);
        __set_salary(Sally, ev, 40000);

        __set_name(Anne, ev, "Anne");
        __set_age(Anne, ev, 20);
        __set_creditLimit(Anne, ev, 1000);

        __set_companyName(myCompany, ev, "ObjectWatch");
        _addPerson(myCompany, ev, John);
        _addPerson(myCompany, ev, Sally);
        _addPerson(myCompany, ev, Anne);
        _printCompany(myCompany, ev);

        stream = FileStreamNew();
        _open(stream, ev, "company.dat");
        company_externalize_to_stream(myCompany, ev, stream);
        _close(stream, ev);

        _somFree(stream);

        _somFree(John);
        _somFree(Sally);
        _somFree(Anne);
}
```

The output from this program is:

```
ObjectWatch

        Name: John
         Age: 22

        Name: Sally
         Age: 24
      Salary: 40000

        Name: Anne
         Age: 20
Credit Limit: 1000
```

We can show that the store is successful by running a restore program and showing that the object it restores is identical to the object just stored. The restore
program is as follows:

```
#include <company.h>
#include <filestrm.h>

main()
{
    company myCompany;
    FileStream stream;
    Environment *ev;

    ev = SOM_CreateLocalEnvironment();

    myCompany = companyNew();

    stream = FileStreamNew();
    _open(stream, ev, "company.dat");
    company_internalize_from_stream(myCompany, ev, stream, ff);
    _close(stream, ev);

    _printCompany(myCompany, ev);
    _somFree(stream);
}
```

The restore program is much simpler than the store, because it doesn't have to know about any of the embedded objects. It just restores the company object; all of the embedded objects are automatically recreated, as demonstrated by the program's output.

ObjectWatch

```
        Name: John
         Age: 22

        Name: Sally
         Age: 24
      Salary: 40000

        Name: Anne
         Age: 20
Credit Limit: 1000
```

7.6 PDS Design Using Externalization

You can probably see where we are heading with all of this. If externalization is going to be the standard mechanism for moving data in and out of objects, then it should be the mechanism POS implementations use when making such data moves. This assumption greatly simplifies the problem of writing PDSs, which is the interface that datastore vendors need to implement to plug in their products. You can imagine how complicated it would be to write a PDS that had no idea how to get data in and out of an object and that had to be prepared to support any of a dozen or more possible mechanisms. Agreeing on a standard protocol is essential if we are to ensure that a given PDS can support the storage of any arbitrary object. We will have much more to say on this topic in this next chapter.

7.7 Summary

Although streams are fascinating and one could spend years discovering all their ramifications, the basic concepts are simple. Object implementors need follow only these rules:

- Objects must be derived from Streamable.
- The object implementations must override externalize_to_stream and internalize_from_stream.
- The object implementations of these methods should expect to have streams passed in and should assume these streams support the operations specified in the StreamIO interface.

Following these rules ensures that the objects can be stored in any of the datastores supported by persistence, as well as support the various nonpersistence operations that build on Externalization. The most important of these are the various flavors of object copying, including the ability to pass objects by value.

The Datastore Vendor
Perspective

There is an underside to the POS that most applications and object implementors will never see. This is the set of interfaces used by vendors to plug in specific datastore products. Although this set of interfaces is not used by applications or object implementors, it is indirectly very important to them. It is the existence of these interfaces that guarantees objects can be stored in any datastore and allows objects to be implemented without having to include datastore-specific code.

In the beginning of the IBM/SunSoft contest (described in Chapter 1), these interfaces were the proverbial line in the sand. Dan Chang and I believed that traditional datastores had to be supported as first-class stores, and Rick Cattell, of SunSoft, believed that object persistence was an issue for object-oriented databases. It was soon obvious that customers would never accept a Persistence Service that excluded traditional datastores. It was the ability to support any and all datastores as full-fledged object data repositories that eventually turned the tide for our proposal.

In this chapter, we look at two examples of datastores to describe the necessary decisions that datastore vendors confront. The first is one of the simplest of the datastores, a POSIX file. The second is a much more complicated example, that of DB2, representative of the relational databases.

The work described for DB2 includes contributions by several people other than me, most notably, Guylaine Cantin, of IBM Toronto, and George Copeland, of IBM Austin.

In this chapter we will look at two datastores. We will start by looking at their characteristics and then look at the work that went into plugging them into POS. We will use them as examples of the type of work one must do to make any datastore a POS-compliant object datastore.

8.1   Overview of POSIX File

POSIX files are close to the lowest form on the evolutionary datastore scale. They support only the most basic of data manipulation mechanisms. Typically, POSIX files can be opened and closed, written to and read from, and repositioned. In a sense, they are literally low on the evolutionary scale, inasmuch as any number of fancy datastore mechanisms can be built on top of these basic POSIX functions.

They have only programmatic interfaces. They are typically hardwired, in that only a program that knows exactly how the data was stored can read the data. The only higher-level datastore functions supported by POSIX files are buffering and formatting. There are many functions supported by POSIX files. We will illustrate only a few here. The following program writes out data to a POSIX file:

```c
#include <stdio.h>
void main()
{
/* Declarations.
   -------------- */
   FILE *fileptr;
   char *name = "Shakespeare";
   char *occupation = "Writer";
   char *fileName = "test.dat";
   int length;

/* Open file.
   ---------- */
   fileptr = fopen(fileName, "w");

/* Write information.
   ------------------ */
   length = strlen(name) + 1;
   fwrite(&length, sizeof(int), 1, fileptr);
   fwrite(name, length, 1, fileptr);

   length = strlen(occupation) + 1;
   fwrite(&length, sizeof(int), 1, fileptr);
   fwrite(occupation, length, 1, fileptr);

/* Close file.
   ----------- */
   fclose(fileptr);
   exit(0);
}
```

The following program reads this data:

```
#include <stdio.h>
void main()
{
/* Declarations.
   ------------- */
   FILE *fileptr;
   char *name;
   char *occupation;
   char *fileName = "test.dat";
   int length;

/* Open file.
   ---------- */
   fileptr = fopen(fileName, "r");

/* Read information.
   ----------------- */
   fread(&length, sizeof(int), 1, fileptr);
   name = (char *) malloc(length);
   fread(name, length, 1, fileptr);

   fread(&length, sizeof(int), 1, fileptr);
   occupation = (char *) malloc(length);
   fread(occupation, length, 1, fileptr);

/* Show what we read.
   ----------------- */
   printf("      Name: %s\n", name);
   printf("Occupation: %s\n", occupation);

/* Close file.
   ----------- */
   fclose(fileptr);
   exit(0);
}
```

This program gives the following output, showing that the read and write are correctly matched:

```
      Name: Shakespeare
Occupation: Writer
```

8.2   Overview of DB2

DB2 is IBM's family of relational databases. Like all relational databases, DB2 organizes data as tables. Tables are composed of columns and rows. Columns represent data types, and rows represent data records. We might organize our employee data in an employee table with three columns, one each for name, social security number, and department. The data for John would then be the row whose column is "John," whose social security number is "111-22-3333," and whose department is "Rumor Control." The table in Figure 20 contains three employees.

Name	SSN	Department
John	111-22-3333	Rumor Control
Amy	222-11-4444	Communications
Jerry	333-22-1111	Review Boards

Figure 20. Employee Table

There are at least four more-or-less standard mechanisms for accessing data in a relational database, all based on the SQL programming language. SQL supports all of the basic data manipulation routines, namely, updating, adding, deleting, and querying data. An SQL statement to find all the data associated with John looks like:

```
select * from Employee where name = "John"
```

There are many good books on programming in SQL, and we will not give a full tutorial here.

The SQL data access mechanisms supported by most relational databases are:

- Ad hoc queries, typed directly into a text interpreter.
- Static Embedded SQL, with SQL commands entered as part of the text in a program that is then precompiled and turned into unreadable C code.
- Dynamic Embedded SQL, with programs manipulating strings that contain SQL statements and are interpreted at run time, similar to ad hoc queries, but without the text interpreter.
- CLI (Call-Level Interface), an industry-standard interface to a variety of datastores.

Each of these data access mechanisms has advantages and disadvantages. Since only the last three are appropriate for programs, we can focus on those.

Static Embedded SQL is very fast. Because it is precompiled directly against the database, it can be turned into optimized C code that can take advantage of indexes and other fast search mechanisms. However, because it is precompiled directly against the database, the generated C code is invalid for other databases and can even go out of date as the characteristics of the database evolve. Its queries are also relatively inflexible, since they must be hand-designed by the programmer.

Dynamic Embedded SQL is very flexible. Programs can run against any database and can contain arbitrary queries. The C code does not go out of date as the database evolves. However, because every query must be reinterpreted every single time it runs, they are usually slower than Static SQL, which is interpreted only at precompile time. If one had a program with a tight loop executing queries, we could expect the Static SQL to perform faster than Dynamic SQL.

The Call-Level Interface (CLI) advantage is portability. Applications written for one CLI supporting datastore can port easily to others. Because of its generality, it tends not to take advantage of any one product's capabilities.

The sample programs in Section 8.1 and rewritten for static SQL are shown next. Notice they are written in a language that is extended C. These files must be preprocessed through the DB2 precompiler, which will generate valid C code. First, the program that writes into the database:

```c
#include <stdio.h>
main()
{
/* Declarations.
   ------------- */
   EXEC SQL INCLUDE SQLCA;
   EXEC SQL BEGIN DECLARE SECTION;
     char dbname[9];
     char name[100];
     char occupation;
   EXEC SQL END DECLARE SECTION;

/* Open database.
   -------------- */
   strcpy(dbname, "database");
   EXEC SQL CONNECT TO :dbname;

/* Write data into database.
   ------------------------- */
   strcpy(name, "William Shakespeare");
   strcpy(occupation, "Writer");
   EXEC SQL INSERT INTO PERSON
     VALUES (:name, :occupation);

/* Close database.
   -------------- */
   EXEC SQL CONNECT RESET;
}
```

Next, the read program:

```
#include <stdio.h>
main()
{
/* Declarations.
   ------------- */
   EXEC SQL INCLUDE SQLCA;
   EXEC SQL BEGIN DECLARE SECTION;
     char dbname[9];
     char name[100];
     char occupation;
   EXEC SQL END DECLARE SECTION;

/* Open database.
   ------------- */
   strcpy(dbname, "database");
   EXEC SQL CONNECT TO :dbname;

/* Read data from database.
   ------------------------ */
   EXEC SQL SELECT NAME, OCCUPATION INTO :name, :occupation
       FROM   PERSON
       WHERE NAME = 'William Shakespeare';

/* Show what we read.
   ----------------- */
   printf("      Name: %s\n", name);
   printf("Occupation: %s\n", occupation);

/* Close database.
   ------------- */
   EXEC SQL CONNECT RESET;
}
```

Comparing these two programs to the POSIX version shows similarities and differences. The overall logic of the two programs is similar. Both go through these phases:

- General declarations
- Datastore opening
- Datastore I/O
- Datastore closing

However, other than overall logic, the programs have little in common. The statements are completely different. Even the next phase of the software development process is different. The POSIX program will next go to a C compiler, and the SQL program will next go to an SQL precompiler.

Clearly any data storage code that needs modification from a POSIX file to an SQL database is going to require radical surgery. This is the basic problem that POS is intended to solve.

8.3   Overview of Plugging in a Datastore

Plugging a datastore into POS is a matter of specializing two abstract classes: the PID and the PDS. The PID (Persistent ID) contains information needed to locate an object's data in some datastore. Its interface is described in Section 5.1 on page 123. The PDS (Persistent Data Service) is an object that understands the protocol used by an object and understands how to move data in and out of some particular datastore. Its interface is described in Section 5.4 on page 142.

8.4   The PID

In this section, I will describe the POSSOM-defined base PID and several examples of PIDs specialized for different datastores. Most of the details here are SOM implementation specific, but similar issues would have to be dealt with in any POS implementation.

8.4.1   PID_DS Interface

In our experience, the generic PID described by the Persistent Object Service (POS) is a little too generic. We have created a PID that seems like a better starting point. It is located in the somPersistencePID module, consistent with the derivation scheme shown in Figure 16 on page 123. We call it PID_DS, for PID for generic datastore. We described its interface in Section 5.1 on page 123.

PID_DS serves these main functions, over and above those inherited from PID:

- It can recreate its data values from a PIDString.
- It allows arbitrary data values to be inserted for use in locating records.
- It defines a miniframework for PID derivation trees to create coordinated PIDStrings.

The first two of these are discussed in Section 5.1 on page 123. The third of these is of concern only to the datastore implementor, and we discuss that now.

One somewhat naive way to implement the PIDstring is to assume each derived PID will override get_PIDstring and set_PIDstring. In practice, this is difficult. One problem is that derived PIDs do not have access to state that is defined in their base classes.

Another naive way to implement PIDstring is to have each PID return a string that represents its own state concatenated with the get_PIDstring of its base class. This almost works. The problem occurs when you pass this concatenated string back into set_PIDstring. The implementation of set_PIDstring has to parse the string into the base part and the derived part. However, it has no way of knowing where the base part ends and the derived part begins. One might be tempted to use a null character to separate the two, since this is the only character that cannot be actually part of a string. However, if a null character appears as a string separator, then the first rule of strings has been violated, namely, a null character has been used for something other than string termination.

Lest you think this is being overly picky, recall that the invoking code of get_PIDString is expecting a string result. It expects to be able to use any of the standard C string manipulation functions, such as strcpy, strlen, and strcat, none of which can handle a string with null separation characters.

Our prototype came up with a solution to this. We have described a mini-framework for coordinating the set/get_PIDString methods among the various derivations of PID_DS. First, let's reexamine the definition of PID_DS, with some added details that are relevant for this framework. These new details are shown in bold.

```
module somPersistencePID {
  interface PID_DS : CosPersistencePID::PID {
    void set_PIDString(in string buffer);
    void updatePIDStream();
    void readFromPIDStream();
    somStream::StringStreamIO get_stream();
  };
};
```

A generic PID class, PID_DS, has an internal stream that can be accessed by the method get_stream. Recall that a stream is an object that supports set and get methods for all the standard CORBA data types. The stream implementation it uses is one that stores the basic data types as ASCII characters. Storing data as ASCII values ensures we will never have to deal with a null byte. Strings are stored as two fields, a length (in ASCII) and a sequence of characters.

In PID_DS, we implement get_PIDstring as follows, shown in pseudocode:

```
string PID_DS::get_PIDstring()
{
  str = instantiate_internal_stream();
  updatePIDStream(str);
  return(get_buffer_from_internal_stream(str));
}
```

Then, each derivation of PID_DS overrides updatePIDStream to do the following:

1. Invoke updatePIDStream on its base class.
2. Add its data into the stream by using standard stream methods.

The magic of runtime method resolution then guarantees that the methods are all resolved properly.

An implementation of updatePIDStream for PID_POSIX, the PID for POSIX files, looks like this, also in pseudocode:

```
PID_POSIX::updatePIDStream()
{
    CosStream_StringStream myStream;
    myStream = _get_stream();

    PID_DS::updatePIDStream(somSelf);
    _write_string(myStream, _pathName);
}
```

As you can see, this makes the implementation of get and set PIDstring relatively easy, especially if you have an example from which to copy.

Our implementation of PID_DS::set_PIDstring that is the mirror image of get_PIDstring is:

```
PID_DS::set_PIDString(string str)
{
    fill_internal_stream_from_str;
    _readFromPIDStream();
}
```

Then, just as each specialization of PID_DS implemented its own updatePID-Stream, each specialization also implements its own readFromPIDStream. The algorithm is to invoke readFromPIDStream on the base class, then retrieve its own data using the standard stream operations. For PID_POSIX, this looks like:

```
PID_POSIX::readFromPIDStream ()
{
    PID_DS::readFromPIDStream(somSelf, ev);

    myStream = _get_stream();
    set_pathName(_read_string(myStream));
}
```

Other implementations of POS, if they choose to allow derivations of PIDs, will come up with their own algorithms for coordinating PIDString activity,.

8.4.2   The POSIX PID

The PID_POSIX represents the simplest PID specialization. The POSIX implementation assumes all of the data from an object will be dumped in a single file. Files directly correspond to objects. Since one and only one object is stored in a file, the only information we need to locate this data is the name of the file in which the data resides. The IDL describing the PID_POSIX is as follows.

```
1.   module somPersistencePOSIX {
2.      /* ... */
3.      interface PID_POSIX : somPersistencePID::PID_DS {
4.         attribute string pathName;
5.         implementation {
6.           pathName : noget, noset;
7.           override: updatePIDStream, readFromPIDStream;
8.           /* ... */
9.         };
10.     };
11.     /* ... */
12. };
```

Let's go through this line by line, just to make sure the purpose of each is clear. Line 1 declares a module named somPersistencePOSIX. In general, it seems easiest to put all the declarations related to a particular datastore implementation into a single module. Line 3 declares this interface to be of type PID_POSIX and says it is derived from the IBM generic PID_DS, which is itself derived from the OMG-defined PID. The PID_DS lives in the module somPersistencePID. Line 4 declares pathName to be a string attribute. Attributes are described in Section 4.9 on page 64. Line 6 is SOM specific and declares the attribute to be one whose set and get methods will be explicitly defined. Line 7 is also SOM specific and says we will override updatePIDStream and readFromPIDStream. This is required to ensure that get_PIDString and set_PIDString work, as described in Section 8.4.1.

8.4.3   The DB2 PID

The PID for DB2 is a little more complicated than the one for POSIX. Knowing the "file" in which this data resides is not enough. One file now contains a virtually infinite number of objects. We need to be more specific. We need a key.

Guylaine Cantin and I went through many iterations trying to decide how to add key information to the PID_DB2. At first we thought we would add one more attribute of type string and named key. However, we wanted the PID_DB2 to work for any type of object with any kind of mapping to DB rows. For some objects, this key might be a string, but for others it could be some other type or even combination of types.

We also considered not putting the key in the PID at all but extracting it from the appropriate object data. This actually works fine for storing objects, when you have an object from which to get the key information. However, on restore, one only has a PID and, in most cases, only a PIDstring. That string has to contain all the information necessary to find the object data, including the keys.

Our scheme was to derive the PID_DB2 from both PID_DS and a stream. The stream from which we derive is the same stream we used inside the PID_DS to create the PIDstring, as discussed in Section 8.4.1 on page 209. This gives us the somewhat odd case where the PID_DB2 both has and is a stream. It has a stream, because it is derived from a PID_DS, which has as a data member a reference to a stream. And of course it is a stream, because the stream is one of its base classes.

Since the PID_DB2 is derived from a stream, it supports all the stream operations. Thus, you can put any basic CORBA type into the PID. This implementation allows us to put any arbitrary type or combination of types of key data into the PID, from whence it can later be retrieved for purposes of constructing database mappings.

8.5   The PDS

From the Persistent Object Service (POS) perspective, the PDS is the end of the line. The abstract PDS as defined in POS is the contract between POS and a datastore vendor. The datastore vendor may choose to implement the PDS as a single simple object or as an entire subframework, perhaps more complex than POS itself.

There are basically two issues the PDS implementor must consider. The first is moving data in and out of the object. The second is moving data in and out of the datastore. If you have M ways of moving data in and out of objects and N ways of moving data in and out of the datastore, then either the PDS must be able to handle MxN combinations or you need MxN different PDSs. This MxN combination can be kept manageable by keeping both M and N as small as possible, preferably one. In practice, it is not difficult to make both M and N exactly equal to 1.

N (the datastore side) is usually 1, because you will probably support only one way of moving data. In our DB2 case, we support only static SQL. And as long as you are willing to assume that objects support externalization (see Section 7.2 on page 173), M (the object side) will also be 1. In the rest of this discussion, we will assume externalization is the only supported protocol for moving data to and from objects.

8.5.1   Externalization Revisited

The Externalization specification defines three interfaces: StreamIO (described in Section 7.2.2 on page 174), Streamable (described in Section 7.2.4 on page 180), and Stream. Only the first two of these are relevant to persistence. The Stream interface is the generic, high-level stream interface. The Stream interface is defined as:

```
module CosExternalization {
  interface Stream : SOMObject{
    void externalize(in CosStream::Streamable obj);
    CosStream::Streamable internalize(
        in CosLifeCycle::FactoryFinder ff);
    void begin_context();
    void end_context();
    void flush();
  };
```

There is an assumption that Stream objects either will support the StreamIO interface or will have a StreamIO attribute, but this is not required. From the perspective of persistence, it isn't even important if "stream" objects support the Stream interface. The only guarantee we rely on is that "stream" objects support the StreamIO interface and that the persistent object supports the Streamable interface. These two interfaces represent the full contract between Persistence and Externalization.

For the purposes of this discussion, when we say "stream," we mean an object that supports the StreamIO interface; we don't care whether or not it supports the Stream interface.

8.5.2   Streams

Since your objects support externalization, you will get data out of objects by creating a stream and telling the object to externalize itself to the stream. You will get data into the object by presenting the object with a stream containing data and telling the object to internalize itself from the stream. Recall that the parameters for store and restore, as shown in Section 5.4.3 on page 144 and Section 5.4.4 on page 144, respectively, include both the object and the (optional) PID. The standard pseudocode algorithm for any PDS store and restore, then, is as follows:

```
SpecializedPDS::store(object obj, PID pid)
{
    stream = instantiate_particular_type_of_stream();
    externalize_to_stream(object, stream);
    store_stream_to_datastore(stream, pid);
}
SpecializedPDS::restore(object obj, PID pid);
{
    stream = restore_stream_from_datastore(pid);
    internalize_from_stream(object, stream);
}
```

Your choice of stream implementations can dramatically impact the overall performance of your datastore. For example, in our POSIX implementation, the stream is just a front for a file. Invocations of put methods on the stream translate directly into writes onto the file. Invocations of get methods on the stream translate directly to reads onto the file.

We have experimented with several ideas for streams optimized for DB2 but as yet have not found anything better than memory-based streams. I have not given up. I am convinced that the implementations of streams optimized for specific datastores will be one of the key differentiators for datastore products.

8.5.3   Open/Close

The PDS is responsible for opening the datastore when necessary and closing it when necessary. It is fairly obvious when the datastore needs opening. The first time somebody tries to read or write to the datastore, it needs to be opened. But it is more difficult to see when the datastore should be closed.

Opening datastores is very expensive. One can usually perform thousands of read and/or writes for the cost of a single open. Therefore, one wants to open the datastore as infrequently as possible and leave it open as long as possible.

Our current assumption is that most PDSs will leave their datastores open until one of two events occurs: The PDS runs out of opens or the PDS itself is brought down.

The PDS runs out of opens when the number of concurrent datastores that are currently in use by the PDS exceeds the total number of datastores the system or the PDS architecture allows to be open at one time. Consider, for example, a PDS specialized for POSIX files. If objects are stored one object per file, one could quickly have open hundreds or thousands of data files. A typical POSIX PDS architecture will most likely limit the total number of files that can be concurrently opened and will use a caching mechanism to open only those that are currently most active. Others will be opened as needed, and those least used will be closed when total opens exceed capacity.

A PDS specialized for relational databases is much less likely to face this problem. Because many objects are stored in a single datastore (database), only a finite and small number of databases need to be opened at once. In this case, the caching is not a big issue, and the database(s) can be left open until the PDS is brought down.

8.5.4   Security

The general issue of mapping object security to database security is not well defined. This issue will become better understood as some implementations of the object security service become available and become integrated into persistence. My general belief is that PDSs will be installed as "superservers," with uncontrolled access to the datastore, and that security will then be provided by the object security service, which will decide which users may invoke which methods on which objects.

8.6 Unmapped vs. Mapped Datastores

When we start thinking about storing objects in specific datastores, we must deal with the possibility that the format of the object's data in the datastore is not the same as the format of the object's data in memory. In these cases, we must have some mechanism for mapping between the two. We can then think of the store/restore process as necessarily including some ability to translate from one format to the other.

We will continue to assume we are simplifying the translation problem by supporting only the externalization protocol. In this case, the problem is really one of translating between the stream format and the datastore format.

A mapped datastore can be thought of us as one where the stream format for the object is different from the datastore format of the object's data and some mapping must be done between the two. An unmapped datastore, then, is one in which the stream format for the object exactly matches the datastore format.

Although we tend to think of datastores as being either mapped or unmapped, the fact is that most could be either. We will look at both cases with a POSIX file, but first, let's review some information about streams. We discussed streams in detail already, but we will give a brief refresher here.

A stream is an object that supports read/write operations for each of the basic CORBA data types. As described in Section 7.2.2 on page 174, a stream can be defined by the following IDL:

```
interface Stream : CosStream::StreamIO {

    short get_short_item();
    void put_short_item(in short item);

    long get_long_item();
    void put_long_item(in long item);

    string get_string_item();
    void put_string_item(in string item);

/* ... */

    void reset();

    implementation {
      releaseorder: get_short_item, put_short_item,
                    get_long_item, put_long_item,
                    get_string_item, put_string_item,
                    /* ... */
                    reset;
    };
};
```

Let's reconsider the memory-based stream described in Section 7.2.3 on page 176 with a modification to set and get the internal buffer:

```
interface MemoryStream : CosStream::StreamIO {
  const long buffLength = 1000;
  string get_buffer();
  short get_buffer_length();
  void set_buffer(in string buffer, in short length);

  implementation {
    string buff;
    long length;
    releaseorder: get_buffer, get_buffer_length, set_buffer;
    override: read_short, write_short,
              read_long, write_long, /* ... */
              read_string, write_string,
              reset,
              somInit;
  };
};
```

The following person object, whose implementation is shown in Section 7.3 on page 181, can externalize itself to any stream, including, of course, a Memory-Stream:

```
#include <somobj.idl>
#include <strmable.idl>

interface person : SOMObject, CosStream::Streamable {
  attribute string name;
  attribute short age;
  void print();
  implementation {
    releaseorder :  _get_name, _set_name, _set_age,
                    _get_age, print;
    name: noset, noget;
    override: externalize_to_stream, internalize_from_stream;
  };
};
```

For reference, the streamable overrides are repeated here:

```
void externalize_to_stream(person somSelf,  Environment *ev,
Stream stream)
{
   personData *somThis = personGetData(somSelf);
   person_parent_Streamable_externalize_to_stream(
      somSelf, ev, stream);
   _write_string(stream, ev, _name);
   _write_short(stream, ev, _age);
}
```

```
void internalize_from_stream(person somSelf,  Environment *ev,
Stream stream, CosLifeCycle_FactoryFinder ff)
{
   personData *somThis = personGetData(somSelf);
   person_parent_Streamable_internalize_from_stream(
     somSelf, ev, stream, ff);
   _name = _read_string(stream, ev);
   _age = _read_short(stream, ev);
}
```

We will now use MemoryStream and person to do some basic I/O with and without mapping. Since without mapping is easiest, let's first look at a program that uses these objects to write out a person to an unmapped POSIX file.

```
#include <person.h>
#include <stdio.h>
#include <memstrm.h>

main()
{
   person John;
   MemoryStream stream;
   string buffer;
   short length;
   FILE *fileptr;
   Environment *ev;

   ev = SOM_CreateLocalEnvironment();

   John = personNew();

   __set_name(John, ev, "John");
   __set_age(John, ev, 22);

   _print(John, ev);
   stream = MemoryStreamNew();
   _externalize_to_stream(John, ev, stream);

   length = _get_buffer_length(stream, ev);
   buffer = _get_buffer(stream, ev);

   fileptr = fopen("test1.dat", "w");
   fwrite(buffer, length, 1, fileptr);
   fclose(fileptr);
}
```

The basic algorithm of this program is:

```
instantiate person;
fill person with data;
instantiate stream;
externalize person to stream;
get internal buffer from stream;
write internal buffer out to file;
```

The output from this program is:

```
        Name: John
         Age: 22
```

This program generates a data file named test1.dat with seven bytes of data. The first four bytes are the ASCII characters J, O, H, and N. The fifth byte is the null character. The sixth and seventh bytes are the numeric value 22.

The following program is able to read this data file:

```
#include <person.h>
#include <stdio.h>
#include <memstrm.h>

main()
{
    person John;
    MemoryStream stream;
    char buffer[1000];
    short length;
    FILE *fileptr;
    Environment *ev;

    ev = SOM_CreateLocalEnvironment();

    John = personNew();

    fileptr = fopen("test1.dat", "r");
    length = fread(buffer, 1, 1000, fileptr);
    fclose(fileptr);

    stream = MemoryStreamNew();
    _set_buffer(stream, ev, buffer, length);
    _internalize_from_stream(John, ev, stream, NULL);
    _print(John, ev);

}
```

The algorithm for this program is:

```
instantiate person;
read buffer from file;
set internal stream buffer with file buffer;
internalize person from stream;
```

This basic form of I/O is called unmapped because we don't care about the format of the file. We can let the format of the file be determined by whatever the internal format of the stream happens to be.

Now let's consider a slightly more complicated situation. First, say we have purchased the person code in binary, so we don't have the ability to change it. Second, say we *do* care about the format of the file, because we have existing programs that need to read the data and that have specific ideas about how the data is laid out. An example of such a program is the following.

```c
#include <stdio.h>
main()
{
    char name[100];
    int age;
    FILE *fileptr;

    fileptr = fopen("test1.dat", "r");
    fscanf(fileptr, "%d", &age);
    fscanf(fileptr, "%s", name);
    fclose(fileptr);

    printf("Name: %s\n", name);
    printf(" Age: %d\n", age);
}
```

Notice this program is expecting the following file layout: an ASCII string containing the age followed by an ASCII string containing the name. This format is quite different from that which our write program will create. First, the order of the elements is reversed. Second, this program expects age to be in the format of an ASCII string, whereas our write program writes in the format of a two-byte number. Suppose this code is representative of millions of lines of corporate-critical code. How do we reconcile our systems?

The easiest way is to have a segment of mapping code that knows both the sequence of data in the stream and the expected format of the file and that maps between the two. We can package this code together into a mapper interface. A generic description of mapper is:

```
#include <somobj.idl>
interface Stream;

interface Mapper : SOMObject {
  void mapped_write(in void *fileptr, in Stream stream);
  void mapped_read(in void *fileptr, in Stream stream);
  implementation {
    releaseorder: mapped_write, mapped_read;
  };
};
```

We can now define a mapper specialized for our person stream and specific required file format:

```
#include <mapper.idl>

interface PersonMapper : Mapper {
  implementation {
    override: mapped_write, mapped_read;
  };
};
```

The implementation of PersonMapper is:

```
#ifndef SOM_Module_pmapper_Source
#define SOM_Module_pmapper_Source
#endif
#define PersonMapper_Class_Source

#include <stdio.h>
#include <stream.h>
#include <pmapper.ih>

void mapped_write(PersonMapper somSelf,  Environment *ev,
void* fileptr, Stream stream)
{
   FILE *file;
   string name;
   int age;
   file = (FILE *) fileptr;

   name = _read_string(stream, ev);
   age = _read_short(stream, ev);

   fprintf(file, "%d", age);
   fprintf(file, "%s ", name);
}
```

```
void mapped_read(PersonMapper somSelf,   Environment *ev,
void* fileptr, Stream stream)
{
   FILE *file;
   char name[100];
   int age;
   file = (FILE *) fileptr;

   fscanf(file, "%d", &age);
   fscanf(file, "%s", name);

   _write_string(stream, ev, name);
   _write_short(stream, ev, age);
}
```

Our PersonMapper is quite specialized. It doesn't know anything about the specific stream being used, only what data items are in it and in what order. It doesn't know anything about Person. In fact, calling it a PersonMapper is a bit of a misnomer. It would be more accurate to call it a PersonStreamMapper. It also knows the exact desired format of the file. If we wanted another file format, we would need another specialization of Mapper, say, PersonMapper2.

We can now modify our store program to user PersonMapper1 to write out a person in the proper format.

```
#include <person.h>
#include <stdio.h>
#include <memstrm.h>
#include <pmapper.h>

main()
{
   person John;
   MemoryStream stream;
   PersonMapper pmap;
   FILE *fileptr;
   Environment *ev;

   ev = SOM_CreateLocalEnvironment();

   John = personNew();
   pmap = PersonMapperNew();

   __set_name(John, ev, "John");
   __set_age(John, ev, 22);
```

```
    _print(John, ev);
    stream = MemoryStreamNew();
    _externalize_to_stream(John, ev, stream);
    _reset(stream, ev);

    fileptr = fopen("test1.dat", "w");
    _mapped_write(pmap, ev, fileptr, stream);
    fclose(fileptr);
}
```

Notice the changes we have made to the algorithm. Now, we don't write out the stream buffer directly but use the mapper to get data from the stream and write it out. We could easily change the format of the generated file by just instantiating a different mapper.

Similar modifications allow the restore program to read a file in the standard company format:

```
#include <person.h>
#include <stdio.h>
#include <memstrm.h>
#include <pmapper.h>

main()
{
    person John;
    MemoryStream stream;
    PersonMapper pmap;
    FILE *fileptr;
    Environment *ev;

    ev = SOM_CreateLocalEnvironment();

    John = personNew();
    pmap = PersonMapperNew();

    fileptr = fopen("test1.dat", "r");
    stream = MemoryStreamNew();
    _mapped_read(pmap, ev, fileptr, stream);
    fclose(fileptr);

    _reset(stream, ev);
    _internalize_from_stream(John, ev, stream, NULL);
    _print(John, ev);

}
```

This program gives the following output, showing the restore was successful:

```
Name:  John
  Age:  22
```

And our corporate-critical millions of lines of code:

```
#include <stdio.h>
main()
{
   char name[100];
   int age;
   FILE *fileptr;

   fileptr = fopen("test1.dat", "r");
   fscanf(fileptr, "%d", &age);
   fscanf(fileptr, "%s", name);
   fclose(fileptr);

   printf("Name: %s\n", name);
   printf(" Age: %d\n", age);
}
```

now work without any modification:

```
Name:  John
  Age:  22
```

This demonstrates the basic technique of mapping. Now let's modify our PDS to do mapping. The basic PDS algorithm for store for an unmapped datastore was this:

```
instantiate stream;
externalize object to stream;
write stream to datastore;
```

For a mapped datastore, this is changed to the following:

```
instantiate stream;
externalize object to stream;
determine which mapper to use;
mapper::write(stream);
```

There is nothing inherent about POSIX files that says they will be mapped or unmapped. This is determined by whether a specific datastore format must be observed, usually for reasons of compatibility with legacy data and software.

When preparing to plug a specific datastore into a POS implementation, a datastore vendor must decide whether or not to support mapping and how that mapping will be communicated to the PDS. In the prototype of the POSIX implementation, we decided not to support mapping. In our experience, few customers storing objects to a file cared about the file format. Our DB2 customers, on the other hand, have typically invested huge sums into existing applications and want objects stored in a manner that is compatible. Our DB2 prototype implementation, therefore, does support mappings.

The mapping code shown here was hand-generated by someone with intimate knowledge of the person stream and the desired datastore format. However, one can imagine tools using an object-oriented user interface to collect information about the mappings and then automatically generating the appropriate mapping code.

8.7 DB2 Schema Mappers

Since DB2 is a typical relational database, it's worth looking at how DB2 implemented the mapping concept. Most of the ideas described here came from joint work between me and Guylaine Cantin, with input from customers and others at IBM, particularly George Copeland. The example shown here was developed by Guylaine Cantin, and I appreciate her permission to reprint it.

DB2 assumes that each persistent class has at least one associated schema mapper. A schema mapper is an object whose type is derived from the DB2-defined SchemaMapper class, which is defined as:

```
module somPersistenceDB2 {
  interface SchemaMapper : SOMObject {

    SOMPsqlca *restore(
      CosStream::StreamIO stream,
      somPersistenceDB2::PID_DB2);

    SOMPsqlca *store(
      CosStream::StreamIO stream,
      somPersistenceDB2::PID_DB2);

    SOMPsqlca *Delete(
      somPersistenceDB2::PID_DB2);
  };
};
```

The schema mapper will be a type derived from SchemaMapper with all three methods overridden. The schema mapper for a given persistent class must have intimate knowledge of three things:

- The internal format of the data in the stream as externalized by the object.
- The external format of the data as stored in the DB2 tables.
- A mapping algorithm for moving data between these two data formats.

Let's look at a simple example. The following IDL defines a dog:

```
interface dog : somPersistencePO::PO, CosStream::Streamable {
  attribute string  TagID;
  attribute string  Breed;
  attribute string  DogName;
  attribute string  OwnerName;
  implementation {
    override: externalize_to_stream, internalize_from_stream;
  };
};
```

The dog has four attributes, all strings. The dog is derived from PO, making it an explicit persistent object, although this discussion applies equally well to implicit persistent objects. The dog is also derived from Streamable and overrides each of the Streamable methods. Thus, it is an object that supports Externalization, the recommended persistence protocol.

The attribute code is not shown. The Streamable overrides are:

```
#define dog_Class_Source
#include <dog.ih>
void externalize_to_stream(dog somSelf,
Environment *ev, CosStream_StreamIO stream)
{
    dogData *somThis = dogGetData(somSelf);
    _write_string(stream, ev, _TagID);
    _write_string(stream, ev, _Breed);
    _write_string(stream, ev, _DogName);
    _write_string(stream, ev, _OwnerName);
}

void internalize_from_stream(dog somSelf,
Environment *ev, CosStream_StreamIO stream,
CosLifeCycle_FactoryFinder ff)
{
    dogData *somThis = dogGetData(somSelf);
    _TagID = _read_string(stream, ev);
    _Breed = _read_string(stream, ev);
    _DogName = _read_string(stream, ev);
    _OwnerName = _read_string(stream, ev);
}
```

After externalization, the stream will contain the following data items:

- A string, which describes the ID on the dog's tag.
- A string, which describes the dog's breed.
- A string, which contains the name of the dog.
- A string, which contains the name of the dog's owner.

In a real object, we would expect to see much more complicated data types, including references to other objects, but this example serves to illustrate the design of a schema mapper.

Let's assume that database stores dogs as rows in a "dog" table, where the dog table consists of four columns, all of fixed length strings, named respectively TAGID, BREED, DOGNAME, and OWNERNAME. Assume the unique ID for the table is TAGID. The dog's schema mapper is defined as:

```
#include <sompdb2.idl>
interface dog_schema_mapper : somPersistenceDB2::SchemaMapper {
    implementation {
        override: store, restore, Delete;
    };
};
```

The overrides for these three methods need to map between the stream data and the database tables. The code for these three methods is:

```
#include "dog_sm.ih"
#include <sqlenv.h>
#include <sqlcodes.h>
#include <dog.h>
EXEC SQL INCLUDE SQLCA;
EXEC SQL BEGIN DECLARE SECTION;
      char      TagID[10];
      char      Breed[15];
      char      DogName[20];
      char      OwnerName[20];
EXEC SQL END DECLARE SECTION;

/*
**************************************************
store
************************************************** */
SOMPsqlca* store(dog_schema_mapper *somSelf,
Environment *ev,
CosStream_StreamIO *objstr,
somPersistenceDB2_PID_DB2 *pid)
{
/* Retrieve the primary key from the DB2 PID.
   --------------------------------------- */
    strcpy(TagID, _read_string(pid, ev));
    _read_string(objstr, ev);
```

```
/* Retrieve dog data from stream.
   ------------------------------ */
   strcpy(Breed,      _read_string(objstr, ev));
   strcpy(DogName,    _read_string(objstr, ev));
   strcpy(OwnerName, _read_string(objstr, ev));
   EXEC SQL UPDATE DOG
       SET BREED = :Breed,
       DOGNAME = :DogName,
       OWNERNAME = :OwnerName
           WHERE TAGID = :TagID;
   if (sqlca.sqlcode == SQL_RC_W100)        /* ROW NOT FOUND */
       EXEC SQL INSERT INTO DOG
           VALUES (:TagID, :Breed, :DogName, :OwnerName);
   return ((SOMPsqlca*) &sqlca);
}
/*
***********************************************
restore
*********************************************** */
SOMPsqlca* restore(dog_schema_mapper *somSelf,
Environment *ev,
CosStream_StreamIO *objstr,
somPersistenceDB2_PID_DB2 *pid)
{
/* Retrieve the primary key from the DB2 PID.
   ----------------------------------------- */
   strcpy(TagID, (char *)_read_string(pid, ev));

/* Retrieve data from database.
   --------------------------- */
   EXEC SQL SELECT BREED, DOGNAME, OWNERNAME
       INTO :Breed, :DogName, :OwnerName
       FROM DOG
       WHERE TAGID = :TagID;

/*  Put data into stream.
   --------------------- */
   _write_string(objstr, ev, TagID);
   _write_string(objstr, ev, Breed);
   _write_string(objstr, ev, DogName);
   _write_string(objstr, ev, OwnerName);
   return ((SOMPsqlca*) &sqlca);
}
```

```
/*
* * * * * * * * * * * * * * * * * * * * * * * * * * * * * * * * * * * * * * * * * * * *
Delete
* * * * * * * * * * * * * * * * * * * * * * * * * * * * * * * * * * * * * * * * * */
SOMPsqlca* Delete(dog_schema_mapper *somSelf,
Environment *ev,
somPersistenceDB2_PID_DB2 *pid)
{
/* Retrieve the primary key from the DB2 PID.
   ----------------------------------------- */
   strcpy(TagID, (char *)_read_string(pid, ev));

/* Delete the record.
   ----------------- */
   EXEC SQL DELETE FROM DOG
        WHERE TAGID = :TagID;
   return ((SOMPsqlca*) &sqlca);
}
```

The advantage of this approach is that it is both simple, for simple cases, and flexible, for complex cases. For very simple schema mappers, we can imagine GUI tools being used for their creation, or default schema mappers, which make runtime assumptions about the mapping between objects and tables.

A given object type can have potentially many different schema mappers, each designed for a specific mapping. We can imagine a whole new profession, database mappers, who read database schemas, documentation of stream formats, and generate or write the code that maps between the two.

DB2 assumes a default schema mapper name for a given class by concatenating the name of the class with "schema_mapper." It also accepts an extended PID type with a schema mapper attribute, which allows a schema mapper to be chosen at run time. Other possibilities for choosing a schema mapper are possible as well.

8.8   Stream Issues

The datastore provider is responsible for finding the best possible implementation of a stream for a particular datastore. In many cases, they will specialize existing streams. In this section, we discuss some of the important factors they should take into account.

8.8.1   Read/Write_Object

The implementation of read/write_object we showed in Section 7.4 on page 193 does not match either of the persistence models (Implicit or Explicit) discussed earlier. Let's reconsider the write_object code.

```
void write_object(FileStream somSelf, Environment *ev,
SOMObject item)
{
    string className;
    string pidString;
    string pidType;
    somPersistencePID_PID_DS pid;
    FileStreamData *somThis = FileStreamGetData(somSelf);

    pid = __get_p(item, ev);
    pidType = _somGetClassName(pid);
    pidString = _get_PIDString(pid, ev);
    className = _somGetClassName(item);

    _write_string(somSelf, ev, className);
    _write_string(somSelf, ev, pidType);
    _write_string(somSelf, ev, pidString);

    _externalize_to_stream(item, ev, somSelf)
}
```

Notice this implementation always writes out the object references. This violates the Implicit Programming Model, which says the Transaction Manager will write out objects when and if they are updated within the course of a transaction. This also violates the Explicit Programming Model, which says that the client program must decided when and if to write out embedded objects.

Both of these problems can be solved by the removal of a single line of code from both read_object and write_object. On the write side, we remove the externalize_to_stream invocation. On the read side, we remove the internalize_from_stream invocation. With these changes, the streams work as desired with the client view of persistence.

8.8.2   Virtual Base Classes

With the new changes in read/write_object, the Stream/Streamable mechanisms we have shown here work extremely well ninety-five percent of the time. There are a few issues, however, that have not been fully worked out. These issues are likely to be hotly contested in the marketplace, with vendors positioning their Persistent Object Service implementation as the one with the best solutions in these areas. One of these is virtual base classes.

Consider the following interface hierarchy:

```
interface person : CosStream::Streamable
{
  attribute string name;
};
interface student : person
{
  attribute string majorField;
};
```

```
interface employee : person
{
  attribute string manager;
};
interface teachingAssistant : student, employee
{
  attribute sequence<string> courses;
};
```

It is clear from this that a teachingAssistant is derived from both student and employee. It has an attribute named courses, which is a sequence of strings. This attribute is defined in teachingAssistant. It has a string attribute named manager, which is part of its employee heritage. It has a string attribute named majorField, which is part of its student heritage.

Beyond this, the situation is less clear. The student part of teachingAssistant is derived from person, which has a string attribute named name. But teachingAssistant is also derived from employee, which is also derived from person. Does a teachingAssistant therefore have one name or two?

The answer to this question is determined by the inheritance model the particular CORBA implementation supports. SOM's implementation of CORBA supports what is called *virtual inheritance*. With virtual inheritance, multiple instances of a base class are folded into a single base class. Our teachingAssistant, which has two instances of the person base class, sees only a single instance. Therefore, the number of names a teachingAssistant has (in SOM) is one.

All of the classes in this hierarchy are Streamable. The person interface is Streamable because it is directly derived from Streamable. The other three interfaces are Streamable because they are derived from interfaces that are Streamable. All must implement the overrides of the Streamable methods.

Pseudocode for the expected overrides of the externalize_to_stream looks like this:

```
teachingAssistant::externalize_to_stream(stream)
{
  student::externalize_to_stream(stream);
  employee::externalize_to_stream(stream);
  add courses to stream;
}
student::externalize_to_stream(stream)
{
  person::externalize_to_stream(stream);
  add major field to stream;
}
```

```
employee::externalize_to_stream(stream)
{
  person::externalize_to_stream(stream);
  add manager to stream;
}
person::externalize_to_stream(stream)
{
  add name to stream;
}
```

This means that person::externalize_to_stream will be invoked twice, once by the employee externalization and once by the student externalization. Similarly, the person::internalize_from_stream will be invoked twice.

Attributes are typically implemented as data members, with set methods implemented as copying parameters into data members, and get methods implemented as returning copies of data members. With these implementations, the double invocation will not be a major problem. Two copies of the person information will be inserted into the stream, but the second will effectively overwrite the first on internalization. However, other implementations of attributes are also possible, and some of these could have problems with the double invocation of the person's externalize and internalize.

In general, any attribute whose set or get method has a side effect will have a problem. An example of a get with such a side effect is an implementation as a read on a database with a lock on the underlying records. The first get will work. The second will find its data locked and fail. An example of a set with such a side effect is an implementation where a new record is stored. The externalization of a teachingAssistant with such an implementation will result in two person records being stored, a possible corruption of the underlying database.

The general problem here is managing parent invocations of virtual base class methods. The management of Streamable methods is just one instance of this problem. Rather than a specific solution for Streamable methods, we would expect a more general solution to the virtual base class method management problem. Until the general solution exists, SOM is working on addressing this as an extension to the StreamIO class.

8.8.3   Distributed Streams

People often raise the issue of performance when discussing streamability. The argument is that we need a long series of method invocations to get data from the object into the stream, and then a long series of method invocations to get data back out. Don't all these method invocations negatively impact performance?

This concern makes sense in a typical, single-process object model, where the cost of method invocation can often be a significant overhead. In a single-process object model, the number of method invocations often inversely correlates to the performance of the system. The more method invocations, the slower the performance.

In distributed object systems, it is not the number of method invocations that slows down performance, but the number of distributed method invocations. In such systems, we can afford a large number of method invocations, as long as those invocations are local. It is only when we start distributing those method invocations that performance is impacted.

Streams can perform well in such systems. Although they do add method invocations to move data in and out of the object, the streams can be implemented such that the data movement methods are invoked locally. Data can be batched up in the stream, then moved efficiently in large packets across the network. The architecture for such a stream might look that shown in Figure 21.

There is still more work to be done in designing distributed streams. However, early theoretical analysis makes us believe in their feasibility.

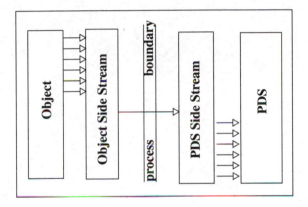

Figure 21. Possible Architecture for a Distributed Stream

8.9   Summary

The Persistent Object Service offers an attractive architecture to datastore providers. They have a well-defined interface that can be specialized to accommodate many different types of datastores, ranging from simple POSIX files to advanced relational databases, and even the new object-oriented databases.

One area not covered explicitly by POS is the protocol used to move data in and out of objects. We recommend a protocol based on the Externalization specification. It is important to standardize on a protocol, because without such a standard, datastore vendors can create general-purpose PDSs. The acceptance of the Externalization specification as such a protocol is likely because of its widespread use in other areas of CORBA.

The Vision

I have now been living with this technology for many years. I have worked closely with experts in the field. I have presented this material before thousands of customers. In this chapter, I will try to solidify my thoughts on why this technology is important and where it is going.

9.1   New Problems

Fundamentally, technology is about doing things better. We can talk about object-oriented programming, distributed objects, and many other ideas, but if these ideas can't be measured in productivity gains, in enabling of new types of applications, and in creating new opportunities for new and existing companies, then this technology is nothing but an interesting, but ultimately useless, academic exercise.

Companies are facing old and new problems. They are still trying to run their business as best as possible and are more and more dependent on computers to do so. They are still trying to deal with applications development backlogs of years. Now they are also faced with a rapidly evolving technology, one that offers a wealth of new opportunities for those companies that can move swiftly and evolve rapidly.

Today's technology is driven by the following factors.

- Almost everybody has access to a computer at home, school, and/or work.
- Virtually all personal computers now have the power and capability to drive highly sophisticated user interfaces.
- Virtually all personal computers now have the ability to communicate with at least one network.
- The bandwidth (bits per second) connecting the computers and networks is increasing dramatically, while the cost of the communication (cost per bit) is becoming negligible.
- Most networks can communicate with most other networks, giving the effect of a single, global network.

This means that effectively any person can communicate with any computer and can do so by using very sophisticated user interfaces on conveniently located computers. This opens the door for a new world of commerce applications undreamed of a few short years ago. We are already seeing on-line banking, advertising on the Internet, and virtual storefronts. Nobody can predict where this technology will lead us in the next five years, but it is clear that the pressure to develop a steady stream of ever-sophisticated applications is only going to get worse.

9.2   New Business Models

This technology is also being driven by another business trend: reengineering. Companies are reevaluating their entire business models and restructuring the relationship between employees and information. Five years ago, information access was organized hierarchically. Frontline employees were seen as data input engines only. Low-level management was given limited authority to access only information that was directly relevant to their place within the organization. As one went higher in the management hierarchy, one's access to information increased proportionately.

The new business trend is to push decision-making authority down to the front lines. Business is now realizing that those closest to customers are in the best position to know what decisions need to be made and what the impact of those decisions is likely to be. This model for business was championed by Michael Hammer and James Champy in their book *Reengineering the Corporation* (HarperBusiness, 1993). This new model for business requires new, creative uses of computer technology. As Hammer and Champy point out, "A company that cannot change the way it thinks about information technology cannot reengineer."

Three recent articles in the New York Times underscored the importance of this new direction in technology.

The first article (November 15, 1995, C1) was titled "77,800 Managers at AT&T Getting Job Buyout Offers." The article described AT&T's need to reduce its middle manager ranks and move decision making down the ranks. The article described a movement begun in the 80s where "...many corporations began to use new information technology as a substitute for supervisory employees."

The second article (November 16, 1995, C1) was titled "New Ideas for U.S. Oil," which described how Texaco has increased production from 150 barrels per day per employee three years ago to 250 barrels today. What caused this incredible increase? New drilling technology? New exploration techniques? Far from it. According to the article,

> ...call it empowerment or plain common sense, but big oil companies are unshackling their field workers from old management restraints. In less than a year, the new policy is already slowing the decline in domestic oil production - and holding out hope of halting it.

Among the many changes made at Texaco was giving employees, for the first time, "unrestricted access to a new central computer that stored data on all aspects of operations from each well's history to underground rock formations."

The third New York Times article (November 15, 1995, C1) was titled "Putting the Squeeze on Small Discounters." This article described the plight of Ames, Bradlees, Hills, Jamesway, and Caldor. The stores were all at one point strong retailers and are all now in trouble. Who is doing well in this competitive business? Wal-Mart. And what is it that distinguishes Wal-Mart? Better locations? Unique merchandise? Nope. Computer technology! According to the New York Times, "by 1990 it [Wal-Mart] was already winning an important technological war that other discounters did not seem to know was going on." While the rest of the discounters were busy investing in real estate, Wal-Mart was investing in the most advanced inventory system in the industry.

So, here we have three totally different industries: communications, oil, and discounting. The success stories all have one common thread: advanced use of computer technology, making that technology available to the widest possible audience and making this technology the technological cornerstone for a new way of conducting business.

What is most interesting about these articles is the time span over which they appeared. Not over a year, a month, or even a week. All three of these feature-length articles appeared in the New York Times within a two-day period. This is a fast-moving world, and only those that can adapt quickly will survive.

9.3   New Technology

Many of us believe that the enabling technology for this new world will be object-oriented programming. Object-oriented programming is characterized by support for inheritance and polymorphism, allowing new objects to be created as straightforward specializations of existing objects. These objects have well-defined and encapsulated interfaces, which allow them to be treated as independent software components. As components, they can serve as building blocks for larger applications. Well-established framework technology allows architectures defining relationships between objects to be defined and implemented.

People often don't understand the difference between object-oriented programming and components. A *component* is a piece of software that can be used through an interface. Object-oriented programming is one technique for developing components. When components are developed by use of object-oriented programming, we call the components *objects*. Objects have the advantage over other types of components in that, through inheritance and polymorphism, they can more easily serve as the basis for further component development.

In an ideal world, we would never write a new object. When we need a new object for our application, we would go to our software catalog, find an object that does what we want, purchase it, and use it as a building block. If the object doesn't exactly meet our needs, we would use inheritance and polymorphism to specialize the object. We would have a steady stream of choices in objects supplied by an established, software-components industry.

We have been predicting a software-components industry for many years and have yet to see one come to pass. This failure is due to the fact that two critical industry requirements seem to be in opposition to each other. Until this opposition can be resolved, the industry will remain in a stalemate. These two contradictory requirements are specialization and generalization.

Any component must be highly specialized in order to be useful. Real-world applications need their components to be distributed through highly complex networks. They need components to interact with databases that use regimented formats and standard languages. They need these interactions to be coordinated with transaction monitors, which use unique programming models and arcane programming technology.

On the other hand, if a component can be sold successfully, it must be very general. It must be useful to the widest possible number of customers, or a components company cannot recoup the development investment. In order to be generally useful, it must solve general business problems. It should limit its code to application-domain issues.

We can see the contradiction between these two goals. On one hand, components are useless unless they can deal with a large number of complex, proprietary, and semiproprietary technologies. On the other hand, every assumption the component makes about an underlying database, an underlying network, or an underlying transaction processing monitor greatly reduces the potential customer list.

9.4   New Solutions

The answer to this dilemma is to provide a set of standard object services and object architectures that can be specially tailored to particular environments, then to build components assuming these services are available. The component then no longer needs to write network-specific code to communicate with distant objects; it assumes the underlying architecture will deal with this issue. It no longer needs to have embedded SQL to store its data to a relational database; it assumes data storage will be managed by the Persistent Object Service. It no longer tries to guess which transaction processing monitor will be used; it assumes that whatever transaction processing monitor is used will coordinate its activity through the Transaction Service.

In order for this solution to work, we need standards both for the underlying object architecture and for the interfaces to the object services. This is exactly the task that OMG (Object Management Group) has taken on. As more object services become defined and more implementations become available, we can expect to see the object component industry start to take off.

Critical to the success of the object components industry will be the Persistent Object Service and the set of related services. It is a rare commercial application that does not have to store and retrieve data. As persistence becomes more tightly integrated with queries, security, transactions, and other services, we will have a powerful enabling technology for a components industry.

We will soon see an interesting shift away from monolithic, closed systems, such as databases and transaction processing monitors. More and more of these functions will be taken over by collections of object services defined with standard interfaces. These services will be plug compatible across vendor products, so that customers will no longer buy whole systems from one vendor but will mix and match service implementations from many vendors to create an environment that is highly optimized for a particular purpose.

This certainly poses a threat to existing technology. Databases and transaction processing monitors will find they have to adapt both to support old applications and to play in this new development environment. Object-oriented databases will find much of their momentum slow down, as customers realize that there are many choices as to where and how data can be stored. There is always some pain when old technology must adapt to new.

Some companies will fail to evolve and will continue to believe in systems development as it exists today. It is hard to see how these companies can remain competitive. They will be selling prefabricated cities in a world that wants Lego® building blocks. They will have software cycles of years in a world that expects overnight change. They will be selling dull monochrome products in a world that expects color and imagination.

But ultimately it is all of us that will benefit. The world of software will become infinitely richer, as new applications can be quickly developed to exploit new ideas. New niches will develop and be filled by existing or new vendors. New relationships will be discovered between existing applications. Customers will find uses for applications that were never dreamed of by their developers. This is the vision.

Index

Object Persistence